William Faulkner

Titles in the series Critical Lives present the work of leading cultural figures of the modern period. Each book explores the life of the artist, writer, philosopher or architect in question and relates it to their major works.

In the same series

William Faulkner

Kirk Curnutt

REAKTION BOOKS

Published by Reaktion Books Ltd
Unit 32, Waterside
44–48 Wharf Road
London N1 7UX, UK

www.reaktionbooks.co.uk

First published 2018
Copyright © Kirk Curnutt 2018

Printed and bound in Great Britain by Bell & Bain, Glasgow

A catalogue record for this book is available from the British Library

ISBN 978 1 78023 998 9

Contents

Portrait of William Faulkner by Carl Van Vechten, 11 December 1954.

Introduction

Q: Some people say they can't understand your writing, even after they
read it two or three times. What approach would you suggest for them?
A: Read it four times.

William Faulkner in *The Paris Review* (1956)

In 1953 *Life Magazine* published a two-part profile of William
Faulkner that promised to unveil 'the man behind the myth'.
Written by Robert Coughlan and reprinted in book form the
following year, its subject considered it an infuriating intrusion.
'I tried for years to prevent it, refused always, asked [reporters]
to let me alone,' Faulkner insisted. 'It's too bad the individual in
this country has no protection from journalism . . . Sweden gave
me the Nobel Prize. France gave me the Légion d'honneur. All my
native land did for me was to invade my privacy over my protest
and my plea.'[1] For the author, biographical background was the
least interesting aspect of art. What mattered, he argued a decade
earlier, was the work itself, not the creator: 'I think that if what
one has thought and hoped and endeavored and failed at is not
enough, if it must be explained and excused by what [the writer]
has experienced, done or suffered, while he was not being an artist,
then he and the one making the evaluation have both failed.'[2]

Most writers in the 1950s would have recoiled at seeing their
name splashed behind the salacious words *The Private World of* . . .
(as Coughlan's article and book were titled). Few of them, however,

were famous for producing as challenging a body of work as William Faulkner had. So formidable was his style and technique, and so labyrinthian the interrelationship of genealogy and setting in his fiction, that *Life* presented his biography as if it were a stepping stone to understanding his core fixations, such as the American South, racial and sexual violence, and the burdens of history. Faulkner was a writer who had elevated his 'little postage stamp of native soil', north-central Mississippi's Lafayette County, into a mythopoeic clash between past and present: knowing where and whom he came from was key to appreciating the aims and ends that he insisted should be self-evident.[3] Faulkner may have believed that 'me as a private individual, my past, my family, my house' were irrelevant to his invented microcosm of Yoknapatawpha County, but for readers now as well as then, that information humanizes the otherwise mysterious process by which life transforms into art, making the writing accessible.[4]

The modernist generation Faulkner belonged to laboured under an unspoken paradox when it came to the writer as a 'private individual'. On the one hand, the innovative techniques by which they dramatized the disorienting newness of the twentieth century aimed to depersonalize writing by obscuring the author's organizing presence. The goal was to make the experience of reading feel as confusing as everyday life, with its seeming fragmentation and loss of cultural cohesion. Modernist writing also intended to demonstrate that the meaning of literature lay in a far broader context than the writer's sensibility. As T. S. Eliot insisted in 'Tradition and the Individual Talent' (1919), a poet's inspiration was merely a catalyst for sparking new compounds that should be valued independently of the creator: 'Impressions and experiences which are important for the man may take no place in the poetry,' Eliot asserted, 'and those which become important in the poetry may play quite a negligible part in the man, the personality.'[5]

This idea worked better in theory than practice. Despite Eliot's claim that art was 'not an expression of personality, but an escape from personality', modernism's emphasis on inventing ground-breaking strategies and devices for combining 'impressions and experiences . . . in peculiar and unexpected ways' relied upon such an ingrained notion of singularity that these unique tools couldn't help but be read as expressions of an authorial ethos, of a particular worldview. As a result, no matter how they depersonalized their writing, many modernists were stereotyped by what the public assumed their style or 'voice' said about them. F. Scott Fitzgerald's twin propensities for audacity and melancholy made him alternately seem such an *enfant terrible* and a disaffected post-adolescent that critics could not recognize his maturity. Ernest Hemingway's blunt confrontation of violence and stoic resolve suggested to detractors a cartoonish masculinity incapable of admitting vulnerability. Gertrude Stein's putatively nonsensical wordplay and repetitive cadences, meanwhile, sounded too much like 'baby talk' for mainstream critics to take her seriously. Satirists of the time, such as Anita Loos and Dorothy Parker, were considered topical comediennes instead of acute assayers of human foibles.

William Faulkner certainly became famous – notorious, even – for a style whose complexity defied readers' ability to feel personally connected to the writer. His fondness for abstract words, multiple and often confusingly commingled points of view and, most of all, his densely packed, exhaustingly long sentences, all conveyed an extreme interiority that suggested little interest in being, in today's parlance, 'reader friendly'. In many ways, Coughlan's unauthorized profile was an attempt to reassure the public that even the most obscure or challenging artist is knowable. The article's intrusiveness almost rebukes its subject for presuming he could 'blue pencil everything which even intimates that something breathing and moving sat behind the typewriter which produced the books', as Faulkner wrote of his desire to avoid publicity in 1949.[6]

Throughout the piece, Coughlan walks readers through the writer's hometown of Oxford, Lafayette's county seat, introducing Faulkner's mother, uncle and brother and, most controversially, commenting on his battles with alcohol. Recognizing how invasive his exposé might appear, the journalist insists that the readers' right to know the 'elusive personality' trumps the writers' right to privacy: '[Faulkner's] books – labyrinthine, grandiose, terrifying, grotesque and beautiful – are no longer his but have become a part of the literary landscape . . . Because he has created them, he does not belong entirely to himself.'[7]

Faulkner was so irate with *Life* that he penned a diatribe called 'On Privacy (The American Dream: What Happened to It?)' The essay laments the loss of 'taste and responsibility' in a culture that exploits public figures 'to sell soap or cigarettes or fountain pens or to advertise automobiles and cruises and resort hotels'.[8] Yet, despite his ire, Faulkner managed to fluster Coughlan's project. As many reviewers observed, for all its research, the profile doesn't really depict its subject in psychological depth or intimate detail. As *The Harvard Crimson* reported, 'The world which Coughlan reveals in his book . . . is not really Faulkner's private world. There is a distinct feeling that [the journalist] is looking in, that he has failed to get beneath the surface of Faulkner's life and is only recording, as fully and as competently as possible, the externals of this world.'[9]

Coughlan admitted the difficulty of penetrating Faulkner's aloof exterior, writing:

He prefers to be an enigma and one can believe that he will always remain one, even to himself . . . His is not a split personality but rather a fragmented one, loosely held together by some strong inner force, the pieces often askew and sometimes painfully in friction . . . He is thoughtful of others, and oblivious of others; he is kind, and he is cruel;

he is courtly, and he is cold . . . he loves the South and feels revulsion for the South.[10]

Subsequent biographers have struggled with a similar feeling that they, too, are recording externals without plumbing inner depths. Joseph Blotner, whose two-volume, 2,000-page *Faulkner: A Biography* (1974) remains the starting point for charting the life, wrote repeatedly of his inability to pin down his subject. Ultimately, Faulkner was an 'impenetrable man', despite working closely enough together from 1957 to 1962 for the writer to regard Blotner as a surrogate son.[11]

Faulkner's elusory character is typically credited to his fondness for personae, for donning masks and guises sometimes flagrant in their theatricality. As another biographer, Frederick R. Karl, has written, 'Intrinsic to nearly everything he did is the quality of role-playing . . . What made him almost "impenetrable" was the fact that the "real" Faulkner – whoever or whatever he was – hid himself under layers of disguise.'[12] At various stages, William Faulkner presented himself as a literary dandy, a shabby bohemian, a humble farmer, a wounded aviator (preposterous, considering he never saw battle), a courtly lover, and a genteel but aloof Southerner, often to the incredulity of family and friends content to consider him just 'plain ol' Bill'. In private and public, he was masterful at making people wonder who he really was. His love of personae was inseparable from the narrative ingenuity that beguiles and baffles readers. First and foremost, Faulkner was a storyteller. He understood that evasion and ambiguity draw readers into human mysteries that may seem deceptively simple. He also understood the allure of another device of mystification in art and life: contradiction. Much as he confounded those eager to know the 'real' person behind the guises, he instilled his characters with conflicting emotions. Many of Faulkner's best-remembered creations are broken by their inability to unify their fragmenting selves and reconcile opposing impulses as they strain to determine 'whoever or whatever' they are. They are often impenetrable to themselves.

Given Faulkner's inapprehensible nature, *Life*'s promise to peer behind the curtain and expose the wizard was wishful thinking. As generations of readers have struggled to appreciate, understanding the relationship of Faulkner's life to his art is not a matter of discovering the 'man behind the myth'.

It is a matter, rather, of learning how the man created the myth.

1

Backgrounds and Futures
(1839–1913)

Accounts of William Faulkner's life rarely begin with his birth on 25 September 1897. Instead, they cycle back to the arrival in 1839 in Mississippi of his paternal great-grandfather, William Clark Falkner (1825–1889), who at some unspecified point began spelling the family name without the 'u'. (Faulkner added it back in 1918.) 'The Old Colonel' or 'W. C.', as this forebear was known, inspired such alternately charismatic and megalomaniacal founding fathers as Col. John Sartoris of *Flags in the Dust* (published in 1929 as *Sartoris*) and *The Unvanquished* (1938), Thomas Sutpen of *Absalom, Absalom!* (1936) and Lucius Quintus Carothers McCaslin of *Go Down, Moses* (1942), men whose hubris exposes the thin line between patriarchal determination and patrimonial delusion. Unlike these characters, this first Falkner was also a writer. Although far from great art, his books encouraged his great-grandson's earliest publishing daydreams by making literature seem glamorous.

The Old Colonel captivated his heir's imagination because he embodied a romantic grandeur that hardly seemed possible in William Faulkner's own time. W. C. belonged to an antebellum generation of self-made gentry for whom airs of nobility and chivalry were rewards for settling the Southern territories. Born in Tennessee during his parents' emigration from North Carolina to Missouri, Falkner ran away to Ripley, in Tippah County, Mississippi, where by sheer grit he became a prosperous lawyer; small-farm operator and slave owner (though never a plantation owner, unlike his fictional counterparts); Confederate colonel; railroad impresario; land, lumber and newspaper investor; as well as aspiring state politician. By 21, he had fought in the Mexican War, serving under future Confederate president Jefferson Davis. In 1851 he self-published an epic poem called *The Siege of Monterrey* and a novel, *The Spanish Heroine*, and a decade later in July 1861 he charged into the first Battle of Manassas wearing a large feather that earned him the grandiose nickname 'The Knight of the Black Plume'. After 1871 he became prominent in the Reconstruction era's railroad boom, amassing a net worth of $100,000 – a millionaire by today's standards. Another decade on, he serialized his most popular novel, *The White Rose of Memphis* (1881), in his own newspaper before selling 160,000 book copies. Subsequent Falkners boasted so heartily of their paterfamilias' accomplishments that when *Life* profiled his great-grandson in 1953 a rhyming caption wryly underscored their reverence: the Old Colonel 'founded a dynasty, became a deity'.[1]

Yet W. C. had a dark streak that made his achievements seem as brutal as romantic. Family lore said he escaped to Mississippi after beating a younger brother so severely with a hoe that he thought he had killed the boy – an explosive rage that, as Coughlan noted, is entirely 'characteristic' of 'Faulknerian violence'.[2] While fighting in Mexico, he lost three fingers on his left hand to a mysterious shoot-out during an unexcused absence from camp. In 1849, shortly before his bride of two years, Holland Pearce, died from tuberculosis, he stabbed an acquaintance named Robert Hindman to death. The pistol-wielding Hindman had accused him of sabotaging his admission to the Knights of Temperance. Acquitted on grounds of self-defence, W. C. three years later shot dead a would-be avenger of Hindman's. A second trial also ended in acquittal.

Nor was the Knight of the Black Plume's service to the Confederate cause unimpeachably patriotic. After incurring

As *Life* magazine wrote in 1953, William Clark Falkner (known as 'The Old Colonel') 'founded a dynasty, became a deity'.

heavy losses at Manassas, the 2nd Mississippi Infantry voted him out of his command. Falkner organized a second, scrappier band of skirmishers but failed to win promotion to brigadier general. Embittered, he abandoned military service and spent the war's latter half, rumour said, trafficking contraband across Union blockades. His business practices, too, raised eyebrows. The Colonel was not above exploiting prison labour to build his rail lines; nor was he averse to manipulating bankruptcy laws to dispatch contrarian partners. And while he built an ostentatious three-storey home in Ripley, dubbed 'The Italian Villa', his second wife, Elizabeth Vance (1833–1910), chose to reside 130 kilometres (80 mi.) away in Memphis – an estrangement perhaps incited by an African American Falkner in the provincial town of 800 named Emeline, whose mixed-race daughters, Fannie and Lena, were likely sired by the Old Colonel.[3] Nevertheless, the sexagenarian W. C. considered himself upstanding enough to run for the state assembly. He was set to win, too, when on Election Day, 5 November 1889, a former business partner shot him in the face with a .44 pistol. Whether Richard J. Thurmond snapped after years of mutual acrimony or fired in self-defence, the result was the same: the first Mississippi Falkner died the following evening. Fifteen months later, as if in ironic payback for W. C.'s own good luck with juries, twelve peers acquitted his killer of murder.

Any author would feel lucky to inherit a legend as ripe for literary picking as the Old Colonel's, but to William Cuthbert Faulkner his ancestor wasn't merely material. W. C. provided a yardstick for measuring the past's influence on the present, a constituent theme of his great-grandson's fiction. Across his nineteen novels and 125 or more short stories, William Faulkner asks how history can feel simultaneously remote and inescapable, how traditions immaterial to contemporary life nevertheless plant the seeds of modern discontent. 'The past is never dead,' reads the most-cited line Faulkner ever wrote. 'It's not even past.'[4] It wasn't said about a fictional version of the Colonel, but the old man's contradictions were his great-grandson's most intensely felt testament to its truth. If W. C.'s rise to wealth and prominence only seemed possible in a bygone nineteenth-century South in which affluence could buy at least the patina of aristocratic standing, the inhumanities the old man defended – slavery and white supremacy, most obviously – were the moral albatrosses his twentieth-century heirs inherited.

Faulkner was born in New Albany (population 600), a depot on the Old Colonel's railroad, and spent his first four years in Ripley, where a marble statue W. C. commissioned of himself shortly before his murder towered over his gravesite on a 4-metre (14 ft) pedestal. Only eight years separated the passing of one generation from another, but to William Faulkner that gulf always seemed much wider, for the Mississippi he grew up in differed vastly from that of his ancestors. The state was still in its infancy when W. C. arrived, having entered the union in 1817. Much of its northern swatch, including Tippah and Lafayette counties, remained frontier; the Chickasaw nation had only recently been forcibly resettled in Oklahoma. The Old Colonel belonged to an emigration wave that tripled the state's population to 375,000 between 1830 and 1840. By Faulkner's childhood, that number had swollen to 1.5 million, and while Mississippi remained a rural state, the culture contemporized in ways that defied its agrarian identity. The Old Colonel certainly witnessed his share of nineteenth-century transformations, including the creation of the cotton plantations that dominated the economy of his day. Yet for all the upheaval the old man lived through – including the Civil War and the emancipation of the slaves – he could look around in senescence and recognize a world cognate with his youth. Despite railroads, travel remained arduous. Rural life was isolated, in-town amenities modest: the Colonel died before electricity lit homes and public squares and when privies were the norm.

In the three decades after his death, technological advances transformed the everyday lives of the younger Faulkner's generation. Historian Dennis J. Mitchell pictures the modern marvels that turn-of-the-century Mississippians spied when they visited even modestly sized population centres like the one in which Faulkner eventually grew up:

> Approaching Oxford in 1900, they saw the new water tank towering over the town and wondered about having water piped into a house. They drove under an archway of trees shading a street lined with what seemed to them immense Victorian homes set back in lawns with flowering plants surrounding them. If they had been able to go inside, they would have seen wonders such as gas, electricity, telephones, indoor toilets, and bathtubs. Hanging in front of the stores on the square were bananas – a fruit never available at [their] country store. After selling their chickens and other produce, they might be granted fifteen cents for a café meal of three vegetables and a meat. They might wander into Neilson's [clothing store] to gasp at the racks of ready-made dresses, shirts, and pants in a bewildering number of colors.[5]

A few years on, Faulkner's peers would see their first automobiles and aeroplanes, two technologies that fascinated the writer. From his first depiction of Yoknapatawpha County in *Flags in the Dust/ Sartoris* to *The Reivers* (1962), the novel published only weeks before his death, Faulkner dramatized the altered senses of time, speed and distance the horseless carriage brought about. Here and in stories such as 'Elly' (1934) car crashes inflict gruesome damage on bodies, exposing humanity's vulnerability in the machine age. As for flight, even before seeing a real-life plane in childhood Faulkner and his brothers jerry-built one from blueprints in a magazine called *American Boy*.[6] By early adulthood, aviation fantasies led Faulkner to claim he flew combat missions in Europe during the First World War. In fact, he never made it out of training with the Royal Air Force in Toronto, Canada – a lie that would haunt him in later decades when biographers came calling. Dreams of daredevilry inspired him to lionize fighter pilots in experimental prose-poems such as 'All the Dead Pilots' (1931). Other short fiction such as 'Honor' (1930) and his eighth novel, *Pylon* (1935), celebrate post-war aerial barnstormers who performed death-defying stunts at airshows. Yet Faulkner's obsession with flying also grieved him deeply when his youngest brother, Dean, was killed in a November 1935 crash piloting a plane Faulkner gave him.

Automobiles and aeroplanes are only two technologies from his childhood that Faulkner writes about. In *The Sound and the Fury* (1929), Quentin Compson obsesses over a pocket watch his father gives him. Although invented centuries earlier, the device only became ubiquitous in the late nineteenth century as transportation and business itineraries came to regulate daily life, these lockstep public schedules conflicting with more private modalities by which people experienced temporality. A 'graphophone' – a handheld gramophone – figures into the cruel joke inflicted on the Bundren children at the end of *As I Lay Dying* (1930) after an agonizing odyssey to bury their mother. In 'Artist at Home' (1933) a hack author's clattering typewriter dramatizes the unceasing mass production of bestselling fiction, which Faulkner dubs 'the typewriting market'.[7] In *The Hamlet* (1940), the wily opportunist Flem Snopes, Faulkner's snakiest symbol of amoral capitalism, sports machine-made white shirts and bow ties to signal his superiority over hardscrabble customers at the country store he takes over. And in 'Shall Not Perish' (1943), a story commemorating the American entry into the Second World War too often dismissed as jingoism, a poor family marvels at how a zipper, an uncommon device even for the middle class before the 1930s, opens and closes a satchel their eldest son, Pete, posts home. The satchel is Pete's final gift before dying in combat. Anxious to preserve their memories of their fallen hero, the Griers poignantly avoid overusing the zipper for fear of wearing it out.

Faulkner also grew up attuned to technology's environmental impact. During his childhood years Mississippi ranked third in the nation for lumber production. By 1909 some 1,700 sawmills operated in the state, employing 37,000 workers. Clear-cutting rapidly depleted hardwoods, while 'skidding', or dragging, felled trees to transport landings shredded groundcover and prevented timberlands from reseeding. Twenty years later, just as Faulkner's career took off, the logging boom ended, leaving behind rutted landscapes of barren stumps and abandoned railway.[8] A lifelong hunter and nature enthusiast, Faulkner raged against deforestation. Several works – most notably the classic novella 'The Bear' (1942) – elegize the disappearing wilderness as a squandered Eden. By the time of *Big Woods* (1955), a compilation of his hunting stories, the lament coarsened into a jeremiad. Here Faulkner condemns that most American of icons, the hearty pioneer, for 'turning the earth into a howling waste from which he would be the first to vanish' and denounces industrial America as a 'gilded pustule'.[9]

Another formative influence was the corrosive racial violence rampant throughout the South of Faulkner's childhood. By the 1890s the minstrel-show-bred stereotype of African Americans as compliantly happy-go-lucky gave way to panicked images of black marauding and rapacity. 'Never before or since,' writes Faulkner biographer Joel Williamson, 'have so many white people believed for so long and so deeply that black people were becoming bestial.' Imagining the fear of hysterical whites, Williamson suggests why their irrational terror flared into organized spectacles of vigilante justice like lynching:

Before the Civil War, the naturally savage potential of the African in America had been held in check only by the very tight reins of slavery. Freed from slavery for a full generation, black people in the 1890s – especially young black people – were falling over the edge of civilization, and hence, must eventually disappear from the American scene. The retrogression was everywhere apparent – in the dissolution of the black family, the degradation of the black church, and the rise of crime, disease (especially venereal), idleness, and improvidence in the black community. Nowhere was it more clear or more threatening than in the alarming increase of rapes and attempted rapes by black men upon white women. It was here, in this crucible, as it were, that a profound confusion of race, sex, and violence occurred in the South.[10]

A major accelerant for this 'profound confusion' was the hatemongering of 'redneck' politicians such as James K. Vardaman and his protégé, the Dickensian-named Theodore G. Bilbo. In the 1880s W. C. Falkner insisted in his novel *The Little Brick Church* that true Southerners 'treat their Negroes with the tenderest humanity'.[11] Vardaman and Bilbo had no use for such niceties; their demagoguery roiled with references to 'niggers', 'coons' and 'orangoutangs', inflamed racist fears of miscegenation, and explicitly condoned lynching. 'If I were a private citizen I would head the mob to string the brute up,' Vardaman boasted about one 1903 murder of a black man.[12] Fed up with the ruling patrician class, disadvantaged whites voted 'The Great White Chief' and his crag-faced crony into long and influential careers. Vardaman was Mississippi's governor from 1904 to 1908 and a u.s. senator from 1913 to 1919, while Bilbo twice helmed the state capitol (1916–20 and 1928–32) before heading to the Senate (1935–47). Some Falkner family members supported the redneck agenda out of political necessity, but Faulkner himself dismissed its crass populism as opportunism. He caricatured the redneck's rise with the aforementioned Flem Snopes and various Snopes cousins who crawl out of the countryside 'like colonies of rats and termites' to gnaw away genteel Southerners' image of themselves as refined and racially benevolent.[13] In this chaotic environment, more lynchings occurred in Mississippi than in any other state, with more than 500 instances between 1890 and 1930. Two such murders occurred in Oxford, those of Harris Tunstal in 1885 and Nelse Patton in 1908. Some biographers speculate that a ten-year-old Billy Falkner witnessed or at least heard details of Patton's lynching; the corpse was genitally mutilated, a gory fate that a living Joe Christmas suffers at the climax of *Light in August* (1932). Faulkner had no interest in reporting on lynching the way John Dos Passos, John Steinbeck and more political peers investigated labour exploitation, but gruesome mob violence erupts throughout his fiction. In addition to *Light*, *Sanctuary* (1931), the stories 'Dry September' (1931) and 'Pantaloon in Black' (1941), and 1948's *Intruder in the Dust* all trace racial hysteria to what Faulkner identified as the 'bitter hatred and fear and economic rivalry of the Negroes' that rednecks incited.[14]

Perhaps in compensation for the rise of this violence, antebellum nostalgia intensified throughout Faulkner's childhood. The myth of the Lost Cause taught his father's generation and his own that the Civil War had been fought for just about every reason under the sun *except* the preservation of slavery: defence of regional heritage, defence of womanhood, defence of (white) liberty from nationalist tyranny. The United Daughters of the Confederacy, founded shortly before Faulkner's birth, lobbied for holidays for Confederate remembrance and raised funds for memorials and statuary dedicated to local troops. Thomas Dixon, Jr's historical romance *The Clansman* (1905) became a bestseller below the Mason-Dixon line, inspiring D. W. Griffith's movie *The Birth of a Nation* (1915) as well as the re-establishment of the Ku Klux Klan, which had been dormant since the 1870s. Faulkner's contact with this Confederate veneration was personal. His first teacher, Annie Chandler, gifted him a copy of Dixon's novel. His grandfather, John Wesley Thompson Falkner (1848–1922), the Old Colonel's eldest son, helped found a chapter of the Sons of Confederate Veterans that hosted reunions for men who served under W. C. There, the Knight of the Black Plume's checkered military record was spun into tall tales of valour and gallantry, fuelling the boy's imagination and training him in the art of storytelling.

Faulkner's childhood is usually described as 'by all accounts . . . happy' or even 'storybook'.[15] He bonded closely with his three brothers, Murry Charles, or 'Jack' (1899–1975), John Wesley Thompson or 'Johncy' (1901–1963) and Dean Swift (1907–1935). After their parents, Murry (1870–1932) and Maud Butler Falkner (1871–1960), moved in 1902 from Ripley to Oxford (population 1,800), the children grew up in an extended family headed by Faulkner's grandfather, J.W.T. Falkner, known as the 'Young Colonel', and his wife, Sallie McAlpine Murry (1850–1906). Like his father, J.W.T. was a prosperous lawyer and entrepreneur, while Sallie came from a prominent Ripley family. They settled in Oxford before the Old Colonel's murder, eventually building a palatial reply to the old man's Italian Villa, known as 'The Big Place' and located near the town square. There the Falkner boys enjoyed the frequent company of at least one cousin, Sallie Wilkins (1899–1974), the daughter of Murry's widowed sister, Mary Holland Wilkins (1872–1946), who had introduced her brother to Maud, her best friend. Occasionally the Old Colonel's widow, the children's step-great-grandmother Lizzie, visited from Memphis, accompanied by her youngest daughter and J.W.T.'s half-sister, Alabama Leroy (1874–1968), with whom Faulkner remained close throughout his lifetime. Additionally, Maud's mother, Leila Dean Swift (1849–1907), resided with Murry and Maud, helping care for the oldest sons, who called her 'Damuddy'. Another constant in the house was Caroline Barr, an aged black domestic known as 'Mammy Callie' whom the boys revered as a surrogate mother. She remained in Faulkner's employ until her death in 1940.

Faulkner's paternal grandparents, John Wesley Thompson Falkner and Sallie McAlpine Falkner, relocated their family from Ripley to nearby Oxford in 1885.

Although Faulkner only obliquely modelled characters on his parents or brothers, the extended Falkner clan appears in his fiction. J.W.T. became Bayard Sartoris, who as a young man struggles with avenging the murder of his Old Colonel-esque father in *The Unvanquished,* and whose old age is rather uncharitably portrayed in *Flags in the Dust/Sartoris*. Lizzie, Alabama (or 'Bama') and Holland inspired such salty Civil War and Victorian-era widows as Granny Rosa Millard in *The Unvanquished* and Aunt Jenny Du Pre in *Flags* and *Sanctuary*. Mammy Callie is remembered as Dilsey in *The Sound and the Fury* and as Mollie Beauchamp in *Go Down, Moses*, which is dedicated to her memory. The traumatic loss of Damuddy in 1907 to uterine cancer may be the most famous inspiration. Faulkner gave Leila's nickname to the maternal grandmother of Benjy, Caddy, Quentin and Jason Compson in *The Sound and the Fury* and borrowed memories of her funeral to initiate the children's loss of innocence.

As close as the Falkners were, patterns of strain between the generations contributed to their poet laureate's depictions of family conflict. The patriarchs could be aloof and yet controlling with their sons. When Holland Pearce died in 1849, the Old Colonel gave an infant J.W.T. to his uncle and aunt, who had taken W. C. in when he arrived penniless in Mississippi. John Wesley Thompson – whose name was handed down through three Falkner generations – and his wife, Justiana, raised the child amid strained relations with his biological father, who in a seemingly ungrateful 1855 act challenged Thompson for a seat in the state senate; W. C. lost. How family resentments affected the Young Colonel is not known, but Ripley was too small to escape his controversial father's shadow, no matter if J.W.T. joined Thompson's law firm or later partnered with a disgruntled former associate of W. C.'s. Relocating to Oxford at the relatively advanced age of 37 was the Young Colonel's symbolic declaration of independence. There he pursued his own business and civic interests, only involving himself with the family railroad as executor of his father's estate. Most significantly, J.W.T. allowed himself to be talked out of avenging W. C.'s murder. Although Southern honour demanded it, confronting his father's killer would have cost him his prestige and perpetuated the family reputation for violence.

The Young Colonel installed his eldest son in various jobs on W. C.'s railroad. Rising from brakeman and conductor to treasurer,

Murry expected to make a career in the family business, but without consulting his son J.W.T. sold off the enterprise in 1902. The reasons remain ambiguous. The railroad was still profitable, and the selling price of $75,000 undervalued the company. Most likely, the Young Colonel felt his duty to W. C.'s memory fulfilled and wished to focus on his own investments. Regardless, Murry felt betrayed and turned moody and apathetic, resenting his wife as much as his father after Maud refused to relocate to Texas, where Murry dreamed of becoming a rancher. (Accordingly, Texas in Faulkner's fiction becomes a land to which characters escape to reinvent themselves, although rarely successfully.) Moving his family to Oxford placed this third-generation Mississippi Falkner squarely under his prominent father's shadow, leaving him dependent and marking him a failure: the house in which his wife and children lived on Second South Street from 1902 to 1906 was the same one where Murry passed his own late adolescence.

Throughout his grandsons' childhood, the Young Colonel financed several businesses for Murry to support his growing family. In particular, Faulkner remembered loitering for hours at his father's livery company, where frank talk, gambling and drinking were the norm even during operating hours. 'I more or less grew up in my father's livery stable,' the writer admitted in 1946. 'Being the eldest of four boys, I escaped my mother's influence pretty easy, since my father thought it was fine for me to apprentice to the business.'[16] The brothers enjoyed hunting and fishing excursions, too, at the Falkner family cabin on the Tallahatchie River, known as the 'Club House'. When automobiles arrived in Oxford, rendering liveries superfluous, Murry drifted indifferently through various vocations, selling coal, oil and hardware. He would not find stable employment until his oldest son was nearly twenty, when the Young Colonel pulled strings to obtain him a modest position in the University of Mississippi's business office. At some point Murry began taking out his resentments on Billy, taunting him for the short stature and slight frame he inherited from his mother's side. Unlike his brothers, who were 6 feet tall and brawny like both colonels, Faulkner barely topped 5 foot 5 and 125 pounds. Murry even called his first-born 'Snake Lips' for his thin, delicate features. Faulkner responded by ignoring his father's authority and looking to the Young Colonel for affection, further feeding Murry's detachment. The generations never reconciled. Shortly before his premature death at 61, Murry boasted that he never read his famous son's writing.

The second pattern that would affect William Faulkner's life and art is his family's history of alcoholism. The Old Colonel's violence was partly fuelled by liquor; some newspapers reported he was drunk and belligerent when R. J. Thurmond fatally shot him. J.W T. and Murry suffered from drinking binges that required stays at the Keeley Institute 24 kilometres (15 mi.) south of Memphis. Opened in 1879, the facility treated alcoholism as a physical dependency rather than a moral failure, injecting patients with bichloride of gold to induce nausea and discourage alcohol intake. As children, the Falkner brothers accompanied the devout non-drinker Maud when she checked her husband into the institute.[17] In adulthood, Faulkner blamed his own alcoholic spells on artistic and financial frustrations, but he attributed Murry's to his passive, purposeless character. Accordingly, drunken fathers are a motif throughout his fiction. As with Jason Richmond Compson, the father of the doomed siblings in *The Sound and the Fury*, they represent a weakening bloodline.

Yet another pattern influencing Faulkner was the marital discord that ran through his family. As previously noted, Lizzie Falkner lived in Memphis apart from W. C. Maud, too, came from a broken home: her father, Charles Butler, abandoned his family in late 1887 when she was sixteen, stealing $3,000 in Oxford tax revenue, never to be heard from again.[18] Among the generations, only the Young Colonel and Sallie enjoyed a companionate relationship, but after her death he entered into a disastrous second marriage that ended with an embarrassing, costly $30,000 divorce. Maud and Murry, meanwhile, were fundamentally incompatible: he a college dropout, she a graduate of the Mississippi Women's College who had worked as a secretary to support her mother. As Murry withdrew, Maud dominated the Falkner home. An avid reader, she encouraged her son's interest in literature and the visual arts while strictly enforcing a Methodist upbringing. In one oft-noted episode from Faulkner's adolescence, she treated Billy's poor posture by insisting he wear a canvas-and-whalebone corset or back brace. The teenager spent two years squeezed into the contraption, disqualifying him from sports and strenuous outdoor activities. Faulkner at times resented Maud's imposing demeanour, but, unlike with Murry, he never stopped craving her approval. The pair remained close until the mother's death in 1960, only two years before the son's own.

Murry and Maud were so mismatched that their differences often tempt commentators into oversimplifying these family dynamics. Describing the couple's oldest son as 'the product of an intellectually ambitious mother and a weak, recessive father, who really preferred "manly" activities, such as drinking', biographers depict the young Faulkner as torn between loyalties: 'The boy identified with the mother's aspirations – the high value she placed on the world of books, of art, of refined things – though still longing for connection to the manly world of the father.'[19] 'Caught' or even stranded 'between the world of women and the domain of men', Faulkner elsewhere is said to have inherited 'two identities' that grew into 'the two sides of his developing creativity: the impulsive masculine side and the shaping side, which was formal, courteous, and controlled – and feminine.'[20] While there is certainly truth to such claims, the gender divisions should not be overstated. Few portraits of Murry have followed up on Joseph Blotner's suggestion, for example, that, however representative of the 'manly world', Faulkner's father was privately a man of 'poetic sensibility if not poetic practice', an unappreciated trait Blotner himself only discovered from diary entries that later family generations showed him in 1979, five years after the publication of his mammoth biography.[21] With a strong, sometimes bawdy sense of humour and a fondness for Western novels (Zane Grey in particular), Murry at the very least was more complicated than the hollow man history remembers him as. And while Maud's refinement undeniably shaped her son's artistic side, her feminine influence inspired little sympathy for femininity itself. Reserved and rarely 'physically demonstrative', Maud handed down to her son 'rules about containing and suppressing feelings of need, weakness, fear, or unhappiness' that left him ill-suited to cope with an eventual marriage to a woman who was far more expressive than her mother-in-law.[22] The stoicism Faulkner inherited from Maud also coloured his judgement of his more tempestuous female characters. Although numerous complex and sympathetic women populate his fiction, he was prone to portray emotional extremes as symptoms of hysteria or nymphomania, making the motives and impulses of more frantic creations such as Temple Drake in *Sanctuary* or Joanna Burden in *Light in August* difficult to diagnose for readers sensitive to stereotype.

The generational and domestic conflicts that shaped Faulkner's writing appear not to have influenced his behaviour much before adolescence. He was an unremarkable but not undutiful student during his earliest years of education. Upon turning twelve, he began skipping school. His truancy forced him to repeat sixth grade, but he revelled in his reputation as an idler. He also developed an interest in fashion. His fondness for skin-tight trousers and stiff collars made him appear pretentiously formal to classmates, who called him 'Count' and 'queer'. Although he played football, baseball and tennis – albeit without much distinction – friends and family noted long instances in which he retreated into lurking silences, refusing to participate in conversations but observing intently, often making others uncomfortable. When Billy did deign to speak he was likely to lie with a flagrancy that made listeners wonder if they weren't the butt of a private joke. Although Maud tried to rein in his rebellion, Faulkner knew his resemblance to the Butler side of the family made him her favourite son, and he learned how to manipulate discipline into doting. Murry, meanwhile, focused his attention on his younger children. He appeared to see in Billy what others in Oxford saw in Murry himself: proof that the Falkner lineage was in decline.

Sometime around 1910, William Falkner – still several years from adding the 'u' to his last name – began to write poetry. If his family questioned his literary bent, he simply insisted he followed in the Old Colonel's footsteps. Exactly what kind of writer he would be took a decade and a half to decide, an artistic apprenticeship notable for both its length and its waywardness. By the late 1920s when Faulkner discovered how to create 'a cosmos of [his] own' by reimagining family history and the environs of Oxford through fiction – a process he called 'sublimating the actual into apocryphal' – he was in his early thirties, already older than the ages at which his two most famous peers, F. Scott Fitzgerald and Ernest Hemingway, wrote their masterpieces.[23]

To most folks in Oxford, the literary life was an excuse to pose and posture, if only for the amusement of provoking their disapproval. Yet the teenaged Falkner was eager to hone his skills. In 1914 he took the first significant steps towards doing that when he realized that to become a writer he needed two things. He needed a mentor, and he needed a muse.

2

Birth of a Faun (1914–21)

The mentor came in the form of an Oxford supporter named Phil
Stone (1893–1967). The scion of a prominent legal and banking
family, Stone returned to his hometown after graduating from
Yale University in mid-1914 to earn a law degree at the University
of Mississippi. A devotee of modern poetry, Phil was not a writer
but an ideas man hoping to foster a Southern literary renaissance.
After learning that J.W.T. Falkner's diminutive grandson dabbled
in verse, he adopted the sixteen-year-old as a protégé and started
him on a reading regime of Greek literature, Algernon Charles
Swinburne, A. E. Housman and others. For almost fifteen years,
Stone would guide William Faulkner's fledgling career, serving
as his editor, patron and publicity agent, as well as providing a
conduit for escaping Oxford – though briefly, because Faulkner
could never stray from home for long.

As crucial as Stone's patronage was, his influence was more
biographical than artistic. Although four years Billy's elder and
much worldlier, Phil did not recognize that fiction was Faulkner's
métier. Thanks to his encouragement, Faulkner churned out
derivative verse deep into his twenties before finding his voice in
prose. Nor did Stone shepherd Faulkner towards the experimental
techniques that made him a modernist writer. Although Phil
probably introduced Billy to James Joyce's *Ulysses* (1922), no
evidence suggests he spurred Faulkner to the Joycean stream-of-
consciousness narration of which *The Sound and the Fury* is the

hallmark American example. Even Phil's part in creating Yoknapatawpha County was modest. After their friendship cooled, Stone claimed the Snopes clan was his idea and that he virtually co-wrote *Flags in the Dust/Sartoris*, though his role was more of a sounding board. Faulkner did borrow details from Phil's life to colour his fiction. Tales from the Stone family hunting camp, Stone Stop, located in an area of nearby Panola County known as the 'Big Bottom', ended up in *Go Down Moses*, most notably the memorable scene recounted in both 'The Old People' and 'The Bear' in which Ike McCaslin's face is smeared with the blood of his first kill at age twelve. (Two of Phil's great-uncles, Amodeus and Theophilus Potts, lent their quaint names to Ike's uncle and father respectively; the young lady to whom Stone lost his virginity, supposedly at the age of ten, likewise found herself immortalized in *As I Lay Dying*: Dewey Dell.)[1] But while Phil insisted he 'drilled into' Billy the importance of 'literature growing from its own natural soil', the fecund turf he described was not the same as Faulkner's 'postage stamp of native soil'.[2] Under Phil's tutelage, Faulkner didn't write about Confederate colonels, sharecroppers and hill people or terrorized blacks. Instead, he borrowed fauns, pipers, damsels and sylvan settings from literary traditions that even in 1914 seemed old and artificial.

In the end, Phil Stone's greatest gift was the assurance he gave his eager pupil. Faulkner's muse during these apprentice years – a woman he would marry in 1929 after many ups and downs – arguably exerted a more lasting literary influence by shaping his attitude towards women and marriage, although not necessarily in positive ways. Billy and Lida Estelle Oldham (1896–1972) first met as childhood playmates alongside the other Falkner brothers, cousin Sallie Wilkins and Estelle's middle sister, Melvina Victoria, or 'Tochie'. A voracious reader and sometime writer, Estelle enjoyed a special bond with Billy that by early adolescence made a romance between them seem as fated as any literary love story. Indeed, a legend Estelle narrated to a reporter in 1951 and then repeated to biographer Joseph

A teenaged William Faulkner, *c.* 1914, around the time aspiring lawyer Phil Stone became his mentor and his childhood playmate Lida Estelle Oldham his muse. The fashion-conscious Faulkner garnered a reputation in Oxford as a dandy.

Blotner claims that she first spotted Faulkner at seven as he rode a pony past her window. 'See that little boy?' she supposedly declared to a nursemaid. 'I'm going to marry him when I grow up.'[3]

If the story sounds too good to be true – it repeats a fable the Old Colonel told about meeting his second wife, Lizzie, when he arrived in Mississippi[4] – it nevertheless suggests the theatrical flair the couple shared. Their relationship intensified around the same time Faulkner met Stone, as Estelle returned to Oxford after an unhappy year at a Virginia finishing school. Strict social barriers prevented them from becoming more than platonic friends, however. Estelle's parents, Lemuel and Lida Oldham, liked Faulkner personally but did not consider him an appropriate suitor, especially after he dropped out of high school in either late 1915 or early 1916. The

Oldhams were Oxford elite; Lem enjoyed a remunerative career as a district-court clerk and had been awarded the honorary title of Major, while Lida, a talented pianist, hosted social clubs in a home even grander than J.W.T. Falkner's Big Place. Murry and Maud were not part of their social circle – Murry's downward career trajectory and drinking made the Falkners déclassé.

A far more acceptable match for Estelle was a fraternity brother of Phil Stone's named Cornell Franklin. He courted the Oldhams' daughter from Honolulu, where he was soon named assistant district attorney. Franklin was one of many gentlemen callers – the vivacious Estelle had a reputation as Oxford's most eligible 'speed', or 'fast girl'.

Neither Phil nor Estelle appreciated the other's importance to Faulkner's development. Stone would insist 'there was no one but me with whom William Faulkner could discuss his literary plans and hopes and his technical trials and aspirations', eliding Estelle's presence in these 'formative years'.[5] Privately, he was even more dismissive, saying she 'was not worth a damn to anybody and never would be, but that she always had lived off the fat of the land and always would.'[6] To Estelle, Stone's support was financial, not artistic. In reality, each played a distinct role. If Phil was Billy's teacher, Estelle was his secret sharer or ideal audience. Faulkner's attachment to his muse was erotic (though not sexual), masochistic and safe – the first because the pair traded poems full of heightened emotions and sensuous language; the second because other men's attention let him play the part of the dejected lover demanded by the Romantic tradition he wrote in; and the third because the Oldhams' disapproval prevented the relationship from becoming too adult too soon. Stone provided Faulkner a literary education, but Estelle supplied him literary material. The one helped him discover forms of expression; the other gave him a content to express.

Phil and Estelle were not Billy's only early allies. Through Stone, he met the poet and future novelist Stark Young (1881–1963), then

Oxford's most celebrated literary son. A professor at Amherst College who would go on to edit *Theatre Arts Magazine* before serving as drama critic for *The New Republic* through the late 1940s, Young critiqued Faulkner's poems whenever he visited family in Mississippi. In 1916 Faulkner also met Ben Wasson (1899–1982). A dozen years later Wasson would serve as Faulkner's literary agent after rescuing *Flags in the Dust* from oblivion when the publisher of his initial two novels unexpectedly rejected it. For now, Ben provided a sympathetic ear for Billy's embryonic ideas of art.

As often as with these literary intimates, Faulkner was spotted in the company of the town drunk. One day he might promenade the square wearing an expensive suit purchased on credit from his favorite Memphis clothier, Phil A. Halle; the next he might turn up in baggy trousers and worn brogues looking haggard and hungover. Wasson's posthumously published memoir suggests how Oxford considered Faulkner an aimless loafer: 'He's not a student and don't, so far's anybody knows, do anything,' an Ole Miss senior explains when Ben arrives at college. 'Lives off his family . . . Shoots craps. Drinks moonshine whiskey when he can get it. Dabbles in things, they say.'[7] At the Young Colonel's insistence, Faulkner trained as a bookkeeper at the First National Bank of Oxford, which J.W.T. founded in 1910. As Faulkner later boasted, he reported to the office mainly to pilfer his grandfather's corn liquor, then framed the janitor for the theft. Soon after he quit, his first publications appeared in *Ole Miss*, the university annual. A trio of drawings featuring dancing couples demonstrated he had inherited Maud and grandmother Leila's illustration skills. The artwork also suggested the influence of Aubrey Beardsley (1872–1898), a British decadent who sparked controversy in the *fin de siècle* Art Nouveau era with his erotically charged illustrations for Oscar Wilde's *Salomé*. Occasionally, Faulkner even dressed like Beardsley, donning a black cape, walking stick and British accent. Although this decadent phase was short-lived, odd, out-of-place references to Beardsley crop up in later fictions. Most curious is one appearing in *Light in August*, when he describes the 'wild throes' of Joanna Burden's nymphomania as shifting her body into 'such formally erotic attitudes and gestures as a Beardsley of the time of Petronius might have drawn.'[8]

Faulkner could get away with such eccentricities, but Estelle was bound by convention. In 1917 her parents discovered her dating a man of mixed blood and insisted she marry Cornell Franklin before she shamed the family. (The incident inspired 1934's 'Elly', which Faulkner adapted from a story his wife attempted.) Estelle resisted the marriage, even hiding the engagement ring her fiancé posted from Hawaii and blaming the houseboy for stealing it. In his highly novelized biography of Faulkner, Stephen B. Oates depicts the even more desperate measure she took to avoid wedding Franklin:

> Estelle came to Billy in tears. Her parents expected her to accept the ring and marry Cornell. 'I supposed I *am* engaged to Cornell now,' she said, 'but I'm ready to elope with you.'
>
> What should [Billy] do? He was sure he loved Estelle; he did not want to lose her. But he did not want them to run away like cowards. He was the grandson of Colonel William Clark Falkner. They must do this the correct way. 'No,' he told her, 'we'll have to get your father's consent.'[9]

Needless to say, the Oldhams did not consent, and the couple did not elope. Oates's depiction of Faulkner's devotion to family honour seems overdramatic here; no other source claims W. C.'s example influenced his reaction to Estelle's plea. Yet the passage differs only in the flagrancy of its licence to presume the twenty-year-old's feelings about the situation. In nearly every depiction of Faulkner's career, Estelle's marriage to Franklin on 18 April 1918 is depicted as the decisive, devastating event of his youth. Most of these accounts quote his brother John Faulkner's 1963 memoir, *My Brother Bill: An Affectionate Reminiscence*: 'His world went to pieces,' John claims.[10]

Other versions speak of romantic 'rejection' and 'betrayal', as if Estelle threw Faulkner over for Franklin. In reality, she ceded to an arranged marriage.

Equally interesting is how these accounts portray Estelle's loss as influencing Faulkner's artistic development. Brother John, for example, claims the marriage ended his older sibling's interest in the visual arts. 'Bill never drew again,' he says, implying the 'devastation' turned Faulkner towards the written word, his true medium.[11] Yet William Faulkner did continue drawing, contributing several more sketches to *Ole Miss* and illustrating self-bound booklets for the next few years, including several presented to Estelle as gifts.

In truth, Faulkner's exact feelings remain a mystery. He presented Estelle with a poem called 'A Song': 'Even though she choose to ignore me, / And all love of me to deny, / There is naught then behind or before me – / I can die.'[12] The verse is so mannered it reads more like a literary exercise than a profession of hurt – which it essentially was, given that Faulkner translated the lines from an obscure French song called 'Obstination'. No diaries or journals from 1918 voice his immediate grief. Faulkner never recorded his pain in a ledger as F. Scott Fitzgerald did when, at nineteen, he described overhearing a wealthy relative of his adolescent love Ginevra King say of him, 'Poor boys should not expect to marry rich girls' – a slight the author of *The Great Gatsby* revisited in story after story about middle-class men trying to prove themselves worthy of upper-crust women.[13] Nor did Faulkner brag in correspondence of curing rejection with 'a course of booze and other women' as Ernest Hemingway did in 1919 after receiving a Dear John letter from Agnes von Kurowsky, the nurse who treated the injuries he suffered as a Red Cross volunteer on the Italian front.[14] Like Fitzgerald, Hemingway repeatedly revisited his jilting in fiction, sometimes punishing versions of himself with gonorrhoea for falling in love (as in 'A Very Short Story'), sometimes killing off the woman who dumped him (as in *A Farewell to Arms*). Faulkner was never so revealing, neither in private nor in fiction.

Instead, as Judith L. Sensibar notes, chatty letters to Maud written before and after Estelle's wedding are 'high-spirited and lively', in no way reflecting a 'distraught, rejected suitor'.[15] For Sensibar, the lack of melancholy or anger suggests losing his muse may not have wounded Bill at all. The fiction arguably corroborates this; in Faulkner the anguish of romantic attachments is usually sharpest not when a man loses a woman but when he *wins* her, as Faulkner would when Estelle later returned to him, divorced, and they married in 1929. From this perspective, Bill's insistence on obtaining the Oldhams' blessing may have been less about respecting tradition than finding a convenient out: he could declare his love for Estelle knowing that because her parents would never approve their union he did not have to prove it. For Frederick R. Karl, such evasion was necessary to preserve his freedom to write: 'Marriage at this juncture would have been destructive to [his] subsequent career. While we cannot predict what he would have done – working, perhaps, in J.W.T.'s bank, scribbling on the side, fathering a child, having family responsibilities, becoming against his will part of Oxford's growth – we do know he needed very badly those apprenticeship years.'[16]

Another biographer, David Minter, goes even further, suggesting that Faulkner *wanted* to lose Estelle: 'William appears almost to have desired his fate – to have decided to know for himself the unrequited love of which he had been making poetry.'[17] In his view, feeling jilted was necessary if Faulkner's verse were to express authentic emotion instead of imitating his literary role models. Other critics dismiss such speculation, insisting, as Philip Weinstein does, that Faulkner compartmentalized his emotions so his letters 'virtually never reveal his more troubling thoughts or feelings': Bill and Estelle's 'failed elopement was indeed a crisis, with reverberations for Faulkner's life and art that would endure indefinitely.'[18] Yet as Weinstein admits, he can no more prove his interpretation than other commentators can. With Faulkner, innermost emotions are always frustratingly elusive.

What is known for certain is that Bill left Oxford before Estelle walked the aisle. Relocating to New Haven, Connecticut, where Phil Stone had returned to Yale for another law degree, he worked for the Winchester Repeating Arms Company filling munitions orders for the First World War, which the United States had entered the previous year. Eager to serve as a combat aviator, he waited in vain for a draft letter from the u.s. Army Signal Corps. His height and weight fell far below minimum standards, however. His only alternative was to enlist with the British Royal Air Force, which operated a pilot training camp in Canada. According to Phil Stone, who also hoped to join the RAF, enlistees had to prove some connection to British citizenry, which supposedly led the pair to hatch an elaborate (and rather far-fetched) scheme. Inserting a 'u' into his surname, Faulkner is said to have passed himself off as the son of an expatriate from Finchley, Middlesex, whose mother had migrated to Mississippi. To sell the ruse he spoke in a strenuously rehearsed British accent and forged a letter of recommendation from a non-existent religious benefactor. How much of this story is embellished remains unclear. Faulkner's letters home tell a more mundane story of meeting a Canadian lieutenant through Stone who referred him to the RAF's New York recruiting office, armed with recommendations from boarding house friends with whom he and Phil played bridge (one of whom just happened to be British).[19]

Whatever, if any, deceptions were necessary worked, though the ultimate plan failed. Faulkner reported for duty to the Jesse Ketchum School in Toronto in July 1918 as a pilot cadet, but the closest he came to an actual plane was practising ignition by 'spinning the propeller of a bolted-down motor inside a tin shed'.[20] Most of his time was spent in the classroom taking notes. This setback did not stop him from fabricating tales. When the Armistice was announced on 11 November, only four months into his training, Faulkner concocted an elaborate story about crashing a plane into a hangar and dangling upside down with a broken nose until he was rescued.

Discharged shortly before Christmas, he returned to Oxford sporting a custom-ordered officer's uniform he was not authorized to wear, affecting a limp. As his brother John remembered, Bill wore 'what we called an overseas cap, a monkey cap that was only issued to our men if they served overseas'. On his breast were a pair of unearned pilots' wings that if anyone bothered to look bore the insignia of the Royal Flying Corps, the RAF's previous name, changed some months before Faulkner even enlisted. Strolling Oxford in his uniform, Bill accepted salutes from actual veterans of the war who 'turned up their noses at our own [U.S. Army] officers who had not been over'. [21] Faulkner did nothing to correct the misperception that he had seen combat. Even more striking, no one called out his audacity. As Ben Wasson recalled, 'None of us who listened to his purported experiences believed half of them . . . "That's the Count for you. Even a war doesn't stop him from telling tall stories," said those that heard him.' [22]

Tolerating a military imposter today seems unimaginable; one marvels in particular at the reaction of Faulkner's other brother, Murry Charles or 'Jack', a Marine who came home in March 1919 with very real shrapnel wounds in his skull and leg from the Battle of the Argonne Forest. While Jack's own memoir, *The Falkners of Mississippi* (1967), states clearly that Bill never saw combat, it reprints a long story told in the older brother's voice of his spurious crash. Jack winks at the fabulation without a hint of indignation or outrage. [23] Nobody, it appears, expected the truth from William Faulkner. For at least two decades to come he spun barely credible variations of his fantasy crash and injury. A 1931 *New Yorker* profile reports that, 'In 1915 he enlisted in the Canadian air force and went to France. He crashed behind his own lines. He was hanging upside down in his plane with his legs broken when an ambulance got to

William Faulkner returned to Oxford from pilot training with the Royal Air Force in Toronto, sporting an officer's uniform he was not authorized to wear and spinning stories about injuries sustained in a plane crash.

him. He heard one of the men say: "He's dead all right," but had strength enough to deny this. After he recovered he transferred to the American air force.'[24] The *New Yorker* clearly had not established its vaunted fact-checking department yet.

But while Faulkner's flagrant inconsistencies seemed to dare someone to debunk his war stories, his habit of telling multiple versions of events would, strangely enough, become a key narrative technique in works such as *Absalom, Absalom!* 'This overlapping of stories, some of them close to the truth, some outrageous,' writes Frederick Karl, 'links with his strategies of relaying information in his major novels. A tale which is told is retold in manifold ways, until the original story has vanished, and what remains is an elaboration which may or may not be close to the truth.'[25]

There is a simpler explanation for why Faulkner indulged in so many 'elaborations' upon returning home: Oxford in 1919 offered little else to do but tell stories. Without employment prospects or any real pressure from Maud and Murry to support himself, Bill reunited with Phil Stone, now home from Yale for good and working in his family's law offices. A heavy gambler and drinker, Stone invited Faulkner on jaunts to Clarksdale, Memphis and the Gulf Coast, introducing him to a colourful array of roadhouse denizens, including bootleggers, brothel owners and borderline underworld figures. One small-time gangster with the euphonious name Reno De Vaux dubbed Bill 'The Poet' and showed him around the red-light district of New Orleans. On another journey into the Tenderloin of Memphis (its red-light district), Faulkner heard disturbing tales about a violent punk nicknamed 'Popeye' for his rubbery facial features. A decade later, Neil Kerens Pumphrey would inspire the sadistic villain of *Sanctuary*, Faulkner's commercial breakthrough. The real-life Pumphrey probably did not rape a female student with a corncob as the fictional Popeye does, but his rumoured sexual proclivities were the talk of local whorehouses, introducing Faulkner to perversions he later forced readers to peek at.[26]

Amid these journeys came initially promising proof that Faulkner was not wasting his time writing. In the summer of 1919 *The New Republic* accepted his loose adaptation of the Stephen Mallarmé poem 'L'Après-midi d'un faune' (The Afternoon of a Faun). The third line included a mildly salacious reference to a maiden's 'lascivious dreaming knees', but for the most part the rhyme scheme and point of view felt inhibited, as if, like the poem's protagonist, the poet suffered a 'nameless wish to go / To some far silent midnight noon' but didn't yet know how to get there.[27]

Despite these faults, Faulkner's apprenticeship in poetry was far from fruitless. Verse writing provided him a love for ornate language that would continue throughout his fiction, particularly with word choices such as 'myriad', 'sibilant', 'suspirant' and 'implacable'.

These abstractions, when juxtaposed against more concrete terms (or tools) specific to rural Mississippi life ('trace chains', 'froe and maul'), elevated his prose above the merely realistic, creating a supercharged world that conveys above all else a sense of having been imagined instead of merely transcribed. The contrast would annoy some contemporaries (Hemingway), win the admiration of others (Thomas Wolfe) and be copied by a few more (John Steinbeck). The frisson between idioms is key to the way Faulknerian rhetoric swoops and soars, rising from the vernacular to the oracular and back, often in a single breath. This quality would not become the trademark it is had Faulkner abandoned poetry for prose at 21 or 22. Without it, his novels might have ended up as leeringly one-dimensional as Erskine Caldwell's *Tobacco Road* (1932) or *God's Little Acre* (1933), two contemporaneous novels that truly delight in demeaning their characters, as Faulkner's early detractors accused him of doing. Whether the tone is biblical or the effect hallucinatory, Faulkner's poetic fervour at its best imbues his prose with a humid, evangelical intensity. (At its worst, it turns into self-parody, as any writer's distinct style will.)

Equally important was the figure of the faun. It provided an image of extreme innocence that influenced the portrait of later characters like the vulnerable Benjy Compson in *The Sound and the Fury.* The faun also provided the basis for bruised romantics such as Horace Benbow in *Sanctuary* and Charlotte Rittenmeyer in *If I Forget Thee, Jerusalem* (or *The Wild Palms*, as it was known up to 1990.) These are figures who feel trapped in the chasm between passion and reality. The faun figure shortly evolved into another persona the young Faulkner dabbled with in verse. Pierrot, a melancholy clown character drawn from Italian *commedia dell'arte*, provided the writer with a mask for channelling his awareness that art was a more satisfying realm of existence than the humdrum world of Oxford.

Because *The New Republic* was a national magazine, and because Faulkner was paid for his contribution (all of $15), his spirits were high in 1919. The acceptance coincided with a visit from Estelle, her first return to Oxford since her wedding. As she and Bill reconnected, Estelle confided her marriage was troubled, despite a newborn daughter, Melvina Victoria or 'Cho-Cho', who travelled with her mother. In response, Faulkner dashed off a sequence of unrequited love poems collected in his first book, *The Marble Faun* (1924).

That September, at his parents' insistence, Faulkner enrolled at the University of Mississippi through a programme admitting military veterans whether they had a high-school diploma or not. He attended classes almost as infrequently as he had in high school, embarrassing Murry, who served as a secretary to the institution's president, a job that provided the Falkners with on-campus living in a former fraternity house. The only aspect of university life that interested Bill was the extracurricular literary and drama clubs. In his freshman year he published roughly a dozen poems in the school newspaper, *The Mississippian*, as well as his first short story, 'Landing in Luck', a version of his plane-crash fantasy. A year later

Faulkner briefly studied at the University of Mississippi in 1919–20, but his interests were more extracurricular. This photo of the local Sigma Alpha Epsilon chapter, to which the writer (far right) pledged, shows how short he was compared to his peers.

he composed a play called *The Marionettes* for a thespian troupe
Ben Wasson had formed. Despite introducing the Pierrot character,
it didn't read well and went unproduced. By then Faulkner had
officially withdrawn from classes, though he remained a campus
fixture. The student newspaper parodied his poetry and caricatured
his affectations, while behind his back classmates called him 'Count
No 'Count'.

By 23, Faulkner could not help but notice his generation's arrival
on the national literary scene. Fitzgerald's debut novel, *This Side of
Paradise*, sparked debates in 1920 over post-war youth's manners
and mores. Edna St Vincent Millay – whose verse play *Aria da Capo*
Faulkner reviewed for *The Mississippian* in early 1922 – published
A Few Figs from Thistles. Its opening selection, 'First Fig', announced
in four sharp lines a new generational ethos: 'My candle burns at
both ends; / It will not last the night; / But ah, my foes, and oh, my
friends – / It gives a lovely light!'[28] Millay's sometime lover Edmund
Wilson was a taste-making editor at *Vanity Fair*, where Dorothy
Parker was already a sardonic contributor. And while John Dos
Passos's first book, *One Man's Initiation: 1917*, garnered little attention
that year, Dos Passos had already completed *Three Soldiers* (1921),
whose uncompromising realism would set the template for imminent
novels about the First World War.

Faulkner's most notable achievement in 1920 was to win a campus
creative writing contest. When the $10 prize ran out, he painted
houses for spending money. Gossip circulated that he had fathered
illegitimate children. Bored and stymied, Faulkner had started the
rumour himself.

3

Foaling Season (1921–7)

Stark Young, the poet who had been informally critiquing Faulkner's early literary efforts for years, provided a solution for Faulkner's stagnation in autumn 1921 by inviting him to stay in New York City. As in 1918, Estelle was a major reason for leaving Oxford. In the summer of 1921 she and her daughter returned home a second time, and Faulkner presented her with a hand-bound poetry collection called *Vision in Spring*. Several passages borrowed from T. S. Eliot's 'The Love Song of J. Alfred Prufrock' (1915), suggesting Faulkner was bringing his Pierrot character into the twentieth century, infusing its Romantic melancholy with contemporary anxieties over alienation and personal insignificance. 'Who am I,' Pierrot asks, 'who am I / To stretch my soul out rigid across the sky?'[1] But if the psychology felt modern, the influences – including not only Eliot but Conrad Aiken, whose *Turns and Movies* (1916) Faulkner reviewed in *The Mississippian* in this same era – remained too obvious. Estelle praised the poems anyway, even pencilling in a title to one unnamed selection as if acting out the role of secret collaborator. Yet she also broke bad news: Cornell Franklin had accepted a diplomatic post in Shanghai, China. This would be her last visit to Oxford for a long while.

Young's invitation not only soothed Bill's disappointment but led to an important professional connection. Stark's landlord, Elizabeth Prall, managed the Lord and Taylor Doubleday bookstore on New York's Fifth Avenue and hired Bill as a clerk. She grew fond and protective of her new employee, whose eccentricities didn't irk her cosmopolitan customers as they did hometown folks. Three years later, Prall married Sherwood Anderson and introduced Faulkner to the author of *Winesburg, Ohio* (1919), who significantly aided his career. While working for her in late 1921 Bill rented an apartment in bohemian Greenwich Village. In a pattern repeated throughout his life, he made little effort to affiliate with the reigning clique of writers that included Edna St Vincent Millay, Eugene O'Neill and Max Eastman. Faulkner preferred to write and drink alone.

Worried his protégé might find a new mentor in New York, Phil Stone conspired almost immediately to bring him home. At Phil's urging, Lem Oldham arranged for a federal patronage job in Oxford paying $1,800 per year. Thus began the unlikeliest of William Faulkner's many careers when, in December 1921, he was named postmaster at the University of Mississippi. For nearly three years he reported to the campus's brick post office to neglect his duties as brazenly as he earlier had at Grandfather Falkner's bank. One day, university officials might find catalogues requested by prospective students piled in a corner, unstamped and unsent; the next, a customer might discover the office closed so Faulkner could play golf or gallivant in his new Model T, which he souped up and painted yellow. Patrons catching him on the clock might wait at the window while he wrote poems at his desk. Other times they watched helplessly as he played bridge or mah-jongg with his brother Jack and pals hired as clerks. Magazines showed up in mailboxes long after their cover date; other deliveries simply disappeared. As one 1931 Phil Stone quote that no biographer can resist citing puts it, William Faulkner 'made for the damndest postmaster the World has ever seen'.[2]

The post may have suffered from indifference, but his writing did not. In 1922 Faulkner attempted fiction for the first time since his debut story 'Landing in Luck' three years earlier. Published in the 10 March edition of *The Mississippian*, 'The Hill' was a short but important exercise about a labourer peering upon a valley after a day of 'strife against the forces of nature to gain bread and clothing and a place to sleep'.[3] While mentioning the 'nymphs and fauns' that populated his poetry, the piece is Faulkner's initial attempt at picturing the Mississippi landscape and the dusty hamlet later known as Frenchman's Bend, the eventual setting in southeastern Yoknapatawpha County for significant portions of *As I Lay Dying*, *Sanctuary* and sundry Snopes tales. 'The Hill' is also Faulkner's early try at a prose-poem, a genre that suited his poetic inclinations well, allowing him to dilate into the dream reveries of favourite poets like John Keats without being confined within rigid metres and rhyme schemes. He would return to this form with 'Carcassonne' (1931), 'All the Dead Pilots', the prefatory chapters of *Requiem for a Nun* (1951) and the late non-fiction essay 'Mississippi' (1954), among other efforts.

Another breakthrough prose piece, 'Adolescence', explores what became two recurring plots, youth's loss of innocence and the expulsion from nature's Garden of Eden. When Juliet Bunden and Lee Hollowell skinny dip in the woods, Juliet's grandmother assumes they are sexually active and ignites a conflict that culminates in revenue officers killing both teenagers' fathers, who are moonshiners. Juliet is the first of many Faulkner females stigmatized for their sexuality; her surname anticipates those of Dewey Dell Bundren in *As I Lay Dying* and Joanna Burden in *Light in August*. The story's idyllic swimming scenes reappear in his first novel, *Soldiers' Pay* (1926), and *The Sound and the Fury*, where they represent children's blissful unawareness of sin and shame. 'Adolescence' also represents Faulkner's first extensive use of vernacular, including rural dialect and epithets decidedly not borrowed from his poetic role models ('slut', for instance).[4] As with Faulkner's other apprentice works, Phil Stone's legal secretaries typed the manuscript, which must have made for interesting office conversation. Although 'Adolescence' remained unpublished in Faulkner's lifetime, it was a formative stepping stone.

Amid these efforts, Bill's beloved grandfather, J.W.T. Falkner, suffered a fatal heart attack. At seventy-three, the Young Colonel was wracked by physical ailments, deafness and alcoholism. His decline would haunt Faulkner half a decade later as he began fictionalizing family history in *Flags in the Dust/Sartoris*. A few months after the March 1922 funeral, Bill consoled himself by striking up a useful literary association. *The Double Dealer*, an emerging New Orleans arts magazine, accepted his poem 'A Portrait'. Modelling itself on H. L. Mencken's glitzy *The Smart Set*, the *Dealer* melded modernism and Southern literature to refute Mencken's bruising dismissal of the South as a cultural wasteland in 'The Sahara of the Bozart' (1917). Nothing in 'Portrait' was especially modernist or Southern, but founders Julius Weis Friend and Basil Thompson wanted to discover young, unknown writers. The same issue Faulkner debuted in featured a poem called 'Ultimately' by Ernest M. Hemingway, 'a young American living in Paris'.

The acceptance inspired Faulkner to visit the Crescent City and introduce himself at Friend and Thompson's offices in the French Quarter. Phil Stone had always discouraged him from joining literary coteries, but Faulkner needed a wider community of support than his mentor could provide. Invited to a party for *Dealer* contributors, he sat in awkward silence, pulling occasional plugs of whisky to soothe his insecurities. When the subject turned to Shakespeare, he blurted out, 'I could write a play like *Hamlet* if I wanted to!'[5] The chutzpah initially amused Friend and Thompson, who liked their writers irreverent and iconoclastic. As time went on, Faulkner's alternately taciturn and braggadocious presence chafed. 'I recall [him] sitting silent and relaxed,' Friend would later say, 'and then at other times talking endlessly, talking about himself and his talents.'[6]

Those talents only slowly gained traction. Writing competed with several diversions for attention. Faulkner was a talented golfer and often closed the post office early to play local links. He also served an unlikely stint as scoutmaster for his youngest brother Dean's Boy Scout troop. For two years he took children camping and taught them woodland skills, a service he both enjoyed and excelled at. He might have volunteered for much longer had his reputation for drinking not upset parents and clergy, who pressured him into resigning.

In mid-1923 Faulkner decided he was ready to publish a book. He submitted a revision of *Vision in Spring* to the Four Seas Company, a Boston-based publisher with an impressive backlist that included Gertrude Stein's *Three Lives* (1909), William Carlos Williams's *Al Que Quiere!* (1917) and *Sour Grapes* (1921), Imagist poet Richard Aldington's *Images of War* (1919) and several volumes by Conrad Aiken, whose work probably led Bill to the imprimatur. What Faulkner didn't realize was that Four Seas was a vanity press and that even famous modernists like Stein and Williams had to pay their own printing costs. After waiting five months without a response, the frustrated poet wrote the company only to learn his acceptance letter had gone missing in the post – no little irony (or karma, perhaps) for Mississippi's most negligent postmaster. He was also irked to discover Four Seas wanted $400 to publish his book. Faulkner declined, claiming he was broke.

A few months later, the Four Seas Company received another letter from Mississippi, this one signed not by William Faulkner but by Phil Stone. June 1924 marked ten years to the month that Phil began coaching his protégé, prodding as often as prepping him for success. As one Oxford acquaintance remembered, 'To say that Phil "encouraged" Bill . . . is a gross understatement. He cajoled, browbeat, and swore at him.' 'If you want to be somebody,' Stone lectured Faulkner, 'you've got to do it yourself.'[7] If manufacturing costs were all that stood in the way of Faulkner becoming a real writer, Phil would foot the bill. Unhappy with *Vision in Spring*, Faulkner decided the cycle of pastoral poems composed in 1919

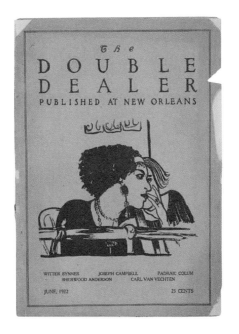

The cover of the June 1922 issue of *The Double Dealer*, which featured poems by both Faulkner and Ernest Hemingway on the same page. Published in New Orleans, the magazine was a crucial training ground for Faulkner as he moved from poetry to prose.

after *The New Republic* accepted 'L'Apres-midi d'un faune' made a stronger artistic statement. In reality, the two manuscripts weren't so different. Both featured laments from a melancholy observer stranded between life and art; whether the figure was the faun or Pierrot was less important than the overall impression of 'a sad, bound prisoner' who, unable to escape alienation, 'marble-bound must ever be'.[8]

Several elements made the eventual volume more curious than the poems it contained. Faulkner borrowed his title, *The Marble Faun*, from Nathaniel Hawthorne's final novel (1860), then insisted to friends he had never heard of that book. The claim did no favours to his bid to be taken seriously as a writer. Nor did the preface Phil contributed. 'These are primarily the poems of youth and a simple heart,' wrote Stone. 'They also have the defects of youth – youth's impatience, unsophistication and immaturity.'[9] The condescending tone appears not to have offended Faulkner. He deferred to Stone on all aspects of *The Marble Faun*'s production and marketing. Phil even arranged for an author photo to be taken in Memphis. As per his instructions, it posed Bill as a modern-day Lord Byron, his shirt collar open and his aspiring gaze cast upward. The only aspect of the collection Faulkner seemed particularly invested in was the author note. 'Born in Mississippi in 1897', it read. 'Great-grandson of Col. W. C. Faulkner, CSA, author of "The White Rose of Memphis".' Whether the 'u' that crept into the Old Colonel's surname was a typo or Bill's way of claiming his ancestor from his family is unknown. The unusual biography ended by dating the poems back to 'April, May, June 1919', hinting the author had already outgrown the contents.

Which Faulkner effectively had. As scattered reviews appeared he could not help but agree with the Memphis *Commercial Appeal*, which asked, 'What has William Faulkner to offer that his master [Swinburne] has not said better?'[10] As if admitting 'not much', Faulkner a few months later published an essay called 'Verse Old and Nascent' that confessed his attachment to verse was immature. As a teenager he wrote poetry 'to complete a youthful gesture . . . of being "different" in a small town' and 'for the purpose of furthering various philanderings' – an apparent boast, since nothing suggests writing paved the way for sexual 'concupiscence' or served as 'an accompaniment to consummation'. The forms and styles he imitated gave him 'a flexible vessel in which I might put my own vague emotional shapes without breaking them', but now he wondered if 'this age, this decade' was 'impossible for the creation of poetry'.[11] The 'pilgrimage' Faulkner traces doesn't end by declaring allegiance to the novel or the short story, but a crossroads is implied. After *The Marble Faun*, verse increasingly became a private gesture, a craft practised for personal satisfaction or as gifts to friends. Interestingly, he sometimes wrote it to woo women, presumably with the intent of 'furthering various philanderings'.

Autumn 1924 saw another transition. Patron complaints about the university post office forced the regional inspector to open a formal investigation, including the charge that Faulkner had 'a book being printed at the present time, the greater part of which was written while on duty at the post-office'. When the inquiry found Bill guilty of dereliction and not embezzling or stealing post, he was allowed to resign without fear of prosecution. He boasted to friends that, while he might die 'at the beck and call of folks with money', he would never again 'be at the beck and call of every son of a bitch who's got two cents to buy a stamp.'[12]

He could be cavalier because, although he didn't know it, he was about to become a professional writer. During a November trip to New Orleans, Faulkner reconnected with Elizabeth Prall. His former bookstore manager introduced him to her new husband, Sherwood Anderson, who was at the peak of his influence and generous in helping fellow writers. Anderson had given a prominent endorsement to Gertrude Stein by contributing a preface to her *Geography and Plays* (1922), and within the year his blurb on the cover of Hemingway's *In Our Time* would establish that innovative short-story collection as a worthy heir to his own *Winesburg, Ohio*. In January 1925 Faulkner moved to the Crescent City, hoping to arrange an extended jaunt to Europe, and he and Anderson spent significant time together through the coming spring.

The older writer's initial affection for Faulkner is evident in his semi-fictional sketch 'A Meeting South', which appeared in *The Dial* that April. Under the alias 'David', the poet is described as a quintessential Southerner, frail and decayed, never far from his liquor, yet warm and convivial despite his tragic aura. The aspiring author is also an inveterate storyteller, spinning tales about a family plantation in Alabama and overseas combat adventures. Anderson slyly wonders whether the stories are true: 'He told me the story of his ill-fortune, a crack up in an airplane, with a gentlemanly smile on his very delicate, thin lips. Such things happened. He might well have been speaking of another.'[13] As he had in 1919, Faulkner passed himself off as a wounded veteran, walking with a stiff limp and claiming he carried a metal plate in his head. As 'A Meeting South' reveals, his New Orleans friends no more called him out on his blatant fibbing than Oxford residents had.

Remaining in New Orleans until July 1925, Faulkner wrote more than he had in the previous ten years combined. To *The Double Dealer* he contributed verse, critical essays and sketches, including an impressionistic, eleven-part prose-poem called 'New Orleans'. Writing in the distinct voices of a priest, a longshoreman, a beggar, a tourist and others, Faulkner experimented with the technique of interior monologue that Joyce had made fashionable among modernists. For the *New Orleans Times-Picayune* he wrote an additional sixteen glimpses of the city, honing his observational eye by depicting sights unseen in his poetry, including poverty and public intoxication. (Unlike *The Double Dealer*, the *Times-Picayune* actually paid.)

At the same time, Faulkner cranked out short stories. 'Nympholepsy' recalled 'The Hill', exploring labourers' inability to escape life's drudgery through dream-visions. 'Frankie and Johnny', a tale about a petty gangster and his moll, drew from his fascination with the underworld. 'Don Giovanni' was a comedy about a would-be lothario whose formulas for seducing women are utter failures. During these months Faulkner even proposed an epistolary collaboration with Anderson called 'Al Jackson' about a half-man, half-alligator. The attempt at a Cajun tall tale fizzled after only two instalments. Unlike his New Orleans sketches, these stories went unpublished, but their varied themes and settings reveal how broadly – how frantically, perhaps – Faulkner attempted subjects and styles in fiction now that he no longer considered himself primarily a poet.

As if these efforts weren't enough, the first half of 1925 saw Faulkner take up the novel. That spring he went uncharacteristically incommunicado with Phil Stone, who prodded him for news. 'WHAT'S THE MATTER?' Phil wired from Oxford. 'DO YOU HAVE A MISTRESS?' Faulkner's reply: 'YES. AND SHE'S 30,000 WORDS LONG.'[14] This was as close as Faulkner would come to announcing his embrace of the genre. Thirty years later he claimed he tried his hand at a novel for 'the sake of writing', as if it were a larkish challenge rather than a conscientious shift in career path. He stuck with it because, to his delight, he 'discovered writing could be fun'.[15] Yet Faulkner knew that long-form fiction was the medium that would garner him the most attention. Rightly or wrongly, he considered the short story a commercial genre, one turned to when in financial need. For a writer with an expansive imagination, the novel offered more possibilities for scope, experimentation and design. Besides, no one in his New Orleans circle had mastered the genre, not even Anderson. As Faulkner wrote in a *Dallas Morning News* essay that April, his new mentor was best at 'sharp episodic phases of people', but his 'halting questioning manner' floundered in larger contexts. No one could write a better tale than Anderson's 'I'm a Fool' ('the best short story in America'), but the abundant defects of his novels *Poor White* and *Many Marriages* made the form a competitive arena – and Faulkner was eminently competitive.[16]

His plot was audacious for a writer flagrantly faking war injuries. As if daring those who knew he had never 'gone over', Faulkner began the manuscript with a disgruntled cadet complaining the Armistice dashed his dreams of aviation heroism, just as it had Bill's. Originally called 'Mayday', the story centred upon a combat veteran, Lieutenant Donald Mahon, who sparks a crisis in his hometown of Charlestown, Georgia, when he returns from the war disfigured by a plane crash. As Mahon's deformities alternately excite compassion and revulsion, characters reveal they are either paralyzed by grief, escaping through dissolution, or, in the case of Mahon's Episcopalian rector father, clinging to spiritual banalities.

As Cleanth Brooks has argued, Faulkner built his storyline upon a set of diagrammatic oppositions.[17] Mahon is a version of the Fisher King myth Eliot popularized in *The Waste Land*, an impotent god whose death will not redeem the land. His counterpoint is one of Faulkner's strangest characters, Janarius Jones, a lustful 'fat satyr' who spouts pretentious literary and philosophical quotations. Two women from Mahon's pre-war life form a second dialectic. The servant girl Emmy is nature incarnate, innocent if not technically pure. (She has slept with Mahon, a childhood friend who no longer recognizes her, and ends up seduced by Jones.) Mahon's fiancée, Cecily Saunders, meanwhile, is the culturally conditioned woman. Worried about appearances, she decides she cannot love a disfigured man and abandons Mahon for another local, George Farr.

If Faulkner had restricted himself to four contrasting characters he might have crafted a taut, focused narrative. Aiming for a social panorama, however, he packed the story with an overwhelmingly large cast. As a result, *Soldiers' Pay* (as it was eventually titled) can feel scattered and improvised. It was not: Faulkner outlined the action on two sheets of paper, checking off plot points as he went along, suggesting his ambition outstripped his abilities. The busyness does a major disservice to the most fully realized female character, Margaret Powers, who is a far more substantive counterpart to Cecily than Emmy – indeed, Margaret is one of the most sympathetic female characters in all Faulkner, though critics rarely pay her attention. A war widow, she alone understands Mahon's pain and does what Cecily refuses to, marrying the soldier so he may die in peace. Not one but two additional veterans intrude in the story to chase her affections, though. As if not distracting enough, Faulkner includes yet another soldier who knows the secret of how Margaret's first husband, Richard, was killed in battle (he was fragged by a local enlistee), and devotes unnecessary time to Cecily's father and her younger brother. The reader has so many characters to track that only the oddest and least realistic, like Janarius Jones, stand out.

The novel's technique feels equally frantic and overstuffed. Amid dialogue bursting with soldier slang and Southern vernacular, Faulkner interpolates letters, song lyrics, conversations staged in the form of theatrical scripts, stream-of-consciousness ruminating and even a choral interlude that pans through the thoughts of Charlestown denizens. This omniscient device is borrowed, most critics say, from Chapter Fifteen of Joyce's *Ulysses* ('Circe') – although its inspiration may have been a novel Faulkner was more apt to cite as a favourite, Melville's *Moby-Dick* (Chapter Forty, 'Midnight, Forecastle').[18]

In the end, the sprawling cast and mishmash of approaches obscure the theme. *Soldiers' Pay* was Faulkner's bid for the *au courant* genre of the 'Lost Generation' novel, beating Hemingway's *The Sun Also Rises* into print by eight months. Yet it is less about the wounds of war than the wounds of sex. For Faulkner, physical intimacy is a fall from innocence that characters cope with either by withdrawing into emotional catatonia (like Mahon and Margaret) or by lecherously indulging the passions (like Jones). When *Soldiers' Pay* was published the following year, Faulkner's apparent antipathy towards carnal knowledge alarmed one reviewer. 'Into his novel he has pumped the most envenomed hatred of sex one can imagine,' wrote E. Hartley Grattan of the *New York Sun*. 'I strongly suspect he felt a relief when he finished the book and knew that to some extent he had freed himself from the burden it was upon him.'[19] It was a canny insight into the sexual and romantic frustrations that would follow the author throughout his life.

Upon completing the manuscript in May 1925, Faulkner asked Elizabeth Prall whether Anderson would recommend it to his publisher. On the novel's outline he originally scribbled the address of Charles Scribner's Sons, suggesting he aimed to submit to the home of F. Scott Fitzgerald, but a personal connection gave him a better shot at acceptance. Up to 1925, B. W. Huebsch had published Anderson's work, but he had recently switched to Boni & Liveright, the leading voice in modernist fiction. Helmed by Horace Liveright, a former toilet-paper factory manager whose father-in-law lent him money to start the company in 1917, the fledgling firm had built a prestigious roster that included Ezra Pound, T. S. Eliot and Eugene O'Neill. Thanks to Sherwood, Hemingway's first book waited in the wings. Anderson, who had read Faulkner's earliest chapters, agreed to the favour, but not with the enthusiasm Bill expected: 'He said that he will make a trade with you,' Elizabeth answered. 'If he don't have to read [the novel], he will tell his publisher to take it.'[20] Faulkner was offended, and the friendship frayed after only six months.

Awaiting Liveright's response, Faulkner had a holiday in Pascagoula on Mississippi's Gulf Coast. There he ardently pursued an artist he had met in New Orleans, Helen Baird, who appears to have been his first serious romantic interest since Estelle. Some biographers argue he fell harder for Helen than he ever did for his adolescent muse; at least this time he was the one raising the possibility of marriage, though his feelings were not reciprocated. As Helen later admitted, she enjoyed the company of bohemian 'screwballs', and Bill fit the category.[21] Faulkner wooed Baird for nearly two years until she married another man, by which point she had significantly influenced his second novel. In Pascagoula that summer he composed a presumptuously erotic sonnet sequence for her called 'Helen: A Courtship'.

In early July Faulkner departed for Europe. Accompanying him was another member of the New Orleans art scene, painter William Spratling, Faulkner's French Quarter housemate that spring. The duo sailed to Genoa, Italy, where, on their first night, Spratling stepped on Italian currency and was arrested for disrespecting the royal family. The incident inspired 'Divorce in Naples', which has raised eyebrows for fictionalizing Faulkner and Spratling as bickering homosexual sailors (Spratling was gay). Eventually Faulkner journeyed alone to Paris, armed with letters of introduction from Phil Stone to leading modernists. He made no effort to hobnob with Stein, Hemingway, Harold Loeb (whose novel *Doodab* was also forthcoming from Liveright) or other expatriate Americans. The closest he came was to spy upon James Joyce at a sidewalk café. Other than Spratling, who visited occasionally, Faulkner's closest acquaintance was photographer William Odiorne, who snapped images of the thick beard Bill grew. Mostly while residing at the Grand Hôtel des Principautés-Unies on the rue Servadoni, Faulkner wrote copiously.

Again following Joyce's example, he attempted a *Küntslerroman*, the biography of an artist à la *A Portrait of the Artist as a Young Man*. Called 'Elmer', the story explored the relationship between eroticism and aesthetics. As painter Elmer Hodge travels through Italy and France, long flashbacks recount his sexual history, including his incestuous childhood attraction to his sister, Jo-Addie, a foreshadowing of Quentin Compson's far more seriously rendered urge to both possess and protect his sibling Caddy in *The Sound and the Fury*. 'Elmer' served Faulkner as a crucible of sorts for how not to use figural language: to dramatize his hero's sexual longings, he peppered passages with Freudian phallic symbols, including cigar stubs, factory smokestacks and 'long tapering whips fixed pliant and slenderly recovering in their sockets on the dashboards of buggies'.[22] They are unartful and obvious. Later he learned to intimate confused desires with more original images, most arrestingly a pair of mud-spattered 'drawers' Caddy exposes when she climbs a tree to peek in on her grandmother's funeral. Faulkner wisely gave up on 'Elmer', but not before producing nearly 40,000 words.

He fared better with a shorter Parisian effort. When not writing Faulkner enjoyed listening to classical music concerts and watching children play in the nearby Jardin du Luxembourg. As he reported to Maud, the setting inspired a 2,000-word vignette, 'poetry though written in prose form', that was 'such a beautiful thing that I am about to bust': 'I haven't slept hardly for two nights, thinking about it, comparing words, accepting and rejecting them, then changing again. But now it is perfect – a jewel.'[23] Five years later, a whittled-down version of this 'jewel' provided the unsettling final scene of *Sanctuary*, in which Temple Drake escapes to Paris after accusing an innocent man of rape, resulting in his brutal murder at the hands of a vigilante mob. In the Luxembourg Gardens, Temple yawns and checks her compact during a brass-band performance, a chilling image of moral detachment. The original Parisian version was an exercise in creating mood through description. It exhilarated Faulkner because, unlike in 'Elmer', the symbolism arose naturally from the pictorial details instead of forcing Freudian meanings onto them.

Sometime that September Liveright officially accepted his novel. Faulkner celebrated his $200 advance by travelling to London, but he found the city too expensive and the British rude. Dribs and drabs of the writing he attempted there appeared in the later story 'The Leg' (1934), but a medieval allegory about a knight searching for his lady stalled after only a few pages. The allegory was given his novel's original title, 'Mayday', when Liveright insisted on changing his book's name to *Soldiers' Pay*. Bill returned to the States shortly before Christmas to prepare for its publication. The novel received generally positive notices in February 1926 but was by no means a critical darling. The most enthusiastic reaction came from Southern Agrarian Donald Davidson, who said as a stylist Faulkner far outshone Theodore Dreiser (who wrote 'as if he were washing dishes') and Sinclair Lewis (who went 'at words with a hammer and saw'). Yet Thomas Boyd – a Marine who survived Belleau Wood to write his own First World War novel, *Through the Wheat* (1923) – criticized the lack of realism, claiming the ornate language broke 'all contacts with the normal world to vault upward into a sort of esoteric sphere'.[24] More wounding than any review was the reaction in Oxford. Maud found *Soldiers' Pay* distasteful, while Murry refused to read it. Ole Miss declined the copy Phil Stone offered to donate to the campus library.

Faulkner looked ahead by submitting short stories to earn money. Neither 'Carcassonne', 'Divorce in Naples' nor two versions of a bootlegging/crime story called 'Once Aboard the Lugger' sold. That summer he returned to Pascagoula to present Helen Baird hand-bound copies of his courtship sonnets and his now-completed medieval 'Mayday' fantasy. When she responded coolly, he announced she would be a character in a *roman-à-clef* he intended as his follow-up to *Soldiers' Pay*. Eventually called *Mosquitoes*, this arch satire of their New Orleans circle, in which Helen appears as the waif-like Pat Robyn, no more impressed her than his poems had. When the book was published in April 1927 she told friends not to buy it, even though it was dedicated to her.

In addition to Helen Baird, *Mosquitoes* features thinly veiled versions of Sherwood Anderson (the novelist Dawson Fairchild), *Double Dealer* editor Julius Weis Friend (Julius Kauffman, referred to as the 'semitic man'), Bill Spratling (the sculptor Gordon) and the local preservationist and suffragette Elizabeth Werlein (the dilettante patron Patricia Maurier). In a metafictional twist, Faulkner makes a cameo appearance when the voluptuous Jenny Steinbauer describes meeting a 'funny man', a 'little kind of black man . . . awful sunburned and kind of shabby dressed' who identifies himself as a 'liar by profession'. When Jenny announces the liar's name, Pat Robyn's reaction seems a self-deprecating admission of Helen's disinterest in the author's affection: 'Faulkner?' replies Pat. 'Never heard of him.'[25]

Much of the plot unfolds around inside jokes like this, including the main scenario. The previous year Sherwood and Elizabeth Anderson invited Faulkner to a party on a Lake Pontchartrain rental boat. The engine gave out, leaving attendees adrift among insects. *Mosquitoes* traps its characters for four days instead of a single afternoon, enough time for their incessant chatter about art and

This drawing of Faulkner by his New Orleans housemate William Spratling appeared in newspapers nationwide in 1926 as an illustration for reviews of *Soldiers' Pay*.

sex to resemble the buzzing of the titular pests. At a more mature stage, Faulkner might have produced a novel as powerful as Hawthorne's *The Blithedale Romance* (1852), another *roman-à-clef* that pokes fun at artists. Yet instead of a detached observer/unreliable narrator like Miles Coverdale, who realizes his moral complicity in an unfolding tragedy, *Mosquitoes*'s most sympathetic character is the unmanly widower Ernest Talliaferro. His lack of sex appeal ('It was unbearable to believe that he had never had the power to stir women')[26] is mocked throughout. Rather than a complex poetess like Hawthorne's Zenobia, whose conflicting political principles and romantic vulnerabilities lead her to suicide, the novel's female protagonists, including Pat Robyn, are cardboard emblems of Jazz-Age attitudes towards sexual liberation. Because the characters are one-dimensional, readers will be forgiven for identifying less with them than with the grounded yacht, the *Nausikaa*: thanks to the continuously wordy exchanges – so typical of a 'novel of ideas' – audiences, too, can feel stuck in the mud.

Mosquitoes was Faulkner's opportunity to work through uncertainties about what type of writer he wanted to be and his relationship to readers. His natural inclination was towards isolation, but the book's most detached artist is its most destructive: Pat Robyn's brother, Theodore, disables the *Nausikaa* by stealing a rod from the navigation room and meticulously carving it into a beautiful pipe. Theodore declines opportunities to market his creativity, turning down a fellow passenger named Major Ayers who is willing to invest in the pipe's mass manufacturing. (And for good reason: by the novel's end Ayers is as content to hawk constipation remedies as he is art.) Yet Theodore is wholly indifferent to the damage his thievery causes the ship; his art-for-art's-sake aesthetic doesn't care whom it inconveniences.

Gordon the sculptor is a far more ideal artist. He abandons marble for clay, an earthier medium, and sculpts a bust of the artist's daffy patron, Mrs Maurier. Gordon's imagination is so intuitive he doesn't need to know the woman's tragic backstory to capture the pain she hides beneath her flighty persona. Yet Gordon is also openly hostile towards consumers of art. He refuses to sell his sculptures to Mrs Maurier and at one point takes Pat Robyn over his knee to spank her for demanding the right to buy his work. (One wonders how Helen Baird reacted to this scene, especially when in Pat's excited delight at being dominated she leaves a wet spot on the sculptor's trouser leg.) Gordon's over-exaggerated masculinity – he works with his shirt off, his pectoral muscles wowing women and men alike – reveals Faulkner's anxieties about the manliness of art. Gordon is last seen entering a brothel clasping a prostitute in a kiss. This is apparently Faulkner's symbol of male self-sufficiency, although how paying for sex is less exploitative than patrons' desire to own his labour is unclear. Talliaferro, meanwhile, suffers the most abuse for being neither artistic nor manly. In the final pages he decides to be 'cruel, hard, brutal, if necessary' with women/audiences, but when he telephones Dawson Fairchild to explain his new resolve, he ends up on the line with a belittling female: 'You tell 'em, big boy,' she ridicules Talliaferro. 'Treat 'em rough' – the final words of *Mosquitoes*.[27]

Before beginning the book, Faulkner congratulated fellow Liveright author Anita Loos on the massive success of her *Gentlemen Prefer Blondes*, then on its way to becoming the second bestselling novel of 1926. The pair met the previous year when Loos visited Anderson in New Orleans while cranking out chapters of her book for *Harper's Bazaar* (whose circulation quadrupled as it serialized the instalments). Unlike most readers, Faulkner was smitten not with Loos's dumb-blonde narrator, Lorelei Lee, but her sardonic sidekick, Dorothy Shaw: 'Please accept my envious congratulations on Dorothy – the way you did her through that elegant moron of a cornflower [Lorelei]. Only you have played a rotten trick on your admiring public. How many of them, do you think, will ever know that Dorothy really has something?'[28] That 'something' was the voice of wisdom that audiences were too busy laughing at Lorelei's malapropisms (the 'Eye-Full Tower') to appreciate. Most successful satires employ a supporting character like Dorothy who cuts through the *faux naif* narration to serve as a moral centre, a Jim to Twain's Huck. Faulkner's problem was he didn't trust any of his characters to be his Dorothy and made all but Gordon Loreleis. The sculptor's refusal to explain his art to other characters – his favorite word is 'No!' – clearly reflects the writer's disdain for 'talk, talk, talk: the utter and heartbreaking stupidity of words' that results when 'ideas, thoughts' become 'mere sounds to be bandied about until they were dead'.[29] But by refusing to allow any character to speak fully for him as Dorothy speaks for Loos, Faulkner leaves readers with nothing but the debunking bite of satire to stand as the central point of view. As Donald Davidson recognized, 'We are chiefly aware that Mr. Faulkner is making all these people the butt of his irony . . . [He] makes us most aware of his own remorseless mind . . . leaving us full of admiration for the skill of the performance, but conscious of some discomfort before the performer.'[30]

Faulkner completed *Mosquitoes* by 1 September 1926. Liveright accepted it without objecting to its running parody of Anderson. Not even a passage in which Dawson Fairchild describes eaves-dropping on a woman in a privy to experience beauty's excremental underside, a gibe at Anderson's homespun earthiness, raised objections. Hemingway had viciously burlesqued Anderson earlier that year in *The Torrents of Spring*, a book Liveright refused to publish, and *Mosquitoes* seemed inoffensive by comparison. Liveright did insist on cutting borderline obscene passages, including a lesbian kiss between Pat Robyn and Jenny Steinbauer. Faulkner mildly protested but backed down. Liveright was always brusque with him, as if he were tolerated as a favour to Anderson and not because his talent was immense.

Faulkner was not done with Anderson, though. That autumn he and Bill Spratling compiled *Sherwood Anderson & Other Famous Creoles*, a parodic guide to New Orleans literati that they published privately and sold to friends as a joke. Faulkner's brief preface rendered Anderson's style windy instead of whimsical. Sherwood took the high road, as he had with *The Torrents of Spring*, and declined to fire back. While Anderson would never truly forgive Hemingway, he helped Faulkner recuperate from a particularly grim 1937 alcoholic binge and always spoke admiringly of his accomplishments.

After the Spratling collaboration, New Orleans held little sway for Faulkner. Returning to Oxford, he reconnected with Estelle, now permanently separated from her husband. Faulkner loved entertaining her two children – Estelle's son, Malcolm, was born in 1923. At the same time, he laboured on two projects, both 'southern in setting', as Phil Stone announced in a press release. The first was 'a saga of an extensive family connection of typical "poor white trash"', the second 'a tale of the aristocratic, chivalrous and ill-fated Sartoris family, one of whom was even too reckless for the daring Confederate cavalry leader, Jeb Stuart.'[31]

The first effort fizzled out after only 25 pages, but it was crucial to Faulkner's future. Called *Father Abraham*, it introduced the scheming Flem Snopes, who flim-flams poor farmers into buying untameable Texas ponies. Faulkner eventually pared the manuscript down to the superb story 'Spotted Horses' (1931) and incorporated another version into *The Hamlet*. Yet *Father Abraham* itself suffered from an overblown preface comparing Flem to Roland, Buddha and Moses's Abraham. For now, the strained analogies rendered the Snopes clan a false start.

He had more immediate luck with the aristocrats than the rednecks. Both *Soldiers' Pay* and *Mosquitoes* illustrated a caution Anderson offered him about his facility with words: 'You can do it too easy, in too many different ways. If you're not careful, you'll never write anything.' The time had come to remember Sherwood's

Boni & Liveright recognized the fledgling Mississippi author as a bright talent and promoted his first two novels in the New York press. The relationship fractured when Faulkner submitted his third novel, *Flags in the Dust*. Boni & Liveright considered him a social commentator and satirist rather than a Southern novelist.

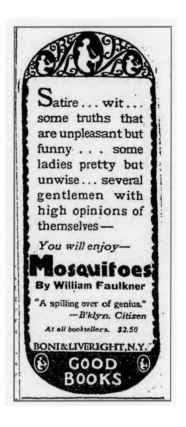

Satire ... wit ... some truths that are unpleasant but funny . . . some ladies pretty but unwise ... several gentlemen with high opinions of themselves —

You will enjoy—

Mosquitoes
By William Faulkner

"A spilling over of genius."
—*B'klyn. Citizen*

At all booksellers. $2.50

BONI & LIVERIGHT, N.Y.

GOOD BOOKS

remedy for this handicap: 'You're a country boy; all you know is that little patch up there in Mississippi where you started from. But that's all right too. It's America too.' As Anderson insisted, 'To be a writer, one has first got to be what he is, what he was born.'[32] For Faulkner, that meant finding his subject-matter in his 'little patch' of Oxford and his family's past. His first two novels took only three months each to write, but this far more personal project absorbed him for the first two-thirds of 1927.

He finished the novel shortly after turning thirty on 25 September 1927, titling it *Flags in the Dust*. To Liveright he dispatched a grandiose letter brimming with confidence: 'At last and certainly, as El Orens' sheik said, I have written THE book of which those other things were but foals. I believe it is the damdest best book you'll look at this year.'[33] As the unusual equestrian metaphor suggests, Faulkner was convinced his long artistic gestation – his own foaling season – was finally through.

He couldn't have been more unprepared for the response.

4

Driving the Nails Straight
(1928–31)

'It is with sorrow in my heart,' Horace Liveright began, 'that
I write to tell you that three of us have read *Flags in the Dust* and
don't believe Boni & Liveright should publish it.' The rejection
said nothing about the ambitious scope of Faulkner's third novel,
which stretched from the Civil War into the First World War's
aftermath. Instead, the book was 'diffuse and non-integral', lacked
'plot, dimension and projection', failed to 'go anywhere' and 'left
a thousand loose ends'. 'My chief objection,' Liveright concluded,
'is that you didn't seem to have any story to tell and I contend that
a novel should tell a story and tell it well.'[1]

Faulkner and his publisher had never truly clicked. 'He's not
the man I can write to frankly and intimately and wholeheartedly,'
Liveright complained to Anderson.[2] That summer the fledgling
writer charged a $200 bank draft to the company to cover gambling
debts, annoying Liveright, whose solvency crises were legendary.
Boni & Liveright's total profit for 1927 was $1,203 – a shockingly
low amount for a firm that routinely dominated the bestseller
lists. Besieged as well by legal conflicts and extramarital travails,
Liveright was too distracted to appreciate a meandering multi-
generational tale about decaying Southern ideals. 'My first emotion
was blind protest,' Faulkner said of the rejection. 'Then I became
objective for a minute, like a parent who is told that its child is a
thief or an idiot or a leper.'[3]

Despite calling its fictional microcosm Yacona instead of Yoknapatawpha County, *Flags in the Dust* planted the seeds of a saga that would blossom for the next 35 years. It also posed interpretive challenges that became synonymous with the experience of reading Faulkner, helping explain Liveright's baffled reaction. First and foremost is the task of keeping genealogies straight. The novel features four different Bayard Sartorises, ranging from a Confederate officer in 1862 to an infant who dies in the 1918 influenza outbreak. Three separate John Sartorises also appear, from a rash Civil War colonel based on W. C. Falkner to his pilot great-grandson killed in the First World War. Additionally, *Flags* marks Faulkner's initial experiments in condensing and confusing chronologies. The novel begins in 1919 with the second-generation Bayard (based on the Young Colonel) learning his namesake grandson has returned from the First World War. The timeframe then shifts back to the unheroic Civil War death of the old man's uncle (the 'Carolina Bayard'), shot in the back by a lowly Yankee cook while seizing anchovies during a raid commanded by General Jeb Stuart, before leaping forward to 1869, when Old Bayard first hears this story from his aunt Jenny Du Pre.

Had Liveright embraced these challenges, he still might have wondered why, after introducing the Sartorises, Faulkner focused on a lawyer named Horace Benbow, or how a subplot about Byron Snopes sending anonymous mash notes to Horace's sister, Narcissa, related to the Sartorises' decline, or why pivotal characters die either in car crashes or plane wrecks. Had he not lost patience, he might have even asked if Faulkner meant to use the word 'sibilant' a dozen times.

Yet *Flags in the Dust* is hardly the inchoate mess Liveright deemed it. Its psychological portraiture and multi-class cast are typical of the nineteenth-century realism that cutting-edge modernists were rebelling against, making it more traditional than either *Soldiers' Pay* or *Mosquitoes*. Yet the book does share with more experimental

1920s novels anxieties over obsolescing values and verities. The Confederate valour that once fed the Sartorises' airs of aristocratic distinction have become at best self-deluding and at worst self-destroying. '[God] must have a name for His pawns,' Faulkner's intruding narrator intones, 'but perhaps Sartoris is the game itself – a game outmoded and played with pawns shaped too late and to an old dead pattern, and of which the Player Himself is a little wearied.'[4] The impulses replacing this 'dead pattern' are even darker, though. The voyeur Snopes, the naive cotton speculator Harry Mitchell and the neurotic Benbow all demonstrate how modern men are driven by lust, pious optimism or, in the case of Horace, incestuous attractions: he sleeps with Harry's wife while feeling a sensual attachment to his sister he can't repress.

Among the Sartorises, resisting the urge to romanticize family history falls to Old Bayard. He feels ambivalent towards his father, whose 1876 murder by his business partner, Redlaw, epitomizes the clan's haughty pursuit of legend. Col. John Sartoris courted death 'to release him of the clumsy cluttering of bones and breath' so he could 'stiffen and shape that which sprang from him into the fatal semblance of his dream[:] to be evoked like a genie or a deity'.[5] The desire to be apotheosized likewise dooms the current generation. As the novel opens, John III has already died in aerial combat, the First World War giving him, as Aunt Jenny decides, 'a good excuse to get himself killed. If it hadn't been that, it would have been some other way that would have been a bother to everybody around.'[6] That 'bother' becomes the prerogative of John's twin, known as Young Bayard, who undertakes risky spectacles to prove his bravery, whether running a stallion to near death or speeding his car through the countryside. Not even a temerarious car ride that causes Old Bayard a fatal heart attack halts this compulsion. After abandoning a pregnant Narcissa, Young Bayard finally gets his wish when an experimental aircraft he pilots disintegrates mid-air.

The defining image of Sartoris vanity appears when Aunt Jenny and the widowed Narcissa unveil unadorned headstones for the family's recent casualties. The simple inscriptions commemorating Old and Young Bayard and John III stand in stark contrast to the 'fustian vainglory' of their ancestor's nearby statue:

> He stood on a stone pedestal, in his frock coat and bareheaded, one leg slightly advanced and one hand resting lightly on the stone pylon beside him. His head was lifted a little in that gesture of haughty arrogance which repeated itself generation after generation with a fateful fidelity, his back to the world and his carven eyes gazing out across the valley where his railroad ran and the blue changeless hills beyond, and beyond that, the ramparts of infinity itself. The pedestal and effigy were mottled with seasons of rain and sun and with drippings from the cedar branches, and the bold carving of the letters was bleared with mold, yet still decipherable:
>
> COLONEL JOHN SARTORIS, CSA
> 1823–1876[7]

Save for minor details, the statue recreates W. C. Falkner's marble likeness in Ripley. Whereas the fictional Old Bayard chiselled 'Fell at the hand of — Redlaw' on Col. Sartoris's pedestal, the real-life Young Colonel never identified his father's killer, R. J. Thurmond, on his ostentatious memorial. That provocative gesture came from the family of Robert Hindman, the Old Colonel's original victim. In 1849 the Hindmans erected a tombstone that, according to legend, read 'Murdered . . . by Wm. C. Falkner' before community pressure forced them to soften it to 'Killed'. (The second marker still stands outside Ripley.) Faulkner's slight revision may represent an attempt to sanitize his great-grandfather's reputation. Yet Col. Sartoris's monument also depicts W. C.'s memorial as an Ozymandias-like symbol of pride and pomposity.

Because Faulkner owed Boni & Liveright for the $200 bank draft cashed in its name, he couldn't legally submit *Flags* elsewhere without permission. Horace Liveright was in no hurry to grant it. Faulkner thus spent much of 1928 in limbo. With nothing to lose, he began experimenting with style and form. Although he maintained 'a kind of stubborn and fading hope of at least justifying the paper I had used and the time I had spent writing [*Flags*]', his new writing took shape without concern for whether it was saleable: 'One day it suddenly seemed as if a door had clapped silently and forever to between me and all publishers' addresses and booklists and I said to myself, Now I can write. Now I can just write.'[8]

The fruits of this creative liberation ripened that April with two coming-of-age stories, 'That Evening Sun' and 'A Justice', and a third manuscript, 'Twilight', which quickly expanded into a remarkable, reputation-making novel. All three focused on the fourth Mississippi generation of the Compson family, who, like the Sartorises, represent the Southern aristocracy's decline. In 'That Evening Sun', siblings Caddy, Quentin and Jason accompany their father to the shack of their black domestic, Nancy, who fears her man, Jesus, will kill her for carrying a white man's baby. Because the children cannot process Nancy's terror, they act out by hitting each other, or, in Jason's case, by crying. 'A Justice', meanwhile, introduced another important Faulkner character, the Native American blacksmith and hunting guide Sam Fathers, later central to 'The Bear'. Sam reveals to young Quentin the mystery behind his mixed parentage by recalling how the Chickasaw chief Ikkemotubbe, known as 'Doom', built a fence to stop a tribesman named Craw-ford from fathering illegitimate children with a married black slave. Later fiction identifies Doom himself, not Craw-ford, as Sam's father, but for now 'A Justice' established pivotal Yoknapatawpha history by explaining how the conniving chief poisoned his uncle to seize control of land later sold to first-generation plantation owners. As Sam's audience, young Quentin cannot comprehend sex and death; much later he

The statue W. C. Falkner commissioned of himself shortly before his 1889 murder still stands in Ripley. Faulkner includes a detailed description of it in *Flags in the Dust* as an Ozymandias-like testament to the pride and pomposity of a fictional clan's paterfamilias, Col. John Sartoris.

understands that passing 'beyond the suspension of twilight' into adulthood initiates him into the complex Southern history of exploitation responsible for Sam's mixed heritage.[9]

'That Evening Sun' and 'A Justice' were dramatically richer than Faulkner's previous fiction. Both stories intimate plot consequences through understatement and implication rather than intrusive exposition, which *Flags* is rife with. 'Twilight', meanwhile, drew from memories of grandmother Leila Butler's 1907 funeral. In all three efforts, sunset represents the murky passage from childhood innocence into adult awareness of moral ambiguity and complicity.

Unlike the other stories, though, Quentin did not narrate 'Twilight'. Instead, Faulkner invented a fourth Compson sibling whose perspective would radically challenge narrative conventions. Writing from the point of view of Benjy, a 33-year-old cognitively disabled man-child, enabled him to dramatize 'the blind, self-centeredness of innocence, typified by children'. Setting out to explore 'the relationship of the idiot to the world he was in but would never be able to cope with', Faulkner created a modern version of the literary character known as the isolato, a figure of extreme alienation who protests the world's loss of humanitarian values – or, in Benjy's case, who cries out for the 'tenderness, the help, to shield him in his innocence'.[10] Inspired by Edwin Chandler, the brother of the teacher Annie Chandler who gifted Faulkner a copy of Thomas Dixon, Jr's *The Clansman*, the youngest Compson sibling was hardly the first mentally impaired character in fiction. Nick Handyside in Charles Brockden Brown's 'Somnambulism' (1805), Mary Murfree's Elijah Price in 'Driftin' Down Lost Creek' (1884) – who smashes a man's head with a sledgehammer – and Charles Dickens's Barnaby Rudge are all prototypical 'simpletons'. Yet these characters are seen externally, usually depicted as quasi-monsters unable to appreciate, like John Steinbeck's later Lenny in *Of Mice and Men* (1937), their capacity to harm. Isolatos who speak in the first person exemplify a related character type Faulkner evokes by labelling Benjy an 'idiot' – namely, the holy fool. Shakespeare's jesters and clowns, Melville's Pip in *Moby-Dick* and Dostoevsky's Prince Myshkin in *The Idiot* all oppose the tyranny of reason by embodying the 'madness' of seeing the world in an idiosyncratic way. Yet Benjy Compson grew into a far more emotionally affecting emblem than previous literary 'idiot savants'. By creating a voice of inarticulate longing and overwhelmed confusion, Faulkner made Benjy a symbol of aching vulnerability representing humanity's inability to understand modern upheavals.

A hallmark of the holy fool tradition is unconventional expression, usually a garrulity or 'babbling' that breaks from orderly norms of syntax to espouse intuitive wisdom. Benjy's perspective allowed Faulkner to extend the linguistic ingenuity of the idiot's voice to new heights of stylistic invention. Through the limited vocabulary of a mentally stunted mind, he radically defamiliarized everyday experiences: golfing is no longer a game of rules but hitting a ball and moving a flag for no apparent purpose. The effect is to recreate in the reader the uncertainty Benjy himself experiences as he witnesses actions without comprehending them. Punctuating the transition between dialogue and an attribution tag with a period instead of a comma ('"What is it now." Mother said.')[11] allowed Faulkner to break down the connective tissue of grammar to suggest how Benjy, unable to ply the logic of cause and effect, can only perceive phenomena in fragments. The most breathtaking stylistic breakthrough involved representing Benjy's sense of time. Bereft of a sense of chronology, the youngest Compson experiences memories as if they occur fresh in his own here and now, dooming him to relive the disappearance of his beloved sister Caddy over and over again.

Benjy's inability to distinguish past and present enabled Faulkner to flout expectations for linear storytelling. Instead, readers must reorder seemingly disconnected scenes from the Compsons' tragic fall with only italics and leitmotifs for cues. Exactly how many timeframes Benjy's narration contains is unclear. Faulkner claimed eight levels, but subsequent critics have discerned as many as sixteen. Ultimately, the inability to agree upon an exact number demonstrates the effectiveness of Faulkner's non-sequential ordering: as a measure of experience, the novel insists, time confuses more than it clarifies.

Despite its technical ingenuity, Benjy's narration was not the element that compelled Faulkner to expand 'Twilight' into the novel eventually titled *The Sound and the Fury*. The turning point came instead with an image of Caddy Compson climbing a tree to spy upon her grandmother's funeral. 'It was . . . a very moving [picture],' Faulkner insisted, 'symbolized by the muddy bottom of her drawers as her brothers looked up into the apple tree that she had climbed to look in the window. And the symbolism of the muddy bottom of the drawers became the lost Caddy.'[12] If the undergarments hint at Caddy's inevitable growth into a carnal being, the mud equates sexuality with filth, suggesting once again Faulkner's sense of childhood as a fall from the purity of innocence into the muck and mire of experience. The fall was not simply sexual. As Philip Weinstein writes, Caddy's muddy bottom intimates 'the menses that have not arrived, but that will eventually launch her on the path of maturation: bleeding, sexual activity, marriage, reproduction, and death'.[13] Because Benjy cannot comprehend this progression of life, he panics when he senses change. In one key episode he grows upset when Caddy tries to wear perfume – a symbol of her blossoming sexuality – because it replaces the natural smell of trees he associates with his sister.[14]

As Faulkner reveals, the Compsons have fallen much further than the Sartorises. Once headed by a charismatic Confederate hero, General Jason Compson, the family has, by 1928, suffered the deaths of both the siblings' alcoholic father, Jason III, and oldest son Quentin. Caddy has been shamed from Jefferson for getting pregnant by the cad Dalton Ames. Her seventeen-year-old daughter (also named Quentin, after her dead uncle) is embarking on the same journey, sneaking around with a fast-talking carny. The family's fear of sexuality is as inhumane as judgemental. As hints reveal, the Compsons had Benjy castrated after he mistook a passing schoolgirl for Caddy, and his reaching out to touch her was interpreted as an attempted rape.

The sexual politics of *The Sound and the Fury* remain controversial. Critics disagree whether the treatment of Caddy's naturally developing womanhood protests or propagates prejudices against female sexuality. Less appreciated is how linking procreation and death by juxtaposing Caddy's muddy drawers to Damuddy's funeral provided Faulkner a structural joist to frame the drama around. If Liveright complained that proliferating storylines left *Flags in the*

Dust centreless, then 'the lost Caddy' served as the core around which the other, interconnected narrative threads ravelled. Exactly when Faulkner decided all three Compson boys should narrate versions of their sister's banishment is unclear. 'I finished it the first time [the Benjy section],' he claimed, 'and it wasn't right, so I wrote it again, and that was Quentin, that wasn't right. I wrote it again, that was Jason, that wasn't right, then I tried to let Faulkner do it [in a fourth, third-person chapter], that was still wrong.'[15] By 'wrong' he meant no single section could stand on its own; only through their juxtaposition do the four parts convey the full pathos of the Compsons' decline.

For Quentin's version, Faulkner developed a perspective obverse to Benjy's: learned instead of stunted, self-conscious instead of guileless, excessively contemplative instead of experiential. The technique dramatizing the anguish that leads the oldest brother to commit suicide on 2 June 1910 is clearly indebted to Joyce's *Ulysses*. Stream of consciousness is more than Faulkner's homage to an influence, though. The device forces readers to experience Quentin's breakdown over the incestuous jealousy he feels towards Caddy's lover:

> do you love him
> her hand came out I didn't move it fumbled down my arm
>   and she held
> my hand flat against her chest her heart
> thudding
> no no
> did he make you then he made you do it let him he was
>   stronger than
> you and he tomorrow Ill kill him I swear I will father
>   neednt know
> until afterward and then you and I nobody need ever know we
>   can take

my school money we can cancel my matriculation Caddy you
    hate him
dont you
dont you[16]

Writing this portion did not flow as smoothly as Benjy's section had.
Faulkner initially began with Caddy's seduction by Ames, the female
Quentin's biological father. Dissatisfied, he started over with the
male Quentin in his Harvard boarding room, fixated by the sound
of his pocket watch. If Benjy is time-deprived, his brother is time-
crippled. 'The mausoleum of all hope and desire,' Quentin recalls
his father declaring when presenting him the watch.[17] The young
man's fatal wade later that day into Boston's Charles River is his
effort to overcome the paralysis he feels from this 'reducto absurdum
of all human experience', as Mr Compson calls the watch (with a
malapropism). Quentin is trapped between knowing that adulthood
(a measure of life) leads only to an oppressive awareness of mortality
(the expiration of one's time) and his father's cynical defeatism.
('"I give [the watch] to you," says Mr Compson, "not that you may
remember time, but that you might forget it now and then for a
moment and not spend all your breath trying to conquer it."')[18]

    For Jason's story, Faulkner returned to conventional first-person
narration. Jason is bitter over losing the banker's job promised by
Sydney Herbert Head, the husband Caddy married to legitimate her
pregnancy before Head realized the baby born seven months after
their quickie wedding was another man's. In revenge, the middle
Compson brother embezzles the child support Caddy provides for
her daughter's upkeep. Faulkner described Jason as 'complete evil'
and 'the most vicious character in my opinion I ever thought of',
but the brother's biting, sarcastic voice is proof of his creator's
own caustic sardonicism.[19] Jason refers to the castrated Benjy as
the 'Great American Gelding', mocks his Ivy League brother's
suicide ('at Harvard they teach you how to go for a swim at

night without knowing how to swim') and dismisses his mother's hypochondria as 'wearing haircloth or probably sandpaper'.[20] Cruel, yes – but funny, too.

For the final section, in which Quentin the daughter escapes with the $3,000 Jason has stolen, Faulkner switched to omniscient narration, gliding between various characters' thoughts. Most notably, he filters through the perspective of Dilsey, the Compsons' black cook, the only character affectionate with Benjy after Caddy's exile. Based on the Falkner family's own domestic, Caroline 'Callie' Barr, Dilsey takes the disabled brother to an Easter Sunday sermon by a famous preacher, Reverend Shegog, where a vision of the Christian afterlife comforts her grief: 'I seed de beginnin,' she sighs, 'en now I sees de endin.'[21] Whether 'endin' is the correct word is questionable. The novel's bleak conclusion offers the reader no resolution to the cruelty of human relations. After admitting that Quentin has run away, Jason beats both Benjy and Luster, the grandson of Dilsey's charged with pacifying the man-child, for navigating the family surrey the wrong direction around the town square. Benjy's only security comes from familiar sequences of scenery, from 'cornice and façade . . . post and tree, window and doorway and signboard', an order that Luster's change of route destroys.[22] Yet that comfort requires avoiding the 'empty eyes' of the square's central landmark, a Confederate soldier statue. The novel thus ends in violence and denial. In our incapacity to control the chaos of memory, time and history, Faulkner implies, we avert our eyes and seek private patterns of meaning that only enforce our alienation.

In theme and technique, *The Sound and the Fury* is obsessed with interiority. What for Benjy and Quentin is extreme alienation (and for Jason and Mrs Compson self-serving solipsism) was for Faulkner a cathartic opportunity for self-invention. Stung by Liveright's rejection of *Flags in the Dust*, he withdrew into a space of private artistry and created a novel that for all its seeming structural and stylistic chaos is unified by conscientiously placed symbols and motifs. Foremost among these symbols are ironic parallels to the Passion of Christ. The showdown between Jason and Quentin the niece occurs during Easter weekend 1928, with Holy Saturday the setting for Benjy's section, which just happens to be his 33rd birthday. The obvious allusion to Christ casts Benjy as a debilitated saviour, unable to save or be saved, giving the family's fall allegorical heft: the Compsons have no hope of redemption or resurrection.

The novel also marked a striking breakthrough in characterization. Years later Faulkner told an interviewer that while labouring over *Flags* he discovered 'writing was a mighty fine thing' because 'you could make people stand on their hind legs and cast a shadow.'[23] *The Sound and the Fury* is the book that truly demonstrates his ability to create characters substantive enough to stand out against the intricate landscapes of his sentences. Especially when Faulkner wants to orate, his authorial voice dominates *Flags,* as in the 'dead pattern' passage describing the Sartorises as pawns in an 'outmoded' game even God tires of playing. In fact, the characters are rarely more than the writer's chess pieces. Restraining his presence in *The Sound and the Fury,* Faulkner collapsed the distance between the drama and the reader, giving the Compsons far more immediacy and presence than the Sartorises. Their vividness also makes them – or Benjy, Caddy and the male Quentin, at least – deeply sympathetic figures.

Immersing himself in the Compsons' world from April to October 1928 did not mean Faulkner had abandoned *Flags in the Dust*. That summer he discovered his Ole Miss friend Ben Wasson now worked in New York as a literary agent. Wasson submitted the book to a dozen different publishers, each rejecting it for the exact reasons Liveright had. Then in September, Harcourt, Brace editor Harrison Smith, an admirer of *Soldiers' Pay*, offered a $300 advance. Taking a swipe at the Jewish Horace Liveright, Faulkner wrote to his

The Lafayette County courthouse on the Oxford square, fronted by a Confederate soldier statue, is the setting for the disturbing final scene of *The Sound and the Fury*.

aunt Alabama, 'Well, I'm going to be published by white folks now.'[24] Founder Alfred Harcourt may have been a gentile, but he had two conditions for acceptance: he wanted the unwieldy novel trimmed by 25 per cent, and he wanted it renamed *Sartoris*.

Busy completing *The Sound and the Fury*, Faulkner had neither the time nor attention to perform the required surgery. Although he stayed at Wasson's New York apartment during the process, he left the cutting to Ben, who removed hefty portions of the Horace Benbow and Byron Snopes subplots. A few years later in a posthumously published essay Faulkner questioned the amputating: 'I said [to Wasson], "A cabbage has grown, matured. You look at that cabbage; it is not symmetrical; you say, I will trim this cabbage off and make it art . . . Very good, I say; you do that then the cabbage will be dead."' He allowed his friend to deliver the punchline: 'Then we'll make sour kraut out of it,' Wasson supposedly replied. 'The same amount of sour kraut will feed twice as many people as cabbage.'[25] The metaphor may have been odd, but it reflected Faulkner's belief that serving a large

audience would compromise his art. For *Sartoris* he was willing –
and he did arguably learn lessons about plot development and
pacing from Ben's cuts, even if he didn't always adhere to them in
later novels. Mostly, though, he assented because he was confident
that the new book he typed in Wasson's living room had already
vaulted his artistry far beyond this retooled one. The day after
Wasson completed *Sartoris*, Faulkner presented him with the
Compson manuscript, saying, 'Read this one, Bud. It's a real son
of a bitch.'[26]

The title came from *Macbeth*: 'Life's but a walking shadow
. . . a tale / Told by an idiot, full of sound and fury, / Signifying
nothing.' Faulkner also proposed an intriguing yet unfeasible
suggestion for guiding readers through Benjy's section: 'If I could
only get it printed the way it ought to be with different color types
for the different times,' Wasson quotes him lamenting. 'I don't
reckon, though, it'll ever be printed that way.'[27] (A special edition
did eventually feature multiple ink colours, but not until 2012.)
In truth, Faulkner doubted the book would be printed at all. He
submitted *The Sound and the Fury* convinced Harcourt, Brace would
decline it.

Sure enough, Harcourt felt the novel's 'unusual qualities' would
preclude 'finding a profitable market'.[28] The rejection came two
weeks after the 29 January 1929 publication of *Sartoris*. As with
Soldiers' Pay and *Mosquitoes*, sales were modest and reviews
encouraging, though hardly exuberant. Critics commended the
depiction of the changing South but cautioned against Faulkner's
stylistic excesses. 'He is for better or worse, eloquent,' wrote Henry
Nash Smith in the *Dallas Morning News*, while Mary Ellen Chase
of *Commonweal* complained, 'Favorite words become intrusive,
"sibilant", "myriad".'[29] From a distance, Liveright's insistence that
the book would not advance Faulkner's career seemed judicious.
Behind the scenes a luckier story unfolded. Faulkner's editor,
Harrison Smith, left Harcourt to start his own company, Cape

& Smith, hiring Wasson as an editor. Within days Faulkner had a contract with the fourth publisher of his short career. Yet the deal for *The Sound and the Fury* effectively stranded *Sartoris* at Harcourt, Brace.

Until now, Faulkner worried little about finances. Odd jobs remained his main support, his cash mostly going to his bootlegger. At 31, he still lived with his parents. Estelle Oldham's impending divorce raised the spectre of obligation, however. They had spent increasing amounts of time together, which in a small Southern town still implied a man's intentions were matrimonial. In a reversal from 1918, Estelle's family – particularly her younger sister, Dorothy or 'Dot' (1905–1968) – impressed upon Faulkner his duty to save her from the stigma of raising two children alone. Compounding the pressure, Estelle's anxieties about supporting herself eroded her stability. A frantic letter to Harrison Smith captures Faulkner's mixed feelings: 'I am going to be married. Both want to and have to . . . I don't think she could fool me in this way; that is, make believe her mental condition, her nerves are this far gone . . . It's a situation which I engendered and permitted to ripen which has become unbearable.'[30]

The Oldhams expected him to find respectable work. Faulkner had other ideas; he would make money writing a 'potboiler' or commercial novel. The decision was a striking departure in self-definition from 1928, when he 'shut the door on all book publishers' to produce *The Sound and the Fury*. Yet when Faulkner visited the local bookstore in Oxford – his friend 'Mac' Reed's drugstore – he watched customers bypass the *Sartoris* copies stocked as a personal favour to him and head for trashy fare with 'either a woman in her underclothes or someone shooting someone else with a pistol on the cover'.[31] If that was what the public wanted, William Faulkner would give it to them – in spades.

Writing had begun by February 1929 when he parted company with Harcourt, Brace. The action drew from trips to Memphis's

Tenderloin district that Faulkner and Phil Stone had enjoyed earlier in the decade when they socialized with roadhouse gamblers and molls. Tone and style were borrowed from the hard-boiled crime fiction of Dashiell Hammett just then leaping from pulp magazines into book publishing. (Hammett's first novel, *Red Harvest*, appeared in hardback that very January.) While crime writers fictionalized notorious gangsters such as Al Capone – the inspiration for both W. R. Burnett's *Little Caesar* (1929) and Armitage Trail's *Scarface* (1930) – Faulkner's villain was inspired by regional bootlegger Neal Pumphrey, nicknamed 'Popeye' for facial features that bulged when he became agitated.

Whether the real-life Popeye was guilty of the heinous crime the novel became infamous for – the rape of Temple Drake with a foreign object – remains doubtful. Pumphrey was purportedly impotent, and his criminal record suggested an incurable bad boy, not a cold-blooded killer. Faulkner's Popeye is a wholly noir invention, stylishly dressed and fastidious, but with a grotesque face ('he had no chin at all. His face just went away, like a wax doll set too near the fire') and a penchant for tightlipped repartee ('Make your whore lay off me, Jack').[32] Unlike Burnett's Rico Bandello, Trail's Tony Guarino or any number of Hammett villains, he never degenerates into a cartoon bad guy, in part because his savagery is as depraved as sadistic: after violating Temple Drake, Popeye forces her to have sex with a fellow gangster, Red, while he watches. As a victim of sexual assault, Temple is a prescient portrait of Stockholm Syndrome, withdrawing into emotional detachment while imprisoned at Miss Reba's Memphis bordello. For the novel's moral centre, Faulkner revived Horace Benbow from *Flags in the Dust*, recuperating some of the storyline Ben Wasson had shorn to form *Sartoris*. Aunt Jenny returned as well, as did Young Bayard's widow, Narcissa, although in far less sympathetic form. This time Horace's sister is a snobby, meddling presence who interferes with her brother's efforts to help a former prostitute, Ruby Lamar, while defending her common-law husband, the bootlegger Lee Goodwin, whom Temple falsely accuses of her rape. Faulkner titled the novel ironically, calling it *Sanctuary* because none of the characters finds refuge from the world's brutality.

Hard-boiled violence was already controversial, but Faulkner pushed Hammett's notion of humanity driven by 'blood simple' primitive instincts to graphic extremes. The original draft of *Sanctuary* opens with a reference to a woman slashed with a razor spewing 'bloody regurgitation' from her 'bubbling throat', describes the bloody excretions from Temple's rape running down her leg and, for comic relief, depicts a funeral for Red at which the wax plugging the bullet hole Popeye plants between his eyes pops free when his casket tips over.[33] Perhaps the most shocking moment occurs when the corrupt district attorney, Eustace Graham, presents the jury with evidence of Temple's assault: 'He held in his hand a corn-cob. It appeared to have been dipped in dark brownish paint.'[34]

When Faulkner finished a draft that May his inner circle was appalled. Estelle deemed the story 'horrible'. Phil Stone insisted Faulkner had misjudged the popular marketplace: 'The day of the shocker is past.' Harrison Smith, busily preparing *The Sound and the Fury* for publication, told him they would both go to jail if the book were printed.[35]

Faulkner let the manuscript lie to focus on more pressing concerns. On 19 June 1929 he and Estelle wed at Oxford's College Hill Presbyterian Church before honeymooning in Pascagoula, where Faulkner had once romanced Helen Baird. The marriage was rocky from the start, with husband and wife both drinking to excess. One night Estelle waded into the ocean in her clothes, apparently intending to drown herself. A neighbour's intervention saved her, and she remained medicated for several days.

Amid this upheaval, Faulkner corrected proofs of *The Sound and the Fury*. Much to his annoyance Ben Wasson had removed the italics signalling time shifts in the Benjy section, replacing them with line breaks. Faulkner objected politely but firmly, insisting that white spaces broke the 'continuous whole' of Benjy's memories. 'Don't make any more additions to the script, bud,' he warned Wasson. 'I know you mean well, but so do I.'[36]

Upon returning to Oxford in August, with *Sanctuary* in limbo, Faulkner had no choice but to find regular work. As night supervisor at the University of Mississippi's power plant, his main duty was to watch over the two black men who fed the dynamo with coal. In later years, he would claim he was the 'heaver' or shovel man. On 9 October, shortly after he joined the plant, Cape & Smith published *The Sound and the Fury*. William Faulkner was truly living parallel lives.

Three reviews were particularly notable. In *Southwest Review*, Henry Nash Smith asked whether Faulkner's treatment of the South transcended regionalism as a tragedy of universal proportions, a question that critics would squabble over for twenty years. In *The Nation*, Clifton Fadiman declared the reader was 'likely to throw the book away in irritation'. Fadiman would soon helm the *New Yorker*'s book review section and establish himself as Faulkner's most vocal detractor. The most perceptive assessment came from novelist Evelyn Scott, whose endorsement Cape & Smith sought before publication. Scott praised Benjy as 'a better idiot than Dostoevsky's' – a line the publisher cited in advertisements – but found Quentin less interesting than his brothers. Overall, Scott declared the novel a 'conquest of nature by art' for wringing 'beauty . . . from the perfect *realization* of what a more limiting morality would describe as ugliness'.[37] Harrison Smith was so excited by the analysis he printed it in pamphlet form and distributed it to reviewers as a primer for understanding the novel. No amount of explaining was likely to help sales, though. A modest print run of 1,789 copies did not sell out for a year and a half. It didn't help that, two weeks after publication, panic on Wall Street crashed the stock market, triggering the Great Depression.

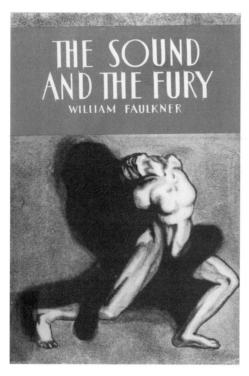

The Sound and the Fury, published by Cape & Smith in 1929, marked an astonishing leap into artistic maturity. 'I don't know whose idea that jacket was, nor who did it,' Faulkner replied, when asked about the symbolism of lightness and darkness on the cover.

One day after Black Thursday (24 October), Faulkner began yet another novel, his fourth in less than three years. The plot of *As I Lay Dying* came to him in the form of a 'deliberate book': 'Before I ever put pen to paper and set down the first word I knew what the last word would be and almost where the last period would fall.'[38] Knowing the complete story arc robbed him of the 'ecstasy' of discovery felt with *The Sound and the Fury*, but deliberateness was necessary to compartmentalizing his new responsibilities as husband, stepfather and provider.

Instead of faded aristocrats or vicious criminals, Faulkner focused this time on Yoknapatawpha County's poor farmers. After the death of their matriarch, Addie, the Bundren family suffers an epic series of mishaps on a ten-day quest to bury the body in Jefferson. Enduring flood, fire, a maimed leg, madness, sexual exploitation and the putrefaction of their mother, the Bundrens are not symbols of noble human endurance as Steinbeck's later Joads are. Rather, they are victims of nature's random indignities. As in *Sanctuary*'s funeral scene, the comedy is black. In one grimly absurd moment, the youngest son, Vardaman, not understanding that corpses don't breathe, drills airholes into his mother's casket, inadvertently boring into Addie's face. In the final scene, the lazy father, Anse, spends the family's last money on false teeth and a replacement wife: 'Meet Mrs Bundren,' he tells his stunned children in the book's final line.[39]

Faulkner insisted that *As I Lay Dying* was such a 'tour de force' not a single word was revised from the first draft – a claim not quite true, though close. The book came easily because he already knew the characters. Despite their poverty, the Bundrens are versions of the Compsons, with a suffering innocent (Vardaman instead of Benjy), an overly sensitive thinker who breaks down (Darl in the Quentin role), two surrogate leaders of the family bowed by responsibility (Cash and Jewel, both more likeable than Jason), a pregnant sister (Dewey Dell) and even an opportunistic seducer (the soda jerk Skeets MacGowan, who, in the Dalton Ames role, trades Dewey Dell a phony abortifacient for sex). Even Anse and Addie are variations on the cynicism and sickliness of Mr and Mrs Compson respectively, although Addie is a far more profound figure.

The socioeconomic gulf separating the Bundrens and Compsons isn't the only reason Faulkner could employ character types without repeating himself. None of the novels produced in this period of astonishing creativity resemble each other in form. Whereas *The Sound and the Fury* divided the narration among four perspectives (including Faulkner's own authorial one), *As I Lay Dying* employs fifteen different points of view throughout its 59 comparatively short chapters, most staged in interior monologue. If the Compsons' story coils around certain unabating memories – Damuddy's funeral, Caddy's wedding – the Bundrens' is kaleidoscopic. Although the plot unfolds chronologically with occasional flashbacks, the juxtaposition of perspectives challenges readers to assess each character's reliability and infer motives both from what they confess and what they can't, not even to themselves.

Thematically, *As I Lay Dying* is the Faulkner novel most concerned with language's limitations. *The Sound and the Fury* may begin with an epigraph that insists life is empty bluster, but the Bundrens' story is the one anxious about words 'signifying nothing'. Minor characters such as neighbour Cora Tull spout hollow pieties. Reverend Whitfield employs shibboleths to avoid confessing publicly that he fathered Jewel during an extramarital affair with Addie: 'He will accept the will for deed,' the minister assures himself of God's forgiveness, 'Who knew that when I framed the words of my confession it was to Anse I spoke them, even though he was not there.'[40] Anse himself is deeply manipulative with language, constantly saying, 'I aint asking,' 'I can do for me and mine' and 'I am not blaming you' to manoeuvre his children and neighbours into doing his bidding. The widower's words are actually not very persuasive; other characters see straight through to his transparent motives but assent to his wishes anyway so they don't have to listen to his blandishments. In this way, Anse parallels the opportunistic MacGowan, who doesn't so much wheedle Dewey Dell into trading sex for possibly worthless pills as he lets her know without stating it explicitly that she has no better option.

Amid this empty rhetoric, the Bundren children break down in various ways. Cash recites carpentry principles to find balance and structure in an upended world. Jewel lashes out in violence, while Darl goes mad and sets fire to a barn storing his mother's casket. By the time his siblings commit him to the state asylum, he is so dissociated he views himself in the third person, laughing and babbling 'Yes yes yes' to any question posed to him. The ten-year-old Vardaman, too young to understand mortality and uncomforted by family, succumbs to linguistic absurdity. His most famous monologue is a single-sentence chapter: 'My mother is a fish.'[41] But the most explicit discussion of meaninglessness comes from Addie herself. In a remarkable dramatic monologue delivered from beyond the grave, she traces her life's disappointments to the false promises words propagate: 'I learned that words are no good; that words don't ever fit at what they're trying to say at . . . motherhood was invented by someone who had to have a word for it because the ones who had the children didn't care whether there was a word for it or not.' As the dead woman declares, words – especially the word 'love' – never fulfil; they are 'just a shape to fill a lack'.[42]

The Bundren who most closely resembles Faulkner is Cash, the carpenter who obsesses over constructing the perfect casket for his mother. Faulkner often compared writing to carpentry, telling reporters that his only artistic goal was 'to drive the nails straight so the cabinet comes out right'.[43] Elsewhere he claimed that he didn't conspicuously plant symbols in his fiction because 'when a good carpenter builds something, he puts the nails where they belong. Maybe they make a fancy pattern when he's through, but that's not why he put them in that way.'[44] Submitting *As I Lay Dying* to Cape & Smith in January 1930, Faulkner turned to the genre whose nails he was still learning to drive: the short story. To professionalize his submission routine, he listed on a piece of cardboard stories he had sent out, first to high-paying slicks such as the *Saturday Evening Post* and *Cosmopolitan* and, when rejected, to less remunerative but more prestigious outlets like *Scribner's* or the *American Mercury*. Over two years this schedule grew to include more than forty titles, with twenty acceptances (and ten additional ones later).

His breakthrough came that winter when *Forum* purchased what became his best-known story, 'A Rose for Emily'. The tale of an aged recluse, Miss Emily Grierson, whose death leads to a macabre discovery that resolves a forty-year-old mystery, 'Rose' demonstrates how Faulkner balanced artistic inclination with magazine editors' demands. The revelation that Miss Emily poisoned her fiancé, Homer Barron, with arsenic and slept beside his corpse for four decades catered for the mass-market taste for Poe-styled Gothic tales. Yet the story also proved Faulkner could dial back his mordant humour so not to alienate general audiences. Nobody bores a drill into Homer's head as Vardaman does Addie's in *As I Lay Dying*, and the odour of putrefaction is treated with a prim decorousness that heightens the comic tone. Faulkner further demonstrated his inventiveness by employing an unusual, first-person plural narration. The story's 'we' speaks the communal voice of Jefferson, one whose unwillingness to insult the gentility of Southern womanhood inadvertently enables Miss Emily to get away with

Five years after Faulkner published *As I Lay Dying*, photographer Walker Evans, working for the u.s. Resettlement Administration, captured the eroded landscape outside of Oxford. The image illustrates the kind of terrain the Bundren family must navigate to bury their matriarch.

murder. So, too, the story's multiple timeframes revealed how the author could blend chronological leaps rather than juxtapose them as he had in *The Sound and the Fury*. 'A Rose for Emily' moves back and forth in time but without alienating or confusing most readers. Overall, the story perfectly distils Faulkner's themes and techniques into an accessible, commercial package.[45]

Shortly after *Forum*'s acceptance, even better news arrived. The crème de la crème of mass-market periodicals, the *Saturday Evening Post*, purchased its first Faulkner story for $750. Although 'Thrift' draws on the author's love of aviation, it is as atypical a story as imaginable, set not in Yoknapatawpha but in Europe during the First World War. Recounting the machinations of a parsimonious Scottish pilot with the unlikely name of MacWyrglinchbeath to profit from military service, the narrative features an exaggerated Scottish brogue and far-fetched incidents indicative of Faulkner's love of tall tales.[46] In addition to its light comedy, the *Post* likely appreciated its message of frugality, a value the middlebrow magazine heavily promoted.

The *Post* became one of the enduring frustrations of Faulkner's career, in part because he often turned to it when in dire financial need, submitting stories unsuitable for its conservative, middle-class tastes (he tried to place 'That Evening Sun' there, for example). Faulkner had worked to win its editors over for three solid years before 'Thrift' sold. His early correspondence reveals his frustration with the magazine's narrow tastes. 'If [these submissions] do not please you,' reads one late 1927 cover letter, 'the *Post* does not know its own children . . . Hark in your ear: I am a coming man, so take warning.' Soon after 'Thrift', the *Post* accepted a second story, 'Red Leaves' – like 'A Justice', a tale about Yoknapatawpha's Native American history of slave-owning – only to then reject eight consecutive submissions. Annoyed, Faulkner dispatched a stern letter reminding the staff that his work had brought the *Post* critical esteem. 'Thrift' was anthologized in 1930's prestigious O. Henry annual of best short fiction, and a prominent British magazine requested permission to reprint 'Red Leaves'. More comically, Faulkner claimed fourteen *Post* readers had written him fan letters: 'Let this be a warning, the *Post* is unwittingly in the way of falling from that high place in letters in which these fourteen people . . . raised it.'[47] In total, Faulkner would submit 32 times to the magazine in 1930 and 1931, with only four acceptances.

Payment for 'Thrift' arrived at a propitious time. That April the Faulkners purchased a century-old two-storey colonial house in south Oxford. Its original owner was a wealthy entrepreneur named Col. Robert Shegog, whose name Faulkner borrowed for the black preacher in *The Sound and the Fury*. The house sat in Bailey's Woods, a favourite childhood playground, and cost $75 a month. It also required extensive renovation. When Bill and Estelle moved in that June there was neither electricity nor running water. Faulkner patched the roof and replaced rotted joists while maintaining a morning writing schedule. Balancing intellectual and physical activity was immensely pleasurable to him. He soon selected a name conveying the two qualities he hoped to find in an estate of his own: Rowan Oak, a Scottish tree symbolizing peace and tranquillity.

Faulkner would live at Rowan Oak for the next thirty years. His attachment to the property is a reminder of the importance throughout his fiction of family manors. *Flags in the Dust* and *The Sound and the Fury* dramatize their atmosphere of antiquation by depicting the once regal homes of the Sartorises and Compsons as dilapidated, while *Sanctuary* opens with a long passage describing the abandoned Old Frenchman Place in Frenchman's Bend where Popeye rapes Temple. The history of this mansion is elaborated later in *The Hamlet*, when Flem Snopes starts a rumour that treasure is buried on the grounds to finance his move to Jefferson. Meanwhile, the working title of both *Light in August* – the first novel written at Rowan Oak – and *Absalom, Absalom!* was 'Dark House'. In these and other works, a house is a projection of a family's standing, its morality

Rowan Oak, the house Faulkner purchased on Old Taylor Road in south Oxford in 1930.

and, often, its soon-to-be-humbled pretensions. Faulkner regarded Rowan Oak similarly as an extension of himself. He might not have the Young Colonel's money, but he now had his own Big Place.

As I Lay Dying was published on 6 October 1930. Titles of reviews suggest the qualms some critics posed regarding the subject-matter: 'Funereal Fiction', 'In the Mire', 'Morbidity in Fiction'. Many commentators exposed their own stereotypes of poor Southerners instead of recognizing the humanity of Darl, Vardaman, Dewey Dell, Jewel and Cash: 'The family of Anse and Addie Bundren suggests inbreeding of the sort that undoubtedly weakens the stock in certain of our backward country districts,' suggested the *New York Times Book Review*.[48] Regional newspapers such as the *Cleveland Plain Dealer* and the *New Orleans Times-Picayune* were more disposed to praise the novel for its Gothic atmosphere. Fellow Southerner Henry Nash Smith defended Faulkner against the presumption he was a 'mere' regionalist by insisting his imagination was Elizabethan: his poetry 'dwells lovingly on vivid color and brave words, and seems almost to yearn for the blank verse which the modern democratic literary tradition has made impossible'.[49]

Faulkner was now a rising star. When Sinclair Lewis won the first American Nobel Prize in literature that December, his acceptance speech praised the author of *As I Lay Dying* for 'free[ing] the South from hoopskirts'.[50] As Chatto & Windus published his novels in England, European critics took note. The *Evening Standard*'s Arnold Bennett insisted that 'none of the arrived American stars can surpass [Faulkner] in style.'[51] Yet with literary recognition came an irritating interest in his personal life. That autumn Sherwood Anderson published 'They Come Bearing Gifts', a bitter essay on the fickleness of literary fame. The piece discusses the quarrels that ruined his friendships with Faulkner and Hemingway; both authors are depicted as petulant and ungrateful, despite praise for their work.[52] Although Hemingway relished public feuds and literary gossip, Faulkner wanted none of it.

That same autumn, after eighteen months in purgatory, a typeset copy of *Sanctuary* arrived at Rowan Oak. Without telling Faulkner, Harrison Smith decided to publish the novel he claimed would send them to jail. His change of heart was a Hail Mary. Having yet to turn a profit, Cape & Smith desperately needed sales, and a scandalous crime story was its best bet.

Two years later in a preface to a Modern Library edition of *Sanctuary* Faulkner described his shock at how poorly the galleys read:

> I saw that it was so terrible there were but two things to do: tear it up or rewrite it. I thought again, 'It might sell; maybe 10,000 of them will buy it.' So I tore the galleys down and rewrote the book. It had already been set up [in type], so I had to pay for the privilege of rewriting it, trying to make out of it something that would not shame *The Sound and the Fury* and *As I Lay Dying* too much.[53]

The preface became one of Faulkner's best-known statements on his writing, mainly because it is thoroughly misleading. It dismisses *Sanctuary* as 'a cheap idea . . . deliberately conceived to make money' and implies 'the most horrific tale I could imagine', originally dashed off 'in about three weeks' (actually six months), had to be elevated to the lofty artistic standards of his other books. In reality, Faulkner did the exact opposite. He de-emphasized the experimental aspects of his first attempt to heighten the pulpier qualities of action and suspense. In doing so, he proved that aesthetic brilliance is as possible in genre fiction as in 'literary' works. Alongside hard-boiled era classics such as Hammett's *The Maltese Falcon* (1930) and Raymond Chandler's *The Big Sleep* (1939) and *Farewell, My Lovely* (1940), *Sanctuary* stands as a definitive example of a crime novel that is great art.

One problem with the original *Sanctuary* was that Horace Benbow overshadowed Popeye and Temple Drake. As Noel Polk notes, the 'early version is, essentially, a heavily Freudian study of Horace's sexual and emotional problems', including his incestuous attraction to his stepdaughter, Little Belle. Faulkner's lawyer isn't a charismatic character, though; his neuroses are too interior. He works far better as a moral reflector of other cast members, a good but weak man defeated by the world's treachery. In Polk's words, placing Popeye centre stage transformed 'Faulkner's primary concern [into] the considerably larger problem of the nature of evil itself: the power of darkness, the insufficiency of light'. [54] The power imbalance between the men is dramatized in the revision's gripping opening scene, in which Horace and Popeye meet by chance at a creek near the Old Frenchman Place and lock gazes across the water for two hours until Horace finally breaks and admits fear. De-emphasizing Horace also enabled several grotesque secondary characters to step forward: the 'feeb' henchman Tommy, whom Popeye murders for protecting Temple; two country boys, Virgil Snopes and Fonzo Winbush, so green they don't realize their landlord, Miss Reba, runs a bordello, not a boarding house; and the corrupt state senator Clarence Snopes, who unctuously helps Horace trace Temple to Miss Reba's. These characters are all present in the original, but the inordinate focus on Horace restricts them to the wings.

The portrait of Temple remains controversial for implying her rape indoctrinates her in evil. Faulkner was far from incapable of sympathizing with female victims; as Horace defends the falsely accused Lee Goodwin, the treatment of *Sanctuary*'s other 'fallen' woman, Ruby Lamar, the mother of Goodwin's illegitimate child, reveals a humane understanding of working-class women's exploitation. Other plot adjustments are equally effective. Faulkner added a frightening capsule biography of Popeye that outlined the evolution of his crimes, from childhood pyromania to violence against pets. A grisly scene of vigilante violence in which Goodwin is burned alive critiques mob mentalities.

Faulkner also restructured the final juxtaposition of Popeye's and Temple's fates. Originally the novel ended with a sheriff's reply to Popeye's last words on the gallows, '"Fix my hair, Jack": *Sure, I'll fix it for you, the sheriff said; springing the trap*.' The conclusion was too hard-edged, though. Instead, Faulkner repositioned two poetic paragraphs first drafted in 1925 in Paris prefacing Popeye's execution. Listening to a brass band in the Jardin du Luxembourg, Temple feels neither regret nor guilt over falsely identifying Goodwin as Tommy's killer and her rapist. As Faulkner later explained, evil 'flowed off her like water off a duck's back'.[55] Temple's emotional withdrawal is her only sanctuary. Readers aren't so lucky. The final image of the sun setting 'prone and vanquished in the embrace of the season of rain and death' suggests that despair and violence are unrelenting and inescapable.[56]

Faulkner revised *Sanctuary* within a single month, allowing his sixth novel to arrive in bookstores on 8 February 1931, barely four months after *As I Lay Dying*. Shortly before it appeared, tragedy struck. On 11 January Estelle gave birth to a baby girl two months premature. The child, named Alabama after Faulkner's great aunt, lived less than ten days. Two events arose from the author's grief, one demonstrating his generosity and the other his penchant for gilding the lily. The hospital in Oxford lacked an incubator, which may or may not have contributed to the baby's fate. Faulkner promptly bought one and donated it to the institution. Around the same time, he circulated a rumour that he shot Estelle's physician, Dr John C. Culley, for medical negligence. The story was untrue, but it became local lore, adding to his burgeoning legend.

The sorrow of Alabama's death was still fresh as *Sanctuary* reviews arrived. Critics shocked by the violence questioned whether the novel was excessive even for crime fiction. The most influential commentary was Henry Seidel Canby's 'The School of Cruelty' in the *Saturday Review of Literature*, which accused Faulkner of inventing characters to torture them: 'He is cruel with a cool and interested cruelty, he hates his Mississippi and his Memphis and all their works, with a hatred that is neither passionate nor the result of thwarting, but calm, reasoned, and complete.'[57] In *Nouvelle Revue Française*, Maurice Coindreau, a French scholar teaching at Princeton, called *Sanctuary* 'an impressive mechanism in which all the wheels mesh with the precision of clockwork'.[58] Coindreau had already translated 'A Rose for Emily' and 'Red Leaves' into French and shortly took on *As I Lay Dying*. He quickly became Faulkner's most important European advocate, persuading the Parisian imprimatur Gallimard to publish his translations. They would sustain the writer's name abroad during his years of American neglect in the early 1940s.

Thanks in part to a breathless review on Alexander Woollcott's 'Town Crier' radio programme – for which Harrison Smith purportedly slipped Woollcott $500 – *Sanctuary* became a *succès de scandale*. Faulkner became a fixture of literary gossip columns, 'the only American who received the distinction of being denounced by J. B. Priestley in the latter's recent lecture here!' according to the *Brooklyn Daily Eagle*.[59] Reporters begged for interviews. The *Memphis Press-Scimitar*'s Marshall J. Smith snapped photographs at Rowan Oak of an obliging Faulkner smoking a corncob pipe, hoeing corn and even stepping into an outhouse, as if mocking his image as a Southerner mucking in mire. Inexorably, the corncob became the symbol most associated with him. When satirist Corey Ford imagined children's author A.A. Milne and two other British novelists visiting the world of *Sanctuary* in a *Vanity Fair* parody called 'Popeye the Pooh', famed caricaturist Miguel Covarrubius depicted Faulkner as an *enfant terrible* in rompers surrounded by cobs. The abrasive British painter and novelist Wyndham Lewis, a modernist godfather, wrote a trenchant dismissal of his style entitled 'A Moralist with a Corn Cob'. As Faulkner lamented to a friend some years later, 'I'll always be the corncob man.'[60]

As Cape & Smith hoped, *Sanctuary* sold briskly, its figures topping more than Faulkner's five previous novels combined. Although *The Wild Palms* (1939) later outstripped its 12,000 hardback tally, *Sanctuary* remained the work for which the writer was most widely remembered until the late 1940s when he was canonized. Faulkner capitalized upon his new-found fame by doubling down on story submissions. As a result 1931 was a banner year for acceptances, with eight major appearances in national magazines and another seven stories debuting that September in his first short-fiction collection, *These 13*.

The stories demonstrate how efficiently Faulkner restrained his love of rhetoric to favour plot structure and suspense. Appearing in *Scribner's*, 'Dry September' critiques the social collusion condoning lynching. Featuring a multi-character cast of white townspeople inflamed by the rumour that a black man may have 'attacked, insulted, [or] frightened' the white spinster Minnie Cooper, the story examines how the South justified racial terrorism.[61] *Scribner's* also published 'Spotted Horses', the tale of a crooked pony auction culled from the abandoned *Father Abraham*. It became the first Flem Snopes story to reach the public. 'The Hound' (published in *Harper's*) recalls Poe's 'The Tell-Tale Heart' with poor farmer Ernest Cotton struggling to dispose of murder victim Jack Houston's body, inevitably giving himself away. 'Hair' (the *American Mercury*) protests small-town gossip by dramatizing Jefferson's prurient interest in the relationship between barber Henry Stribling (nicknamed 'Hankshaw') and the teenaged Susan Reed. The story reveals Faulkner's annoyance with Oxford's snobbish sanctimony. 'Hair' also marked the first published appearance of lawyer Gavin Stevens, who became a versatile, recurring character. Stevens would star in occasional Perry Mason-like detective stories with which Faulkner failed to establish a revenue stream (collected in 1949's *Knight's Gambit*). More seriously, from *Light in August* through *Go Down, Moses* and into *Intruder in the Dust*, Faulkner uses Stevens's propensity for ponderous rhetoric to poke holes in Southern rationalizations of racial inequality. By the 1950s the lawyer served as not only a foil but something of an alter ego, channelling his creator's feelings towards old age and loneliness in *The Town* and *The Mansion*.

For every tale taking place in Jefferson, Faulkner produced a non-Yoknapatawpha story. Set in 'old Carolina', 'Fox Hunt' (*Harper's*) uses the rituals of the sport that will obsess Faulkner in his final years to illuminate marital jealousy and control. 'Dr Martino' (also *Harper's*) is a Hawthorne-like narrative about the apparently mystical spell an older man casts over a young woman. As in 'Hair', appearances are not what they seem.

Dealings with editors reveal that Faulkner was already so associated with his mythical county that periodicals didn't always appreciate his non-Mississippi offerings. When he submitted a prose-poem tribute to First World War aviators called 'All the Dead Pilots' to *Scribner's*, assistant editor Kyle Crichton asked instead for another Flem Snopes story: 'We regret that it has not been possible to accept more of the stories you have offered us, but on Flem Snopes we are clear. He is our character and think that in your hands he will become one of the great characters of

Already publicity averse, Faulkner reluctantly supplied an author photo for a United Press article on *Sanctuary* in 1931. Taken by his preferred portraitist, J. R. Cofield of Oxford, it has since become one of the most widely reproduced images of the writer, capturing him in his prime.

literature.'[62] The assumption that the only good Faulkner story was a Yoknapatawpha story meant atypical efforts such as 'Ad Astra' – another First World War tale featuring the doomed Bayard Sartoris III from *Flags in the Dust/Sartoris* – ended up in fleeting, pittance-paying outlets such as *American Caravan*.

With so many stories in magazines, following *Sanctuary* with a collection of them was a natural next step. The title *These 13* was a curiously declarative choice; a more marketable name might have been *A Rose for Emily and Other Stories*. Hedging his commercial bets, Harrison Smith listed the contents on the book jacket and reminded readers that William Faulkner was 'the author of *Sanctuary*'. The story selection was likewise curious. Faulkner included a sextet of his strongest efforts: 'Red Leaves', 'A Rose for Emily', 'A Justice', 'Hair', 'That Evening Sun' and 'Dry September'. Yet he sandwiched these Jefferson tales between two other sections, one devoted to First World War stories (a topic that was hardly groundbreaking in 1931) and one gathering experimental efforts. To lead the collection Faulkner stitched several abandoned manuscript fragments into 'Victory', which, like his *Saturday Evening Post* breakthrough, 'Thrift', concerned a Scottish soldier – an odd, even risky choice. A cast-off portion of 'Victory' also became 'Crevasse', the section's closing selection. Three previously unpublished efforts, all set outside the United States, closed the book: 'Mistral', 'Divorce in Naples' and 'Carcassonne'. *These 13* demonstrated Faulkner was more than a regionalist. The collection sold surprisingly well, entering a second printing less than two weeks after its 21 September publication.

A month before *These 13* appeared Faulkner began his seventh novel – his fourth in three years and, more impressively, his fourth straight masterpiece. As previously noted, he originally titled it 'Dark House'. An afternoon conversation with Estelle at Rowan Oak inspired a more evocative title: 'Does it ever seem to you,' Mrs Faulkner reportedly posed of her husband, 'that the light in August is different from any other time of year?'[63]

The novel did not gel as easily as previous ones had. His initial protagonist, a disgraced minister named Gail Hightower, obsesses over the Civil War heroism of a grandfather who, like Col. John Sartoris, was modelled on W. C. Falkner. After some false starts, Faulkner refocused on a different character, a young country woman named Lena Grove, who, like Dewey Dell in *As I Lay Dying*, is pregnant. (Faulkner later claimed 'light in August' was a Southern colloquialism for childbirth.) Searching for the baby's father, Lena is mistakenly directed to a lonely bachelor named Byron Bunch, who falls in love with her.

As Faulkner meandered into the backstory of the unborn baby's biological father, Lucas Burch, he discovered his true focus with the invention of Burch's ethnically ambiguous bootlegging partner, Joe Christmas. Christmas is a 'parchmentcolored' drifter convinced he is a 'nigger', though Faulkner neither confirms nor denies his exact racial identity. Instead, *Light in August* interrogates the negative cultural connotations of black skin that fosters animus towards African Americans. 'That Evening Sun' and 'Dry September' had forayed into this subject, but the spatial breadth of novels provided more depth for psychological analysis.

Writing *Light in August* wasn't the adventure *The Sound and the Fury* had been. As Faulkner later recalled, he 'would sit down to it each morning without reluctance yet still without that anticipation and that joy which alone ever made writing a pleasure to me. The book was almost finished before I acquiesced it would not occur.' The reason was that he 'had read too much' and was too attuned to the 'possibilities and probabilities' role models such as Balzac and Joseph Conrad offered him: 'I had reached that stage to which all young writers must pass through, in which he believes that he had learned too much about his trade.'[64]

Despite this admission, *Light in August* betrays no hint of overlearning. The technical devices are dazzling without being distracting. For whole stretches, Faulkner tells the story

in third-person present tense, which, save for rare examples
(Katherine Ann Porter's 'Flowering Judas'), was uncommon in
this era. The device not only vivifies character psychologies, which
are densely plumbed, but dramatizes the key theme of how one's
past predetermines choices in one's present. Repeatedly, characters
rifle through options that might deliver them to a positive path,
only to succumb to a strict fatalism that makes their tragedies seem
preordained. Nowhere is this better stated than in Joe Christmas's
vision of time as a 'flat pattern . . . going on, myriad' and yet 'familiar'
because 'all that had ever been was the same as all that was to be,
since tomorrow to-be and had-been would be the same.'[65] As *Light
in August* developed, Faulkner sharpened this defeatism into a raw
rebuke of racism, sexual repression and religious zealotry, all by-
products of the Calvinist influence on the American consciousness.
Lena and Byron's love story offers the only counterbalancing hope.

Faulkner completed a first draft within his now-standard six
months for novels in February 1932. That he managed to do this
is remarkable given the distractions of fame and his own growing
susceptibilities. In late October 1931, only two months into the
manuscript, he rather reluctantly attended the inaugural Southern
Writers Conference held at the University of Virginia. Conferees
included Ellen Glasgow, James Branch Cabell and the husband–wife
team of Allen Tate and Caroline Gordon, among others. Although
Thomas Wolfe declined his invitation, Sherwood Anderson eagerly
signed on. Faulkner had not belonged to a literary coterie since his
New Orleans era, six years earlier. Then he soothed authorial
insecurities with a facade of eccentricity. Now he coped by binge
drinking.

Most biographers quote Anderson on Faulkner's behaviour
during the festivities: 'From time to time he appeared, got drunk
again immediately, and disappeared. He kept asking everyone
for drinks. If they didn't give him any, he drank his own.'[66] Other
accounts depict him heckling Glasgow's keynote address, declaring

'I agree!' even as she took thinly veiled potshots at him, declaring, 'The substitute for genius in American literature is brutality.'[67] At another point he either spat or vomited on Gordon after a wayward swallow of booze. (Either way, Gordon remembered, 'There was a geyser I was engulfed in.')[68] He also undermined the entire enterprise, assuring a scoop-hungry reporter that Southern writing was 'not very significant in itself'.[69] Tales of his inebriation circulated widely. William Faulkner might be a genius, gossips whispered, but he was also clearly a drunk.

To stabilize his famous author, Harrison Smith whisked Faulkner to New York. He also had ulterior motives. Smith's partner, the British publisher Jonathan Cape, had forced their firm into receivership, disgruntled with his American subsidiary's negligible sales. Cape's main objection, though, was the work of William Faulkner, which he found pointlessly obscure. Smith intended to start a new firm with a more congenial partner, Robert K. Haas, a founder and former president of the Book of the Month Club, and he wanted to retain Faulkner. To fend off other interested parties, Smith sent the writer on a boat trip to Florida with a handler named Milton Abernathy. When Faulkner couldn't dry out, Abernathy drove him from Jacksonville to Chapel Hill, North Carolina, where he and a partner, Anthony Buttitta, published a left-wing journal called *Contempo.* In his inebriation Faulkner gave them an excerpt from *Light in August* for a special issue on his work, infuriating Smith. By the time Abernathy delivered the writer back to New York, the diversion was all for naught. As Smith's rivals began circling, Faulkner complained to Estelle they treated him like 'some strange and valuable beast'.[70]

Prospective publishers included Harold Guinzburg of the Viking Press, Bennett Cerf of Random House and Alfred A. Knopf, whose imprimatur bore his name. Among the trio, Cerf made the greatest inroads, wooing Faulkner with plans to include *Sanctuary* in the Modern Library, a prestigious and profitable imprint founded, ironically enough, by Faulkner's former publisher Harold Liveright. Through Random House, Cerf also produced a limited edition of a minor non-Yoknapatawpha story, 'Idyll in the Desert', set in Arizona. The project initiated an important relationship, despite the dedication Faulkner scribbled on the manuscript: 'Fuck You, Bennett'. Cerf wisely took the expletive as a drunken joke, and his persistence paid off. Five years later Random House became Faulkner's publisher until his death. As Cerf understood, the profanity bespoke the writer's stress over the barrage of offers he received, from adapting *Sanctuary* into a stage play to writing a movie for Tallulah Bankhead.

If Cerf benefited the most from meeting Faulkner, Knopf suffered the worst. On one occasion, alongside Dashiell Hammett – a star Knopf author – Faulkner crashed a dinner party at the publisher's apartment. He briefly outlasted his drinking companion (Hammett was a notorious alcoholic) before both lay passed out on the floor. At another event Faulkner offended Knopf by refusing to autograph first editions of his novels the publisher collected. Concerns over Faulkner's drinking so intensified that by late November Smith summoned Estelle to New York. Considering she binged as prodigiously as her husband, the strategy wasn't the smartest. Twice in the city, first with Cerf and then with Dorothy Parker witnessing, Estelle threatened to leap from a window.

Despite his drinking, Faulkner maintained a steady writing routine. *Light in August* remained his top priority, but he also produced a short story that opened important doors for him. Through the fabled Algonquin Round Table he met Robert Lovett, a banker and sometime *New Yorker* contributor who had served in the Royal Naval Air Service during the First World War. Lovett – later U.S. Secretary of Defense under Harry S. Truman – shared stories of the Coastal Motor Boat units, three-man torpedo vessels sent on virtual suicide missions to penetrate German minefields and engage Axis Power vessels. To an aviation fan who idolized pilots, the boat crews' valour was eye-opening. The resulting story, 'Turn About', depicts air- and seamen paying mutual tribute to each other's courage under fire. Published in March 1932 in the *Saturday Evening Post*, the story caught the eye of Hollywood. Under the title *Today We Live*, it became the first Faulkner adaptation to reach the silver screen, beating *The Story of Temple Drake*, a controversial rendering of *Sanctuary*, by two months in spring 1933.

For all his flirtation with other publishers, Faulkner followed Harrison Smith to his new venture, despite Cape & Smith's dissolution costing him $4,000 in royalties from his scandalous potboiler. Smith was 'my one friend in the North, one man I like', he insisted.[71] What he meant was Smith would publish anything he submitted, and without editorial meddling. *Sanctuary*'s lost income nevertheless caused severe financial stress. Upon completing *Light in August* Faulkner half-heartedly hoped for a serialization deal, though he knew no periodical would consent to his two conditions: '$5,000 . . . and not a word to be changed'.[72]

The latter request would have been an impossibility in 1932. As the fatal catalyst for Joe Christmas's self-loathing self-destruction, Faulkner has his racially ambiguous anti-hero embark on a taboo affair with Joanna Burden, a white woman known in Jefferson as a 'lover of negroes'. The couple's lovemaking is clearly sadomasochistic, with Christmas intent on sparking some proof of racial bigotry in her Christian amity. Joanna's motivations are more ambiguous, in part because Faulkner ascribes them to 'the wild throes of nymphomania'. As the descendant of Yankee abolitionists – two of whom Col. John Sartoris will kill in *The Unvanquished* – Joanna seeks to abnegate white culpability for oppression, not through repentance (at least not at first) but by 'damning herself forever to the hell of her forefathers, by living not alone in sin but in filth'.[73] Scenes from this complex racial-sexual dynamic would have been too incendiary in an age when vice squads and watch and ward societies patrolled newsstands for obscenity, especially when Faulkner describes 'wild' Joanna screaming 'Negro! Negro! Negro!' in orgasmic passion.

The violence was equally censorable. As Joanna emerges from her sexual 'mania', she aspires to help Christmas by reforming him, thus denying him the hatred he craves from her. In a fury, he slices her throat with a razor, nearly severing her head. Yet that gruesome act would not be the novel's bloodiest moment. That would come when Christmas is cornered in Reverend Hightower's kitchen for the crime and a state national-guard captain named Percy Grimm castrates him, screaming, 'Now you'll let white women alone, even in hell,' as Christmas dies.[74] In a masterful chapter leading up to the mutilation – a common atrocity during lynchings – Faulkner depicts the psychological resentments and the social militarization of white violence that normalizes such savage brutality in the name of preserving law and order. Grimm is a chilling portrait of the fascist mind; as Faulkner said of the character years later, 'I didn't realise until after Hitler got into the newspapers that I had created a Nazi before he did.'[75]

Faulkner knew *Light in August* was as complex a statement on race as any white American had ever produced. But he also knew it would not make him money. Recognizing he had only one realistic option, he contacted Ben Wasson and agreed to an offer he had rejected in New York.

He would go to Hollywood and, for $500 a week, write for the movies.

5

Rushing from Pillar to Post
(1932–8)

Faulkner's reluctant Hollywood career began on 7 May 1932. According to legend, he reported to Metro-Goldwyn-Mayer dishevelled and with a gashed forehead from a drunken mishap. He stayed just long enough to learn his first assignment was a wrestling feature called *Flesh*, whereupon he disappeared into Death Valley for a week. Upon returning, he submitted plot ideas, all flimsy and none filmable. Six weeks and $3,000 later, MGM realized William Faulkner had no viable ideas, nor any real interest in the movies.

Yet for the next six years he contracted with studios a half-dozen times out of financial desperation. Among writers in the 1930s who looked to Hollywood for a livelihood, Faulkner is considered the second most illustrative example of the incompatibility of literature and cinema. F. Scott Fitzgerald remains first only because he dramatized his ambivalence towards the film industry in his unfinished novel *The Last Tycoon* (1941). Faulkner admitted his inadequacies at scriptwriting, but he never poured his resentment into fiction. He set exactly one short story – 'Golden Land' (1935) – in Los Angeles. That it is not overtly about moviemaking may be the best evidence of his disinterest in Hollywood. While critics routinely compare his literary devices to film techniques, Faulkner's fondness for ornate language, tangled syntax and non-linear plots clashed with the unadorned, instructional format of scripts. Whether Faulkner was incapable or merely uninterested in adapting his style to Hollywood's remains debatable.

Despite his rocky start at MGM, Faulkner benefited from something Fitzgerald never did: a close friend and protector. Without director Howard Hawks, his tenure in Tinseltown might have ended quickly, whether by his choice or the studio's.[1] MGM was uninclined to renew his contract until Hawks, eager to adapt the story 'Turn About', lobbied executives. In the first of many humiliations Faulkner felt Hollywood heaped upon him, MGM halved his salary to $250 a week.

While in California news arrived on 7 August that Murry Falkner had died from a heart attack at 61. Faulkner assumed responsibility for his mother's well-being. Two months later financial anxieties relaxed, if only briefly, when Paramount Pictures bought the rights to *Sanctuary* for $6,000. The windfall allowed Faulkner to return to Oxford. Through Hawks's continued intervention, he received rare permission to work from home. Pleased with Faulkner's script for 'Turn About' – filmed as *Today We Live* – Hawks persuaded MGM that Faulkner deserved a pay raise. Faulkner would earn $2,400 a month until May 1933, an unusual interim of affluence (adjusting for inflation, the pay equates to $44,000 per month today).

Amid funerals and cross-country treks to and from Hollywood, *Light in August* was published on 8 October. The first novel from Faulkner's fifth publisher in seven years included a glaring error on the jacket that referred to 'Lee' Christmas instead of 'Joe'. Fortunately, reviewers focused on the content instead of the packaging, most saying the book improved upon *Sanctuary*. 'There are still moments when Mr Faulkner seems to write of what is horrible purely from a desire to shock his readers or else because it holds for him a fascination from which he cannot altogether escape,' wrote J. Donald Adams in the *New York Times*. Yet Faulkner also 'permits some of his people . . . to act sometimes out of motives which are human in their decency . . . In a word,

Faulkner has admitted justice and compassion to his scheme of things.'[2] Genre may have influenced such responses. Numerous critics took Faulkner to task for bragging of writing *Sanctuary* strictly for money in his Modern Library introduction. Because *Light in August* confronted a specific social problem, its intentions seemed nobler than hard-boiled sensationalism. Unfortunately, reviewers saw the racial hatred the novel critiques as a Southern rather than American crisis.

For the first time, reviewers also worried that Faulkner's stylistic habits might degenerate into tics. Techniques like conjoining words ('womanfilth', 'allembracing', 'laborpurged') struck them as mannerisms rather than experiments. Sentence structures seemed needlessly complex, and to some the flashbacks sapped the action's crescendo. Decades later Faulkner was still defending his decision to follow Joe Christmas's climactic castration with a thirty-page chapter on Reverend Hightower's failed career as a Presbyterian minister. When a student at the University of Virginia in the 1950s asked why that subplot wasn't integrated more dramatically into earlier scenes, the author replied, 'Unless a book follows a simple direct line such as a story of adventure, it becomes a series of pieces . . . It takes a certain amount of taste and judgment to arrange the different pieces in the most effective place in juxtaposition to one another.'[3] The quote explains why *Light in August*, along with *As I Lay Dying, The Hamlet, If I Forget Thee, Jerusalem* and *Go Down, Moses*, is constructed modularly. Faulkner considered plot threads components positioned in patterns instead of woven into a seamless whole.

The story of Joe Christmas capped an amazing three-year run. Between *The Sound and the Fury* and *Light in August*, Faulkner set a pace for innovation that no American writer before or since has matched. The streak startled contemporaries who debuted earlier but stumbled in their second stretch. Ernest Hemingway was silent in this period except for a smattering of unremarkable stories. Two

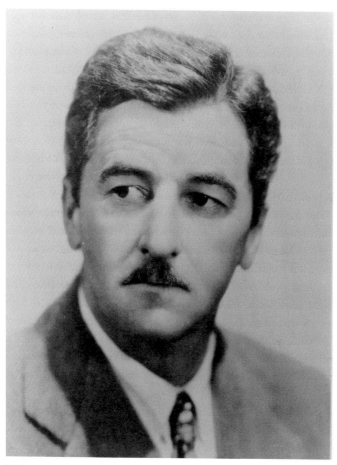

Hollywood's image of the famed novelist as a screenwriter in the 1930s: matinee-idol handsome and impeccably professional. The truth was far messier.

weeks before *Light* appeared, he published his first book since *A Farewell to Arms*, which pre-dated *The Sound and the Fury* by one month in 1929. *Death in the Afternoon* was not a novel – Hemingway would need six more years to produce another of those. A bombastic treatise on bullfighting, *Death* exposed its author's anxiety over

Faulkner's emergence. In a mock dialogue on contemporary letters, Hemingway claimed *Sanctuary* opened publishing doors to books about 'the finest whorehouses in the land' and 'the most brilliant society there found'. He also sniped about the speed of Faulkner's output, the first of many potshots to come: 'Madame, you can't go wrong on Faulkner. He's prolific, too. By the time you get [his books] ordered there'll be new ones out.'[4]

Light in August was far from a commercial failure, but sales didn't match *Sanctuary*'s. Buoyed by Hollywood money, Faulkner spent freely anyway. In February 1933 he began flying lessons with pilot Vernon Omlie, whose wife, Phoebe, was also an aviation pioneer. That autumn Faulkner celebrated earning his solo licence by purchasing a 210-horsepower Waco cabin aeroplane, an indulgence even for a man bragging to journalists of earning $35,000 from Hollywood, though it was 'a rotten way to make a living'.[5]

Flying distracted him from his MGM obligations. Throughout the winter and spring of 1933, he toiled over various aviator scripts, the most promising of which was *War Birds*, the story of a real-life First World War pilot who, like John Sartoris III, was downed over France. Faulkner's adventures with Omlie should have engaged him with the storyline, but he made little effort to convince MGM that he was worth his salary. During a May location shoot for a New Orleans swamp romance called *Louisiana Lou* directed by Todd Browning – whose nightmarish circus-sideshow movie *Freaks* (1932) made *Sanctuary*'s grotesquery seem tame – his employment was terminated.

Faulkner could have remained employed had he relocated back to Hollywood, but family matters bound him to Oxford. On 25 June Estelle gave birth to a daughter named Jill. Faulkner proved an attentive, doting parent, taking the baby on flights before she was three months old. Yet Jill's birth strained romantic relations with Estelle, whose upbringing had not prepared her to deal with the frugality that living off art requires. Faulkner grew impatient with his wife's spending habits. They were no more profligate than his, but as breadwinner he considered her wardrobe and furniture less important than his aeroplane. Estelle's parents now lived in reduced circumstances and often required help. Other family obligations kept Faulkner financially frazzled, including flying lessons for his youngest brother, Dean. When Harrison Smith gently asked when a new novel might arrive, he listed the pressing needs that made focusing on fiction difficult: 'I have my own taxes and my mother's, and the possibility that Estelle's people will call on me before Feb. 1, and also my mother's and Dean's support, and occasional demands from my other two brothers which I can never anticipate.' Exhausted, Faulkner concluded, 'I seem right now to rush from pillar to post and return.'[6]

Amid the bustle he came up with a great title – *Requiem for a Nun* – only to realize he lacked a viable plot. (Twenty years later he found one.) In other cases, he demurred on projects he lacked the energy to complete, such as a novel about the Snopes clan. Slowly, however, an idea took shape. The genesis was another formidable short story, 'Wash', published in *Harper's* in February 1934. The title character, Wash Jones, squats on the estate of Thomas Sutpen, who at sixty brazenly impregnates Wash's teenaged granddaughter. Overhearing his benefactor compare Milly to a horse, Wash murders Sutpen, then the girl and her child. Setting fire to his shack, he commits suicide by proxy by rushing the local sheriff with the same scythe that teaches Sutpen a fatal lesson in 'white trash' pride. The story bloodily rebukes the 'hoop skirts and plug hats' nostalgia of genteel Southern fiction.[7]

Fascinated by Sutpen's bristling hubris, Faulkner elaborated upon the character's patriarchal grandiosity under his favourite working title, 'Dark House'. As he told Smith, 'The theme is a man who outraged the land, and the land then turned and destroyed the man's family.'[8] 'Wash' was not his first exploration of Sutpen's outrages. The unpublished 1931 story 'Evangeline' depicted Sutpen's son, Henry, killing his brother-in-law, Charles Bon, after discovering Bon is a bigamist whose first wife is black. The novel whips miscegenation taboos into pure melodrama, speculating that Charles himself is half black *and* Sutpen's son.

The real breakthrough came when Faulkner reinvented the narrative frame. Instead of two chatty friends telling a pseudo-ghost story in 'Evangeline', Sutpen's fall is reconstructed by Quentin Compson shortly before his 1910 suicide in *The Sound and the Fury*. 'I use his bitterness which he has projected on the South in the form of hatred of it and its people to get more out of the story itself than a historical novel would be,' Faulkner explained to Smith.[9]

He optimistically believed he could finish the novel by the autumn, but the writing proved the most agonizing of his major works, requiring almost three years of on-again, off-again labour. At summer's end 1934 he invented a new title, *Absalom, Absalom!*, an allusion to the son of King David who kills his half-brother for raping their sister. Yet conveying the sociocultural and mythic import of Sutpen's rise and fall required a creative focus pressing cash concerns didn't allow. The title came, for example, after a three-week assignment producing a treatment for a novel adaptation about the 1848 California Gold Rush that Howard Hawks wanted to direct. The $1,000 a week that Universal Studios paid was welcome money, but returning to Hollywood afforded no time for fiction.

Despite this momentary bonanza, short fiction remained Faulkner's main means of generating income. In 1934, eleven of his stories were published, along with his second collection, *Dr Martino and Other Stories*. Neither sales nor reviews matched those of *These 13*. Part of the problem was the table of contents lacked any discernible unity. Barnstormer stories mingled with marriage tales; nineteenth-century bloodshed sat alongside present-day murder mysteries. The juxtapositions dramatized the many genres Faulkner attempted, from war stories to detective fiction to supernatural tales. Not even geography was consistent: for every Yoknapatawpha tale, another story took place in New York City, Oxford, England or even Latin America. To reviewers *Dr Martino* was a 'mixed sheaf' or just 'Another Batch of Faulkner Stories'.[10] Many critics dismissed the stories as potboilers instead of polished work.

That judgement is unfair, for the collection demonstrates Faulkner's diversity. Highlights include 'There Was a Queen', a sequel to *Flags in the Dust/Sartoris* that depicts Narcissa Benbow Sartoris trading sexual favours to an insurance investigator to recover embarrassing love letters Byron Snopes anonymously sent her; 'Death Drag', which features exhilarating descriptions of a wing walker dropping from an aeroplane rope ladder into a moving car; and 'Elly', a miscegenation tale that ends with a fatal car crash – it began life as a story by Estelle called 'Selvage'. In addition to 'Turn About' – retitled 'Turnabout' – the most gripping entry is the post-Civil War thriller 'Mountain Victory', in which a one-armed Confederate major, Saucier Weddel, and his black manservant, Jubal, encounter a murderous family of Tennessee Unionists. Faulkner never advocated for *Doctor Martino* as a collection, but he regarded highly the stories within it. All but one are included in *Collected Stories of William Faulkner* (1950).

In addition to stand-alone stories, he also attempted a short-story sequence, a series of tales featuring recurring characters that across monthly issues of a periodical read like instalments of a serialized novel. The *Saturday Evening Post* was fond of this genre, especially when the stories formed a coming-of-age narrative in which individual entries initiated the main character into successive stages of maturation. For his sequence, Faulkner returned to the Civil War and Reconstruction-era boyhood that haunts Old Bayard Sartoris in *Flags in the Dust/Sartoris* and produced three stories. 'Ambuscade', 'Retreat' and 'Raid' feature Bayard and his sidekick, the slave Marengo 'Ringo' Strother, as Tom- and Huck-styled innocents outfoxing Union troops. Raising the boys while Col. John Sartoris commands a motley band of irregulars is Bayard's wily maternal grandmother, Rosa Millard. The plots involve comic set-ups, with Bayard and Ringo hiding under Granny's skirts to elude the Yanks, or getting their mouths washed out with soap for using a profanity, or a Union miscalculation inadvertently enriching the trio with silver and mules. The stories tapped a literary nostalgia for the Confederacy popularized by old friend Stark Young's contemporaneous bestseller, *So Red the Rose* (1934). This nostalgia soon culminated in Margaret Mitchell's *Gone with the Wind* (1936), which appeared before Faulkner could publish his series in book form as *The Unvanquished* (1938).

Faulkner dismissed the Bayard and Ringo tales as 'pulp' and 'trash'.[11] The best he eventually said of them was that their accessibility made them congenial primers for his more challenging works. That the series was conceived for money is evident from Faulkner's instructions to his new agent, Morton Goldman, who took over marketing his short fiction when Ben Wasson left publishing for Hollywood the previous December. Faulkner wanted $10,000 for six instalments, a hefty amount considering the *Post*'s top price for his stories was $900. Editors balked, then annoyed the author by questioning character motives in the fourth entry, 'The Unvanquished' (later retitled 'Riposte in Tertio').

Although the *Post* accepted this story and a fifth, 'Vendée', before the year ended, they were not published until late 1936. By then the sixth instalment had appeared out of sequence in *Scribner's* in April 1935. Rejected by the *Post*, 'Drusilla' (later 'Skirmish at Sartoris') only brought in $250. That price was still better than earnings for the concluding seventh entry, 'An Odor of Verbena', which no periodical bought. In the end, magazine sales of the stories barely netted $5,000, half of what Faulkner considered their worth. *The Unvanquished* would not pay off until early 1938, when MGM offered $25,000 for movie rights.

Writing these stories, Faulkner was all too aware that two years had passed since *Light in August*. Spinning his wheels with *Absalom, Absalom!* he decided he could finish a non-Yoknapatawpha novel quicker. Earlier that year, he and Vernon Omlie attended the inauguration of New Orleans's Shushan Airport. Before their arrival, a stunt pilot was burned alive participating in the Pan-American Air Races held there. Despite barnstorming's dangers, Faulkner, Omlie and Dean Falkner began sponsoring aerial exhibitions outside of Oxford. Known as the Faulkner Flying Circus, the events featured parachuting, stunts and races. Inspired by the spectacle, Faulkner dashed off a narrative about aviation daredevils. Entitled *Pylon* (1935) after the tall ground markers used for race perimeters, the story was loosely modelled on the New Orleans fatality, though Faulkner renamed the city 'New Valois' and set it in the state of 'Franciana'. 'The story and incidents and the characters as they perform in the story are all fictional,' he informed Harrison Smith. 'But someone may read it and see into it what I didn't.' Faulkner asked whether the real-life figures inspiring his characters could sue for libel. He also wondered aloud 'whether a suit would help sell the book'.[12]

Libel concerns are understandable. Protagonists Roger and Laverne Shumann are clearly based on Vernon and Phoebe Omlie, except in one shocking regard: accompanying the couple is parachutist Jack Holmes, who may be the father of Laverne's son, also named Jack. The threesome's polyamory exemplifies the modernity of the barnstormer existence, a point Faulkner underscores through an unnamed reporter fascinated by the unapologetic *ménage à trois*. The reporter realizes that by risking their lives pursuing airspeed, the Shumanns and Holmes – along with their alcoholic mechanic, Jiggs – cannot be harnessed to social norms on the ground.

For most reviewers, *Pylon* again demonstrated Faulkner's luridness. In one startling flashback, Laverne insists that Roger make love to her in an aloft cockpit. During a post-coital parachute jump, her dress flies above her torso, exposing her vagina to a countryside of men rabid with lust.[13] Sex and barnstorming to Faulkner may have symbolized the same modernist fury for speed and thrills, but audiences only saw sensationalism. According to their biographer, the Omlies were appalled: 'Publicly, [Phoebe] said nothing except when asked about the veracity of the characterizations. Then she simply noted that she and her husband "disapproved of Bill's *Pylon*". When Vernon privately admonished Faulkner with the comment that "aviation people are not like the way you portray them, I doubt that it will be accepted by the majority of people," the author allegedly replied he was more interested in selling books than portraying historical accuracy.'[14]

Faulkner's eighth novel is about more than daredevilry and sex, though. Published in March 1935 – two years into the New Deal, before recovery efforts took hold – *Pylon* is as close to a proletarian novel as the movement-averse Faulkner ever produced. As barnstormers chase prize money from exhibition to exhibition, municipal authorities exploit and cheat their labour. Faulkner even compares a meeting with airport management to a 'conventional conference between millowners and the delegation from the shops', a stock scene in Depression-era strike novels like Sherwood Anderson's *Beyond Desire* (1932).[15] Yet *Pylon* is not protest fiction. There is no statement of solidarity or assertion of worker dignity. The novel ends with a newly pregnant Laverne abandoning little Jack to her dead husband's parents to continue vagabonding with Holmes. Technology is less a path to progress than unremitting motion, says Faulkner, taking us nowhere fast.

Pylon was written from October to December 1934, more quickly than any Faulkner novel except *As I Lay Dying.* Unlike with that classic, the haste shows. The book is Faulkner's single greatest missed opportunity: it could have elevated aviation fiction to the heights of art as *Sanctuary* did the hard-boiled crime genre. Critics have drawn parallels between *Pylon* and *Air Birds*, *War Birds*, *Sky Birds* and other flyer magazines, but Faulkner doesn't engage their tropes as his previous pulp foray does those of *Black Mask* and comparable crime rags. For starters, he is too busy sowing literary allusions: the book's penultimate section is called 'Lovesong of J. A. Prufrock', and *Waste Land* imagery and Joycean devices stick out, unassimilated, more than in any work since *Soldiers' Pay* and *Mosquitoes*. The novel also contains curious repetitions that stymie the theme, including two long, detailed descriptions of alcoholics vomiting.

But the main reason is style. If *Light in August* hinted that Faulkner's expressive habits could erode into mannerisms, *Pylon* is his first mature book to be roundly criticized as self-indulgent. As Laurence Stallings cleverly wrote, his 'rush of prose engender[s] enormous technical friction which invariably overheats the oil of narration'. John Crowe Ransom called the style 'frenzied and bad; the wildest prose he has ever written' and insisted Faulkner was 'spent'. The book nevertheless sold well, undoubtedly thanks to its racy content. The pulp magazine *Snappy* even recommended it 'for torridity seekers' as a 'Torrid Tome'.[16]

Creatively, *Pylon* primed the pump for *Absalom, Absalom!* Five days after the former's publication, Faulkner began the latter's final draft. To maintain a steady output, he followed the same composition process as his aviator novel. Rather than send Harrison Smith a completed manuscript, he submitted it section by section. Occasionally bills and debts forced him to stop to churn out short stories. The most important of the quartet published in 1935 was 'Lion', a moving hunting story pitting a scrappy dog against a legendary bear named Old Ben that introduced a major character, Boon Hogganbeck. A rough-hewn handyman with Chickasaw blood, Boon grieves over both animals' deaths and nature's mortality in general. Six years later Faulkner revised 'Lion' into a core section of 'The Bear'. Selling intermittent stories to *Harper's* or the *American*

Mercury wasn't enough to finance *Absalom*, though. By autumn Faulkner owed $1,700 to various Oxford merchants and grocers. Only by negotiating a loan from Smith & Haas – who had already advanced him $2,000 for the book – could he write without distraction.

Then on Sunday, 10 November, tragedy struck. During an air show in Pontotoc, Mississippi, 40 kilometres (30 mi.) east of Oxford, the Waco cabin-cruiser Faulkner purchased from *Sanctuary*'s movie rights plunged 610 metres (2,000 ft) and crashed, killing Dean Falkner and three passengers. So Maud might see her son's body before burial, Faulkner spent the night with an undertaker reconstructing his brother's mangled face. In an eerie coincidence, the writer's recently published story 'Uncle Willy' (the *American Mercury*) ended with its titular hero dying in a similar plane crash.

Blaming himself for his brother's death, Faulkner moved into Maud's house to comfort her and Dean's pregnant widow, Louise. Erasing the boundaries between fiction and family, he selected for Dean's gravestone the same epitaph *Flags in the Dust/Sartoris* borrowed from Exodus for his fallen First World War pilot John Sartoris iii: 'I bare him on Eagles' / wings and brought him / unto me.'[17]

By December the need for income outweighed any comfort he could provide his family. He returned to Hollywood for another stint with Howard Hawks, who persuaded Twentieth-Century Fox to hire Faulkner for $1,000 a week. In California he commenced an affair with Meta Carpenter, Hawks's 28-year-old script girl. Born in Mississippi and raised in Memphis, Meta was worldlier and more sexually assertive than most Southern women. She found Faulkner's gentility charming, his loneliness touching. As he confessed, intimacy with Estelle had evaporated after Jill's birth; at Rowan Oak they slept in separate rooms. Whether this was true is unclear. Regardless, according to Meta's memoir, *A Loving Gentleman* (1976), she unleashed a previously unexpressed erotic vigour in Faulkner.

Inscriptions to his mistress in books thanked her for offering 'for him his love's long girl's body sweet to fuck' and calling her 'my April and my cunt'.[18]

The relationship was not merely sexual. Faulkner relished romantic gestures such as holding hands as they walked Sunset Boulevard. The couple openly socialized with industry people, fuelling speculation, which Faulkner encouraged, that he intended to divorce Estelle. Despite the ardour Meta awoke in him, one susceptibility remained unhealable: she could not stop his drinking.

Grief over Dean's death and constant financial stress ignited a gruelling cycle of self-destructive bingeing. Faulkner was in California barely a month before landing in a hospital to dry out. When a fellow screenwriter questioned his whisky consumption, he replied, 'There's a lot of nourishment in an acre of corn.'[19] (He did not eat when bingeing.) Back at Rowan Oak in late January 1936 his behaviour grew so erratic that Estelle checked him into a sanitarium in Byhalia, Mississippi, 80 kilometres (50 mi.) north of Oxford. Eerily, the facility was the same one where, 26 years later, Faulkner would die.

Relations with Estelle, meanwhile, grew vindictive and violent. Friends reported finding Faulkner with his face scratched, Estelle with bruised arms. Irate over her spending, Faulkner famously took out ads in both the Oxford *Eagle* and the Memphis *Commercial Appeal* declaring he would 'not be responsible for any debt incurred or bills made, or notes or checks signed by Mrs William Faulkner or Mrs Estelle Oldham Faulkner.' The ads attracted national attention; *Time* magazine printed Faulkner's unconvincing explanation that the notices were a legal manoeuvre to protect himself from debtors, not a sign of discord at Rowan Oak.[20]

While at home, Faulkner pined to return to Hollywood, or at least to Meta. Yet his alcoholism precluded steady employment, leaving him bouncing for short bursts between MGM and RKO. Inexplicably, when he went west that July for his third 1936 contract, he brought

Estelle and Jill with him. Whenever Estelle was incapacitated, Faulkner took his daughter on picnics and beach trips with Meta. In another hurtful episode, he arranged to attend a dinner party with his wife where his lover was also present, supposedly as Ben Wasson's date. Estelle was not fooled and berated Wasson (who was gay) for colluding in the deception. The incident suggests how cruelly Faulkner used Meta to punish Estelle for their mutual unhappiness. Estelle insisted that if he divorced her she would take Rowan Oak and Jill. Meta realized her lover would never leave his wife.

Amid this turmoil, *Absalom, Absalom!* was finally published on 26 October. Its long incubation was worth the exhaustion. As Faulkner intuited, the novel was his masterwork. In Thomas Sutpen he created his version of the uniquely American story of the individual who rises from nothing only to fall from hubris. As such, Sutpen is kin to Hawthorne's Judge Jaffrey Pyncheon, William Dean Howells's Silas Lapham, Fitzgerald's Jay Gatsby and Steinbeck's Adam Trask, among others. In the novel's keyword, Sutpen concocts a 'design' for establishing a dynasty after suffering the insult, in adolescence, of a black servant turning him away from the front door of a Tidewater, Virginia, mansion. Seeking his fortune first in Haiti, Sutpen marries and fathers a child, only to discover his wife is half-black. Abandoning her, he builds in Mississippi his Sutpen's Hundred plantation, becoming Yoknapatawpha County's wealthiest landowner and fathering two white heirs, Henry and Judith. His standing is threatened when his first-born son, Charles Bon, reappears, intent on claiming his own legacy by marrying Judith. Preserving his design means Sutpen must destroy his family by pressuring Henry to murder Bon. After the Civil War devastates the plantation, a widowed Sutpen twice more attempts to realize his design. He offers to marry his sister-in-law if she first bears him a son; then he impregnates the adolescent squatter Milly Jones.

In utter disregard for his megalomaniacal vision, the child is a girl. As in 'Wash', Sutpen meets his end by the blade of Wash Jones's scythe.

While critiquing the slide that unchecked American ambition often takes into tyrannical self-delusion, *Absalom, Absalom!* also offers a masterclass in the systems of economic exploitation from which Southern plantation owners like Sutpen derived their enormous wealth. Debunking all pretences of class nobility and racial beneficence, the novel reveals, as Sutpen's disillusioned father-in-law, Goodhue Coldfield, is credited with acknowledging, the South 'erected its economic edifice not on the rock of stern morality but on the shifting sands of opportunism and moral brigandage'.[21] Those 'shifting sands' are, in essence, the complex and unstable power dynamics between capital, labour and value that cannot be regulated by or even contained within simple acts of acquisition and accrual, no matter how those acts are mythologized in legends of human ambition or folly – not even in literary parables of hamartia, or the 'fatal flaw' that provides a convenient psychological explanation for Sutpen's rise and fall. ('His trouble was innocence,' one of his contemporaries decides, invoking that most mythic of American attributes.)[22] At all points Faulkner shrouds the plantation owner's story in ambiguity, contradiction and even impossibility. The future colonel first attains status, for example, by putting down a slave revolt on a Haitian sugar plantation in 1827. As a reward, he is allowed to marry the plantation owner's daughter, Eulalia, who bears him the son, Charles, he repudiates for possessing black blood. As many critics have noted, a revolt in Haiti could not have happened given that the island nation had been a free republic liberated from both slavery and colonial rule since 1804. Whether Faulkner's anachronism is a mistake, artistic licence or a carefully planted clue to an entire chain of anomalies remains a matter of unresolvable contention.[23] About the only thing critics can agree upon is that the impossible story is but one of many details springing from motives, both authorial and characterological, that readers must struggle to rationalize.

The 'shifting sands' of the novel are not just economic but narratological. One remarkable aspect of *Absalom* is the distance Faulkner keeps Sutpen from readers. We see him in striking moments: insulted by the slave at the mansion door; pursuing an escaping French architect he forcibly brings with him from the West Indies, along with a pack of slaves, to design and build the most lavish estate in Yoknapatawpha County; pelted with dirt clods by townspeople as he marries Ellen Coldfield; stripped to the waist and sweating as he fistfights his own slaves for sport in front of his children (including Clytie, whom he sired with a slave); pressuring Henry to kill Bon to protect the family reputation; cracking Wash twice in the face with a whip before the scythe 'tech[es]' him the ultimate lesson; and, in the final indignity, his body sprawled in a ditch in his Confederate regalia after the mules pulling his coffin wagon bolt and spill him, 'sabre plumes and all', into the dirt.[24]

Despite such details, Sutpen is never so much a character as an object of speculation. His ambitions are constructed through guesses, assumptions, hand-me-down recollections and outright hearsay by the novel's four main interlocutors: his sister-in-law, Rosa Coldfield; Quentin Compson and his father, Jason; and Quentin's Harvard roommate, Shreve (surnamed MacKenzie in *The Sound and the Fury*, but here called McCannon). Crucial plot twists that should explain events are also hypotheses. Readers never know whether Charles Bon is indeed Sutpen's first-born son, or if Sutpen really urges murder upon Henry, or whether Bon actually has black blood. These are Shreve's and Quentin's conclusions. Shreve badgers Quentin to confront their implications, assuming the fear of race mixing is the obvious explanation for *any* white Southern planter's actions. (More logical even than the incest taboo: '*So it's the miscegenation, not the incest, which you can't bear,*' the roommates imagine Bon taunting his presumptive half-brother over his half-sister.)[25] Judging by Quentin's famously defensive non-defence of the South that concludes the novel ("'I don't hate it," he said. *I don't hate it he thought . . . I don't! I don't!'*),[26] fear of miscegenation is the only possible motive for him, too. Remarkably, few readers question whether Shreve and Quentin are wrong about the causes of Sutpen's fall. Just as some critics describe Joe Christmas in *Light in August* as a 'mulatto' – forgetting that the novel never establishes his actual racial identity – readers speak of Bon's blackness as if it were a textual fact, not the roommates' best guess.

To put it another way, *Absalom, Absalom!* is a defiantly indeterminate text. It excites anxieties and defers certainties. Had Faulkner told the story straightforwardly, he might have produced a Southern melodrama akin to Kate Chopin's famous story 'Désirée's Baby' (1893), works that impugn audiences' ability to define racial categories by facial features and skin colour. *Absalom* takes that challenge deeper, undermining the certainty that any racial differences exist. The novel implies that because definitions of white and black are subjective they can only be defined against each other, interdependent to the point of indistinction. As Frederick R. Karl writes, Faulkner 'appears on the edge of suggesting that the resolution of the South's (and the nation's) racial dilemma was in a single race, one that would transcend black and white by becoming black-and-white'.[27] Shreve predicts this outcome to Quentin: '[I]n a few thousand years, I who regard you will also have sprung from the loins of African kings.'[28] Insisting miscegenation is inevitable was as radical a stand as a white Southerner could take in 1930s America – one so radical that Faulkner eventually backed away from it.

Suffice to say, *Absalom, Absalom!* demands a reader with enormous patience. The interpretive dedication it requires would largely go unrequited until the late 1940s and 1950s when academics promoted the practice of close reading known as New Criticism. This analytical approach taught generations of college students to dissect symbols and image patterns with scientific rigour. Without such scrupulous attention, *Absalom* feels like a whirlpool of repetition. Yet its form is actually the inverse, a Yeatsian gyre. The circularity of repetition spirals uncertainties centrifugally rather than winnowing implications centripetally.

Until that audience was created, Faulkner had to weather exasperation. For many reviewers in 1936, the radical structure of *Absalom*, along with the gymnastic sentences, seemed pointlessly convoluted. Mary-Carter Roberts in the *Washington Evening Star* described Faulkner as 'fighting with his own prose like a man slashing his way through a forest of falling velvet curtains armed only with a dull knife'. Max Miller of the *San Diego Union* decided that 'if the secret of great writing is to write in a cross-word puzzle code that only the writer can decipher then Faulkner this time certainly should have the boys and girl buffaloed into the epitome of admiration'.[29] By far the most infamous dismissal came from Clifton Fadiman in the *New Yorker*, who called it 'the most consistently boring novel' he ever read: 'This is a penny dreadful tricked up in fancy language and given a specious depth by the expert manipulation of a series of eccentric technical tricks. The characters have no magnitude and no meaning because they have no more reality than a mince-pie nightmare.'[30] A minority of reviewers, including a young Wallace Stegner, defended the experimentation, dismissing detractors as 'impercipient and probably lazy'.[31] Nevertheless, most responses that weren't outright contemptuous were ambivalent.

Absalom, Absalom! appeared under the imprimatur not of Smith & Haas but of Random House. In early 1936 Faulkner's publishers sold their company to Bennett Cerf and Donald Klopfer, who had long promised Faulkner they could win him a wider audience. To make the novel comprehensible they encouraged Faulkner to add a chronology and genealogy outlining the action and clarifying character relationships. The novel even came with a fold-out map of Yoknapatawpha County. Faulkner's sixth publisher in eleven years (and his final one) heavily promoted *Absalom*, even fibbing to booksellers: '10,000 copies are the least that have been sold of any Faulkner novel published in the past six years,' read one industry ad.[32] Other copy celebrated the novel as a 'best-seller', an optimistic assessment at best. *Absalom* ended up selling roughly 8,000 copies. Yet its difficulty doomed prospects for Faulkner's next book, which, ironically, was far more accessible and should have broadened his audience.

That book was *The Unvanquished* (1938), whose sequenced stories Faulkner began revising in early 1937. Still in Hollywood, still lackadaisical about script assignments, still incapable of salting away his salary, despite downsizing from the lavish, furnished Pacific Palisades home he and Estelle rented the previous summer to a modest Beverly Hills address. By summer's end Faulkner had earned nearly $22,000, most of it freely spent on servants, dining out and entertainment. Despite the large paycheck, he was unhappy. That spring Meta Carpenter left him for the German concert pianist Wolfgang Rebner, sinking him into a woe that inspired a novel begun a few months later, his most fiercely passionate. When his studio work ended he returned briefly to Rowan Oak, only to race that September to New York. The ostensible purpose was to meet his new editor, Saxe Commins, the replacement for Harrison Smith, who had left Random House. The real motive was to see the Rebners as they returned from their honeymoon. In Manhattan, Faulkner's drinking worsened; in one November incident he passed out on the toilet at the Algonquin Hotel and severely burned his back slumping against a steam pipe. A procession of friends nursed him through his pain, including Sherwood Anderson, with whom Faulkner reconnected for the first time since 1931.

Returning to Oxford, he immersed himself in the novel Meta's loss inspired, calling it *If I Forget Thee, Jerusalem*. Years later Faulkner claimed he wrote about a doomed love affair 'to stave off what

I thought was heart-break'.[33] Harder to stave off was his financial recklessness. In February 1938 MGM bought the rights to *The Unvanquished*, earning Faulkner $20,000 after commission. Combined with the previous year's salary from Twentieth-Century Fox, he had earned the equivalent in 2018 of $861,922, a sum that should have sailed him through years (if not decades) of novel writing. Yet in quick succession he bought the forest surrounding Rowan Oak known as Bailey's Woods, along with Greenfield Farm, 320 acres of land located 27 kilometres (17 mi.) northeast of Oxford. There his brother John – an aspiring novelist himself – oversaw cotton, hogs, corn and mules. The farm was meant to provide a steady income, but it drained his resources. Mainly, it allowed Faulkner to present himself to the public as a humble farmer who just happened to write.

Random House had high expectations for *The Unvanquished*. Shortly before its publication, Bennett Cerf's partner, Donald Klopfer, wrote to a colleague, 'I feel we will do well with it, although it is a hell of a job to break down the resistance caused by confusion in ABSALOM, ABSALOM. Here's hoping Faulkner will get his real audience.'[34] The company capitalized upon the popularity of *Gone with the Wind*, explicitly comparing *The Unvanquished* in advertising to Margaret Mitchell's epic. The resistance Klopfer worried about was too formidable, however. Despite favourable reviews – most commentators welcomed the book's comparative simplicity – sales petered out at 6,000 copies, less than the far more Byzantine *Absalom*. Although the movie rights made up for the loss of projected income, Random House still faced the challenge of reinventing Faulkner from a prestige to a popular author. Klopfer's reference to his 'real audience' raises questions about just who the company thought should be reading him but wasn't.

The Unvanquished remains controversial for glorifying the Lost Cause and for simplifying Faulkner's themes and style into commercial form. When read as popular fiction, the stories demonstrate the writer's talent for humour, suspense and character

Despite the domestic discontent at Rowan Oak, the Faulkners hosted a mock hunting party for friends in 1938. Faulkner stands in profile, fourth from right, with Estelle at the centre, in a white dress.

development, with the treatment of Bayard Sartoris's ambivalence towards his father's violent brand of honour, in particular, redeeming Bayard from his sometimes pejorative depiction in *Flags in the Dust/ Sartoris*. As many critics complain, Ringo's portrayal as a surrogate brother idealizes white–black relations and perpetuates the fallacy that under slavery African Americans were treated affectionately as extended family members. Yet Faulkner allows Ringo to step out of this cliché at several points by speaking in a decidedly modern voice laced with sarcasm and irony. The most powerful of these moments occurs in the penultimate entry, 'Skirmish at Sartoris', when the young man voices his awareness that not even emancipation will allow African Americans to forge their own identities: 'I ain't a nigger no more,' Ringo tells Bayard after the South concedes defeat. 'I done been abolished.'[35]

'Skirmish' also features one of Faulkner's most fascinating heroines, Drusilla Hawk, who after her fiancé's death at Shiloh dons 'the garments not alone of a man but of a common private soldier' to fight alongside Col. John Sartoris. After the war, Drusilla's cross-dressing is both a 'flouting and outraging [to] all Southern principles of purity and womanhood' and she is pressured into marrying Col. Sartoris to preserve the values for which the Confederacy claims it fought.[36] The best story, 'An Odor of Verbena', dismisses these codes as hoary and outmoded through Faulkner's most in-depth fictionalization of his great-grandfather W. C. Falkner's murder. When Col. Sartoris is shot dead by his business partner, Ben Redmond, Drusilla tempts Bayard to avenge the killing with visions of glory. Bayard does confront Redmond (who was called Redlaw in *Flags in the Dust/Sartoris*), yet unarmed, as the Colonel was at the time of his death, tired of violence. Symbolically casting off the burden of honour and revenge, the son allows his father's murderer to leave Jefferson unscathed. 'Maybe you're right,' one of the Colonel's men tells Bayard. 'Maybe there has been enough killing in your family.'[37] As such, *The Unvanquished* suggests the need for new Southern codes, even while nostalgically lamenting the passing of the old Confederate ones.

Faulkner was nonchalant about the commercial disappointment of *The Unvanquished*. He was too preoccupied with *If I Forget Thee, Jerusalem*, struggling to work amid painful skin grafts to heal his burned back. 'I still am not able to tell if the novel is all right or absolute drivel,' he admitted to Robert Haas. 'To me, it was written just as if I had sat on the one side of a wall and the paper was on the other and my hand with the pen thrust through the wall and writing not only on invisible paper but in pitch darkness, too, so that I could not even know if the pen still wrote on paper or not.'[38]

Random House felt no such concerns. The new novel was raw and unrelenting in its debunking of romantic love. Its treatment of adultery marked Faulkner's third engagement with pulp fiction following *Sanctuary* and *Pylon*, challenging the tropes of romance and sex pulps as those earlier novels had hard-boiled detective fiction and aviator exploits. The manuscript's only drawback was its biblical title, which Cerf, Klopfer and Haas all felt was too literary for a mass audience.

Three years earlier Faulkner complained he lacked the commercial instinct for 'writing trash'. Popular fiction was 'probably hard work', but 'I seem to be so out of touch with the Kotex Age here that I cant think of anything myself.'[39] The Kotex reference was a dig at women's fiction, but *The Wild Palms* (1939), as the novel was retitled, demonstrated Faulkner was as fascinated with female desire as romance fiction was. Like Temple Drake and Laverne Shumann, his latest heroine, Charlotte Rittenmeyer, is a woman defined and ultimately defeated by the relationship between her sexuality and her corporeality, a relationship immeasurably defined by voyeurism and invasion. As one reviewer declared, Faulkner had produced yet another novel in which 'the decadent, the sensational and the merely brutal are found side by side.'[40]

This time, readers flocked to it in droves.

6

'The Best in America, By God' (1939–45)

On 23 January 1939 *Time* magazine featured Faulkner on its cover, giving his career a boost like that enjoyed by Eugene O'Neill, Willa Cather, Kathleen Norris, Ernest Hemingway and two dozen other writers profiled in the 1930s. Photographed by Eric Schaal, the author gazed upon *Time*'s readership with neither Noël Coward's sophistication nor John Dos Passos's cigar-chomping swagger in their cover portraits. Between his open-collar shirt and galluses (braces), the stark backdrop and his dour expression, Faulkner looked like a stoic cotton farmer humbled by a failed crop. The profile itself described him as equally inexpressive: 'In Hollywood, he has a reputation for silence and eccentricity; in Manhattan literary circles, he is considered antisocial. People who meet him in Memphis find him unbending a little.' Even in Oxford 'he talks eloquently, intently in sentences that sound old-fashioned and literary.'[1] Except for an anecdote about reading the funny papers to Jill and a picture with her that captured 'one of the broadest grins ever to adorn his face in a published photograph', the profile did little to humanize the enigma that for most audiences – those who had heard of him, anyway – was William Faulkner.[2]

Then again, the essay was not a personality profile as Hemingway's *Time* cover story had been fifteen months earlier. Nor did it seek the real person behind the celebrity image as Gertrude Stein's had in 1933. As reporter Robert Cantwell later remembered, his aim was to demonstrate that Faulkner was readable: 'While I felt uneasy about introducing the deepening involutions of Faulkner's style to readers, the fact that his writing was growing steadily more obscure suggested that the difficulty might be greater in the future, and unless the story were done quickly it might not be possible to do it at all.'[3] *Time* originally commissioned the essay to coincide with *The Unvanquished* but replaced it at press time with a feature on the Westminster Dog Show, of all things. Cantwell's thesis probably fit Faulkner's current novel, *The Wild Palms*, better anyway. As he wrote, the 'short, reticent Southerner, sharp-eyed as a gambler' was a 'social historian' capturing the changing South with 'scenes of murder, suicide, insanity, [and] horror, giving as unsparing a picture of social decay as any U.S. novelist has ever drawn'. Two asides describing his style as 'turgid and confusing' and 'muddled [and] undisciplined' went unelaborated. Nor did Cantwell examine the stream of consciousness and temporal experimentation of *The Sound and the Fury* or the multiple perspectives in *As I Lay Dying*. Those works were simply 'formless' and 'bitter'.[4] *Absalom, Absalom!* went entirely unmentioned.

Cantwell represented one side of a growing divide over Faulkner's significance. His 'social historian' interpretation almost diametrically opposes that of Conrad Aiken, who later in 1939 defended the author's 'passion for overelaborate sentence structure'. A poet whom Faulkner had both imitated and reviewed during his apprentice years, Aiken was a kindred literary spirit who understood the value of experimentation. He viewed Faulkner's 'baroque and involuted' style as reinventing narration into a 'continuum . . . a medium without stops or pauses' rather than a plot-driven story. Faulkner's world was 'fluid and unfinished', built from 'certain relatively abstract words' like 'myriad' and 'sonorous' whose repetition directed readers' attention 'inward and downward' to an 'image-stream'. Here, meaning existed 'all inside and underneath', not in events. While Cantwell insisted that Faulkner's plots were full of 'melodrama', Aiken argued that the author was disinterested in 'the novel as revelation, the novel as slice-of-life, the novel as mere story'. Instead, he practised *form*, 'the *use* to which the circumstances [of a plot] are put, the degree to which they can be organized'. As a result, Faulkner was not 'a mere "Southern" writer': 'The "Southernness" of his scenes and characters is of little concern to him,' Aiken insisted. Regionalism was simply his content; his true métier was innovation. While admitting that Faulkner's ambitions often led to 'blunders . . . bad habits and . . . willful bad writing', Aiken declared him a 'genius' and equated him with the ultimate aesthetician of American letters, Henry James.[5] In doing so, he set the agenda by which later academics resuscitated Faulkner's reputation by defining him as a high modernist, not a 'social historian' as Cantwell did.

Of course, another major difference separated Cantwell's and Aiken's essays. The former appeared in a newsweekly with a seven-figure circulation, the latter in the more discerning *Atlantic Monthly*, which reached one-tenth of *Time*'s one million subscribers. Thanks to *Time*'s exposure, *The Wild Palms* (originally titled *If I Forget Thee, Jerusalem*) sold better than any Faulkner novel since *Sanctuary*. Indeed, *Palms* outsold its predecessor – no small accomplishment given its unconventional structure, which interlaces two only marginally connected stories. Cantwell praised the second of the narratives, 'Old Man', as 'a kind of hysterical Huckleberry Finn, its humor at once grotesque and shrewd, its moral at once grim and humane'.[6] While commending this tale of a convict caught in the Great Mississippi Flood of 1927, he was less sold on the 'sick, squalid, miserable sequence of events' in the first. In 'The Wild Palms' two adulterous lovers, Harry Wilbourne and Charlotte Rittenmeyer, roam the country striving to maintain sexual passion amid the numbing demands of domesticity and poverty. Cantwell's synopsis is surprisingly explicit: 'When [Charlotte] becomes pregnant [Harry] performs an abortion, as a result of which she dies and he is jailed for life.'[7] The message to readers was clear:

'The Wild Palms' was the tawdry Faulkner, the Faulkner of rapes by foreign objects and castrated penises, the 'outrageous' Faulkner. One doubts a *Time* cover would have spiked sales of the comparatively mild *The Unvanquished* to a thousand copies a week – 16,000 in total – had Cantwell's profile run in 1938 as first planned. For the moment, the Faulkner in which the public was most interested was the sensational one, not the devoted artist.

The irony of the popularity of *If I Forget Thee, Jerusalem* – since Noel Polk's 1995 'restored' edition, critics have referred to Faulkner's eleventh novel by his original title – is that its interwoven stories, even more than *Sanctuary*, are fraught with contempt for the mass market. Unlike *Sanctuary*, Faulkner never claimed he wrote it for money; if anything, the adultery plot was so personal he worried his sorrow over losing Meta Carpenter had literary worth. The peaks and valleys of Harry and Charlotte's affair ask how sustainable the sexual passion he and Meta enjoyed would have been had Estelle divorced him. The answer is not very. As Harry and Charlotte discover, crushing realities inevitably sap sexual desire: money, certainly, but also biology, whose price for pleasure is either pregnancy or death.

Bitterly admitting these realities, Faulkner assails both the idea of romance and the media that promulgate it. As critics note, *If I Forget Thee, Jerusalem* mocks the power of 1930s' pulp fiction to instill fantasies in readers. In 'The Old Man' the convict is imprisoned because he fell for adventure stories featuring outlaws such as Diamond Dick and Jesse James. In his naivety he tried to rob a train to impress a girl. In 'The Wild Palms' Harry briefly supports himself and Charlotte by cranking out romance tales, aware he invents salacious scenarios without real-world consequences. The lovers imagine themselves protesting the idealized desires in popular fiction. As Charlotte declares, 'It should be the books, the people in the books inventing and reading about us – the Does and Roes and Wilbournes and Smiths – males and females but without the pricks or cunts.'[8]

Unfortunately, Faulkner's ire at starry-eyed aphrodisia veers into misogyny. The convict's story ends with his discovery that the woman he went to prison trying to impress has married one of his prison guards, leading him to exclaim, 'Women, shit.'[9] Oddly, Random House censored this expletive ('Women, –,' the story originally concluded) while letting the 'pricks and cunts' line into print. More intriguingly, 'The Wild Palms' ends with exactly the sort of romantic sentimentality that the narrative itself debunks. Incarcerated for Charlotte's botched abortion, Harry chooses not to commit suicide with a cyanide pill – a pulp device if ever there was one. '*Between grief and nothing*,' he thinks, '*I will take grief*.'[10] The line has become the second most quoted of Faulkner's career, cited out of context and employed to illustrate a defiant romanticism the novel portrays as impossible.

At the time, reviewers cared less about this bleak vision of love than about the novelty of intercutting two disparate storylines in one volume. Faulkner claimed the contrapuntal form allowed him to highlight the motifs of flight and retreat 'as a musician would do to compose a piece of music in which he needed a balance, a counterpoint.'[11] While scholars have traced how antithesis operates in the rotating chapters, the juxtaposition also sparked disagreement over which story is better. Early reviewers were split; then for years, opinions broke along the popular vs literary divide. During the golden age of paperbacks (from the late 1940s to the 1970s) 'The Wild Palms' story was published on its own and appeared in drugstore racks with salacious covers. While 'Old Man' occasionally appeared in paperback form, with the title often tweaked to *The Old Man*, the story was also reprinted alongside 'Spotted Horses' and 'The Bear' in a 1958 Modern Library edition called *Three Famous Short Novels*. Despite this dubious title – only 'The Bear' is famous, and whether any of the three is a novel or 'short' is debatable – this collection was for decades a classroom staple, giving *Jerusalem*'s second story the upper hand in prestige. Recent critics argue the treatment of gender and abortion in 'The Wild Palms' gives it the edge because of its usefulness in understanding Faulkner's attitudes towards womanhood. The author himself was unequivocal about his preference: the lovers' story was his main interest and the convict's tale merely a mirror for reflecting its themes. He was so partial to Harry and Charlotte that in the late 1940s when the Modern Library planned to reprint *The Sound and the Fury* and *As I Lay Dying* in a single volume, he argued – unsuccessfully – that 'The Wild Palms' story deserved the spotlight alongside the Compson novel.

Amid the novel's brisk sales, Faulkner received additional good news. After several rejections – including one from the always fickle *Saturday Evening Post* – his story 'Barn Burning' sold to *Harper's*. Handling the deal was Harold Ober, his new agent. Faulkner dismissed Morton Goldman for demanding commission on *The Unvanquished*'s $25,000 movie rights, reluctantly paying him $1,000 to end their relationship. With a clientele that over three decades included Jack London, Pearl Buck and F. Scott Fitzgerald, Ober was the premier literary agent in America. Once again living off short stories, Faulkner needed Ober to boost his currency among magazine editors.

'Barn Burning' was an auspicious start to their partnership. A coming-of-age drama about a ten-year-old boy, 'Sarty' (named after Col. John Sartoris), suffering divided loyalties between his father, Ab Snopes, and his sharecropper family's landlord, Major de Spain, it became Faulkner's second most anthologized story after 'A Rose for Emily'. It is also a powerful critique of the Southern sharecropping system. Even readers who find Major de Spain more likeable than Snopes will side with Ab's resentment towards tenant farmers' economic exploitation. How they feel about Ab's preferred form of protest – torching his landlords' property – affects their sympathy for Sarty's confused feelings for his father. In the end

Sarty runs away from Yoknapatawpha County, but whether he can outrun his Snopes blood remains ambiguous.

'Barn Burning' was conceived as the first chapter of the long-gestating Snopes novel. Actually, Faulkner had enough tales for three novels about the redneck clan. First would come *The Peasants*, focusing on Flem Snopes's 'beginning in the country, as he gradually consumes a small village until there is nothing left in it for him to eat'. The second instalment, *Rus in Urbe* (a term meaning an illusion of countryside in an urban setting), would follow him to Jefferson, where Flem would blackmail his way into a bank presidency. The concluding book, *Ilium Falling*, would follow Snopes's cousins into town, where they would tear down the colonial homes and 'chop up the lots into subdivisions'.[12] The titles of all three books eventually changed.

Completing the second and third volumes took twenty years, but the first one coalesced quickly. Faulkner wove together several previously published Snopes tales, assimilating some whole, recasting others to meet new needs. The homicidal protagonist of 1931's 'The Hound', Ernest Cotton, turned into Flem's embittered cousin Mink. The generic 'Pap' of 1936's 'Fool About a Horse' became Sarty and Flem's father, Ab, transformed from the violent sharecropper of 'Barn Burning' into the comic dupe of a horse-trading scam. (Ab also makes a less than heroic cameo in *The Unvanquished*.) Two key Flem stories – 1931's 'Spotted Horses' and 1932's 'Lizards in Jamshyd's Courtyard' – went into the manuscript with fewer conceptual changes, just elaboration.

Because it incorporated existing stories, *The Hamlet* (1940), as the book was retitled, can strike readers as episodic, a collection of tall tales instead of a tightly structured novel. The overall plot follows Flem from poverty into middle-class affluence, culminating in a scam to sell his estate, the Old Frenchman Place that Faulkner first introduced in *Sanctuary*, through rumours of buried Confederate treasure (a swindle first hatched in 'Jamshyd's

Courtyard'). Other sections focus on colourfully named Snopes cousins, including I. O., Ike, Eck and Wallstreet Panic Snopes. Another portion details the Venusian charms of Eula Varner, whose father marries her off to Flem when another man impregnates her. Nowhere is the novel's garrulous style and loose structure better illustrated than in the incorporation of 'Barn Burning'. Instead of opening *The Hamlet*, the story is reduced to a passing anecdote told by a travelling sewing-machine salesman, V. K. Ratliff, whose idling fondness for spinning yarns is the opposite of Flem's conniving acquisitiveness. Gone are both the original's dramatic intensity and its main protagonist (Sarty is only indirectly mentioned), replaced by Ratliff's genial narrative ambling. More than any other Faulkner work, *The Hamlet* revels in oral storytelling traditions, celebrating local sagas, rural legends and folkloric fables. As such, the novel harkens back to pre-industrial American literature. Like Washington Irving's 'The Legend of Sleepy Hollow' (1819) or *Narrative of the Life of Davy Crockett* (1834), it offers communal story-sharing as an antidote to America's relentless success-striving, which Flem's cupidity satirizes.

Predictably, reviewers in April 1940 fixated on the bawdiness. Nearly every commentator warned readers about Ike Snopes's misplaced affection for a cow. The *Southern Review* called *The Hamlet* 'Faulkner's latest explosion in a cesspool', bemoaning not just the Benjy-like Ike's bovine sodomy but a passage in which Eula's school teacher 'kisses the warm seat of the chair which [she] has vacated'.[13] *Newsweek* titled its review 'Rural Scum', while the *San Francisco Chronicle* headlined its article 'Faulkner Again Writes Strongly About Extremely Nasty People'. Among positive notices, Malcolm Cowley in *The New Republic* cited 'friendliness' as a new authorial quality: 'He likes [the denizens of Frenchman's Bend's] back-country humor, he likes the clean look of their patched and faded shirts, he likes the lies they tell when swapping horses. In a curious way, he even likes the invading tribe of Snopeses.'[14] And Stephen Vincent

Benét in *Saturday Review* commended *The Hamlet*'s 'earthly force': 'Reading [it] is like listening to the gossip of a country store, with its cruelty, extravagance, its tall stories, and its deadly comment upon human nature – but a gossip translated, heightened, and made into art.'[15] Although Benét warned the book would prove 'repellant to many readers', *The Hamlet* sold nearly 7,000 copies – thanks, most likely, to the lingering popularity of *If I Forget Thee, Jerusalem*.

Characteristically prolific, Faulkner was already mulling his next book. In January 1940 he completed 'A Point of Law', a story introducing Lucas Beauchamp, a 67-year-old trickster whose moonshining flusters his landlord, Roth Edmonds, and the judicial system. Soon after, Faulkner's beloved Mammy Callie Barr died. The passing of this 'hundred-year-old matriarch' compelled the author to examine black–white relationships more intently than he had since *Absalom, Absalom!* He quickly produced two additional Beauchamp instalments, 'Gold Is Not Always' and 'The Fire on the Hearth', the latter featuring Lucas's wife, Mollie, who resembles Mammy Callie. On hand by spring was a much darker story, 'Pantaloon in Black', in which a grieving black widower named Rider – another resident on Edmonds's plantation, but unrelated to Lucas and Mollie – is lynched for killing the white boss who cheats him at dice. Faulkner flippantly referred to this quartet as 'four stories about niggers' but felt they could form 'a book like *The Unvanquished*'.[16] Eventually titled *Go Down, Moses*, its depiction of race is more complex and sensitive than his glib use of the N-word might suggest. This last great work of Faulkner's career also experiments more with form than Bayard's and Ringo's Civil War adventures, leading to debates over whether it is a collection of interconnected stories or a novel.

Faulkner first envisioned arranging the stories into a 'more or less continuous narrative', but their unity eluded him.[17] Similar in tone to 'Pantaloon', 'Go Down, Moses' begins with an unrepentant criminal, a sort of black Popeye, awaiting execution for killing a

Chicago policeman. Named Samuel 'Butch' Beauchamp, he identifies Molly, his grandmother, as his next of kin; the story then details Molly's determination in Jefferson, aided by lawyer Gavin Stevens and other whites, to bury his body with dignity. (The other stories spell her name as Mollie, with the 'y' appearing only in this one.) A more slapstick story, 'Almost', follows a pair of antebellum bachelor brothers, Uncle Buck and Uncle Buddy, pursuing an escaped slave named Tomey's Turl. Narrating it was none other than Bayard Sartoris.

This tantalizing connection to *The Unvanquished* suggests Faulkner planned to revive, or at least recall, important characters from earlier works. Molly in 'Go Down, Moses,' for example, was first called Rosa Coldfield Sutpen. Borrowing the name of the spinster from *Absalom, Absalom!* for a different protagonist promised to confuse readers, though, and her creator quickly renamed her. Internal evidence in 'The Old People', meanwhile, implied its anonymous narrator was Quentin Compson. Although Faulkner deleted the evidence when Ober sold the piece to *Harper's*, Faulkner likely invoked Quentin remembering an earlier hunting story, 1935's 'Lion'. It, too, soon found its way into *Moses*.

A November 1940 hunting trip inspired another key story, 'Delta Autumn'. By now lumbering had decimated the once-thick woods surrounding Oxford, requiring Faulkner and friends to travel more than 240 kilometres (150 mi.) into the Mississippi Delta to track game. Faulkner had controlled his drinking since his despair over losing Meta Carpenter, but on this trip he binged himself unconscious. His party rushed him home, where doctors discovered internal hemorrhaging severe enough to warn he was hours from death. Some critics consider this medical emergency the turning point at which the ravages of addiction began to diminish his imagination.[18] Yet at the time Faulkner rebounded quickly enough to finish this latest story. Unlike *Pylon* or 'Golden State', 'Delta Autumn' makes no mention of alcoholism's crippling effects. Rather, the theme is nature's ruin, its protagonist an old man, 'Uncle Ike' McCaslin. As Ike rests in camp, a light-skinned African American woman appears seeking Dan Boyd, the father of her illegitimate child. Appalled to learn Boyd is paying the woman to disappear, Ike counsels her to marry within her race and avoid white men's abuse. Her response became another of Faulkner's most quoted lines: 'Old man . . . have you lived so long and forgotten so much that you don't remember anything you ever knew or felt or even heard about love?'[19] The encounter upsets Ike, and he compares miscegenation ('Chinese and African and Aryan and Jew, all breed and spawn together until no man has time to say which is which nor cares') to the so-called 'progress' that has 'deswamped and denuded and derivered' his beloved woods. Faulkner's ending is deeply problematic, undermining sympathy for Ike. Unlike Shreve's insistence in *Absalom, Absalom!* that whites will eventually spring 'from the loins of African kings', the old man laments race mixing instead of accepting it as inevitable. Although regrettable, Ike's soliloquy taps into a feeling as prevalent among modernists as Southerners that miscegenation was a sign of modernity's confusions, not its evolution.

However quickly Faulkner completed these stories, he delayed compiling them until mid-1941. Selling them to magazines was too exhausting. For every 'A Point of Law' that brought in a fast $1,000 from *Collier's*, a 'Gold Is Not Always' or 'The Old People' earned a comparatively modest $400 from the *Atlantic Monthly* or *Harper's*. Some stories ('Almost', 'The Fire on the Hearth') never appeared in periodical form, and one of the best, 'Delta Autumn', landed in the small-circulation *Story Magazine* for $40. As always, the *Saturday Evening Post* was particularly frustrating. For the moment it only seemed interested in whodunits. Since 1932's 'Smoke', Faulkner intermittently called upon the lawyer/sleuth Gavin Stevens to solve crimes, Perry Mason-style. The *Post* purchased two Stevens potboilers, 'Hand Upon the Waters' and 'Tomorrow', in 1939 and

1940 but rejected the darker, more literary *Moses* tales. (Selling detective fiction was not guaranteed, however: after accepting 'Tomorrow' the *Post* rejected another Stevens story, 'An Error in Chemistry'.) Faulkner also knew the project needed a centrepiece, 'a novella, actually,' he wrote Ober in July 1940. Yet a longer work was impossible when 'I have got to write something short and quick to sell.'[20]

The main reason for postponing the collection, though, was that Faulkner could not decide how to connect them. As usual with Yoknapatawpha County's fictional history, the answer was bloodline. In spring 1941 Faulkner charted a genealogy that bound Lucas Beauchamp and Issac McCaslin as grandsons of Lucius Quintus Carothers McCaslin, a Sutpen-like plantation patriarch who sires two families, one white and one black, one legitimate and one illegitimate, but both haunted by slavery's violent legacy. Combining his three Beauchamp stories under the tweaked title 'The Fire and the Hearth', Faulkner reinvented Lucas from a Br'er Rabbit-like conniver into a conflicted emblem of 'impenetrable' dignity. Lucas's fierce pride in his McCaslin lineage troubles his white cousins, who predictably consider their slave cousins illegitimate. Yet Lucas's self-regard also threatens his marriage to Mollie, who files for divorce when her husband obsesses over uncovering gold on the plantation.

Revision transformed Isaac McCaslin, meanwhile, from a bitter old man into an ambiguous symbol of penance and exile. Employing 'The Old People' and 'Delta Autumn' as bookends, Faulkner drew an extended parallel between the decimation of nature and Ike's discovery of family sins that compel him to renounce his inheritance, leaving the same cousins Lucas confounds to manage the McCaslin plantation. *Moses*'s irresolvable question is whether repudiation expatiates slavery's sins or simply isolates Ike.

The centrepiece of Ike's sequence, 'The Bear', is a towering contribution to American literature. Written between July and

Illustrations from the magazine version of 'A Point of Law', published in *Collier's* in June 1940, suggest how Faulkner's initial depiction of Lucas and Mollie Beauchamp and their family perpetuated African American stereotypes. As the author revised this and other stories into *Go Down, Moses* he transformed the Beauchamps into far more complex characters.

December 1941, it elegizes the American Eden that 'The Old People' celebrates as eternal. In that story, Faulkner reinvents the half-Chickasaw, half-black Sam Fathers from 'A Justice' into a master hunter who grants Ike a glimpse of an elusive buck. The spiritual manifestation of nature's grace ('not proud and not haughty but just full and wild and unafraid'),[21] the buck is a corollary of Sam himself, who after slavery abandons the human world to hunt the Big Bottom in solitude. Altering the history outlined in 'A Justice', Faulkner reveals that Sam's father, Ikkemotubbe, the Chickasaw chief who sold Lucius McCaslin his plantation land, also sold Sam and his half-black mother to the patriarch.

In 'The Bear' a sense of doom now pervades the lessons Sam teaches Ike. Civilization's encroachments are inexorable, and the Yoknapatawpha men who have for decades tracked the near-mythical bear called Old Ben recognize its reign in the woods and in their imaginations will soon end. For Ike this means that escaping the McCaslin legacy as Sam has is no longer possible.

Faulkner surrounds the suspense of tracking Old Ben with complex symbolism. A paradoxical line describes Old Ben as creating 'a corridor of wreckage and destruction' with 'the ruthless and irresistible deliberation of a locomotive'.[22] The odd comparison of a natural predator to a man-made machine suggests that even woodsmen like Ike can no longer think of the natural world without resorting to images of human technology. The line also suggests the human imagination can only project destruction upon the landscape. After Boon Hogganbeck regretfully kills Ben trying to save his mongrel Lion, this moral indictment becomes the focus of the story's dense fourth section. Studying ledgers in the McCaslin commissary, Ike at 21 learns that his grandfather bore a daughter from one slave, Eunice, and then fathered a son – Lucas Beauchamp's father – from that daughter, Tomasina.[23] His lineage tainted by rape and incest, Ike renounces his inheritance (or most of it; he lives off a small family stipend) and withdraws into a long life of denial.

Faulkner had yet to begin his ornate treatment of Ike's discovery when money pressures halted work on 'The Bear'. With the *Saturday Evening Post* in mind, he produced a commercial version of the hunt for Old Ben, straightening the chronology and removing Ike's name so the protagonist was a more universal 'the boy'. While Sam Fathers's mentoring remained, this version climaxed not with Boon killing Old Ben – since that story had already been told in 'Lion' – but with the boy's first encounter with the bear. The child cannot understand why he and Sam hesitate to shoot Ben. In the novella, the scene affirms that Old Ben knows he is mortal and has chosen Ike as a worthy witness to his passing. In the story, the decision marks the boy's commitment to preserving the American values Ben represents:

There was an old bear, fierce and ruthless, not merely just to stay alive, but with the fierce pride of liberty and freedom, proud enough of that liberty and freedom to see it threatened without fear or even alarm; nay, who at times even seemed deliberately to put that freedom and liberty in jeopardy in order to savor them, to remind his old strong bones and flesh to keep supple and quick to defend and preserve them.[24]

Remarkably, Faulkner includes a version of this passage in the novella, but only as a memory Ike recollects when rejecting his inheritance: 'Courage and honor and pride, and pity and love of justice and of liberty,' Ike's cousin Cass Edmonds told him after Ben died. 'They all touch the heart, and what the heart holds to becomes truth, as far as we know truth.' For the adult Ike, such sentimentality covers up the 'injustice . . . ruthless rapacity and . . . at times downright savagery' American history is built on.[25] But in the commercial version, the boy's father speaks Cass's words as a means of exhorting his son to preserve and defend American ideals. His call resonated politically as the United States debated entry into the Second World War. Barely one month before the bombing of Pearl Harbor, the *Post* accepted the patriotic version of 'The Bear', asking Faulkner to emphasize this message even more. The magazine editors either did not know or did not care that Old Ben's demise had appeared in a rival periodical six years earlier. Faulkner happily complied, though he had to rewrite from memory because the *Post* had his only copy of the manuscript. His $1,000 paycheck financed the book's finishing.

When *Go Down, Moses* was published on 11 May 1942 (two days after 'The Bear' appeared in the *Post*), its dedication paid tribute to Mammy Callie Barr. Faulkner commemorated her 'fidelity' to his family 'without stint or calculation of recompense' and the 'immeasurable devotion and love' she gave him in childhood.[26] Two significant changes to 'Delta Autumn' undermined this message of racial harmony. First, Dan Boyd, the character that Ike originally discovered pays off his black mistress to disappear with their illegitimate child, became Roth Edmonds, Cass Edmonds's grandson and the latest manager of the McCaslin estate. (Roth is Lucas's foil in the Beauchamp stories.) Roth's treatment of the woman reveals that Ike's sacrifice taught his family nothing, for white McCaslins continue to exploit African Americans. Second, Faulkner has Roth's lover announce that she, too, is a McCaslin descendant, the granddaughter of Lucas Beauchamp's long-lost brother Jim, who abandoned the plantation a half-century earlier. This twist can strain credulity, heavy-handedly underlining the 'sins of the father' theme. Yet it makes irrefutable Faulkner's point that whites recapitulate slavery's oppression from generation to generation, and that black bodies bear the wounds.

Reviewers interpreted *Go Down, Moses* as an exorcism of Southern demons, as if the racial animus it bewails were irrelevant to the North. That assumption overlooked the fact that in the title story Butch Beauchamp is executed for crimes committed in Chicago, the terminal of the Great Migration that had already proven as hostile to blacks as Mississippi. (A point demonstrated in fellow Mississippian Richard Wright's *Native Son*, a novel Faulkner commended.) Ultimately, the Pharaoh that Jefferson's black community condemns when they mourn Butch's death by joining Molly in singing the slave spiritual that gives story and novel alike its name is America – not a New Canaan but an Egypt cankered with greed, lust and inhumanity.

Condemning America as racist would have been unpatriotic in 1942, with thousands of American soldiers embarking for the Second World War. Accordingly, critics debated genre instead of theme. Faulkner was irked when Random House subtitled *Moses* '*and Other Stories*'. As one reviewer rightly recognized, the contents were best understood 'as part of a whole. They are like a fugue with repetitions and variations on a central theme.'[27] Seven years later

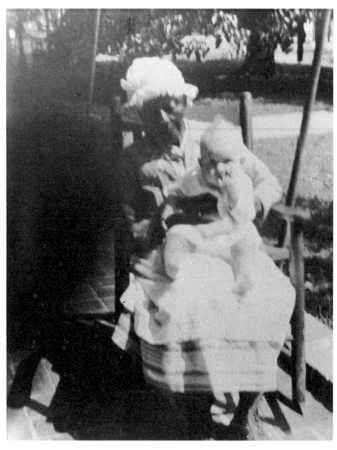

The Falkner family's beloved domestic, Caroline 'Mammy Callie' Barr, shown here with youngest brother Dean, c. 1907, remained in Faulkner's employ until her death in 1940. He dedicated *Go Down, Moses* to her.

when Random House republished the book, Faulkner struck the phrase from the cover, insisting *Moses* was a novel. Yet he was inconsistent on the matter, sometimes even contradictory. Addressing Ole Miss English majors in 1947, he claimed *Go Down, Moses* was unified as 'seven different facets of one field', then described it as 'simply a collection of short stories'.[28] Subsequent critics have found that categorizing the book is no easy matter.

Writing to Harold Ober in June 1942, Faulkner found himself at a crossroads: 'I have been buried here [in Oxford] for three years now for lack of money and I am stale.'[29] He had sold only ten stories in that period, forcing him to live on advances from Random House that his book sales didn't recoup. His lack of frugality wasn't the only reason he remained broke; Faulkner was also remarkably generous, even when he didn't have money. In March 1939 he cashed in an insurance policy and borrowed against future royalties so his old mentor Phil Stone could avoid bankruptcy with a $6,000 loan. The favour was striking considering the pair hadn't been close for a decade. In 1934 Stone had even criticized Faulkner's writing in a short-lived hometown journal called *Oxford Magazine*. Nor would the loan soften his opinion.

Despite this generosity, Faulkner resented demands on his pocketbook. For a decade he had provided either 'sole, principal [or] partial support' for Estelle, Jill, his two stepchildren, his mother, his widowed sister-in-law and niece, and his brother John and family, including 'food, shelter, heat, clothes, medicine, kotex, school fees, toilet paper and picture shows'.[30] Random House and Ober wired emergency loans when business wisdom allowed, but they were invested in his art, not his earning potential. When Faulkner begged for larger advances, Robert Haas gently reminded him of his modest sales. The situation grew so bleak Faulkner could not afford basic amenities. 'I have 60c in my pocket,' he raged, 'and that is literally all.'[31]

His only hope was Hollywood, but studios were leery. Desperate, Faulkner committed the biggest mistake of his career by encouraging competing agents to find him work. He should have relied on Ober's seasoned West Coast associate, H. N. Swanson, but a novice freelancer, William Herndon, opened unexpected doors at Warner Bros. When Swanson tried to negotiate particulars, Herndon

threatened to sue. After acrimonious exchanges, Faulkner felt
honour-bound to the terms the younger man struck: $300 a week,
a junior writer's wage, one-fourth of his peak salary. What Herndon
failed to explain was that Warner Bros could option his services
for seven years – something Faulkner, accustomed to short-term
contracts, had no reason to suppose before reporting for work in
July 1942. The deal amounted to indentured servitude for a novelist
who considered himself 'the best in America, by God'. At least
Warner Bros's cut-throat chief, Jack Warner, agreed: 'I've got
American's best writer for $300 a week,' he boasted.[32]

Faulkner toiled at Warners for three years, contributing to some
seventeen screenplays, about two-thirds of which were produced.
His only screen credits were adaptations of competitors' novels. He
helped relocate Hemingway's *To Have and Have Not* (1937) from its
original Key West/Cuba setting to Martinique, where it became a
story of resistance fighters instead of rum runners and Communist
revolutionaries. Thanks to the presence of Humphrey Bogart, the
final 1944 product bore more than a passing resemblance to
Casablanca. Faulkner also co-adapted Raymond Chandler's
The Big Sleep, with Bogart as detective Philip Marlowe. Directing
both movies was Faulkner's guardian angel, Howard Hawks.

Aside from these classics, he mostly bided his time. He worked
on patriotic war pictures and was among the many screenwriters
who took a crack at James M. Cain's *Mildred Pierce* (1945), though
almost nothing of his draft made it to screen. Aside from his
collaborations with Hawks, his only notable contribution was
to Jean Renoir's *The Southerner* (1945). Because the film was not
a Warner Bros production, he was not credited.

The only fiction attempted during this limbo began as a
collaboration with producers William Bacher and Henry Hathaway.
'It is a fable,' Faulkner reported to Ober in late 1943, 'an indictment
of war perhaps, and for that reason may not be acceptable now.'[33]
Faulkner spent a decade allegorizing Christ and his disciples as

mutinous First World War soldiers in *A Fable* (1954). The most torturous of his novels to complete, it is, to many, the most tortuous to read.

During these years, Faulkner lived at cheap residential hotels and fellow screenwriters' guestrooms. He drank heavily and recommenced his affair with Meta Carpenter, now divorced and working again as Hawks's script girl. When Meta suggested they cohabit to conserve his salary, Faulkner demurred. 'You are not easy to know, Bill Faulkner,' she told him. Her memoir paints a picture of a man ardent in passion but uncomfortable with bodily processes:

> I had almost forgotten until our renewed intimacy Faulkner's curious physical tidiness when he was with me. He was obsessed with keeping from me the grossness of his physical self, running the water in the bathroom to cover the evidence of his animality, bathing each time we made love. Always the sleeved handkerchief was drawn out to suppress a cough or contain a sneeze. Once . . . he had become ill from tainted food and I recall his agonizing attempts to muffle the sounds of his violent retching.[34]

Estelle and Jill briefly relocated to Hollywood, but not even family boosted his spirits. His unhappiness is evident from 1944 photographs Alfred Eris captured of him on his hotel patio, shirtless, in shorts and out of sorts: 'His facial expression is tight and seems to be one of complete disdain for everything in his sight, an anguished disdain that asks the question *What am I doing here?*'[35]

As Faulkner complained, writing for Hollywood was akin to working in 'the salt mines'.[36] During this nadir, conversations about his fiction were often laced with bitter resentment. When the *Saturday Evening Post* published 'Shingles for the Lord' in February 1943, a reader named Dean F. W. Bradley wrote to him questioning certain facts. Faulkner shot back angrily: 'I just took what I thought was a minor liberty in order to tell the story. I didn't consider the liberty important and still don't. But I regret sincerely having offended anyone's sense of fitness . . . I hope you got some pleasure from the story to balance some of the irritation.'[37] Positive or negative, letters from readers were few and far between. The *Post* occasionally asked Ober why they no longer received Faulkner submissions, but most editors considered him spent.

A gradual turnaround began in spring 1944 when Malcolm Cowley, a frequent Faulkner reviewer in the 1930s, asked for biographical information for a re-estimation of his work. Entitled 'William Faulkner's Human Comedy', the article appeared in the *New York Times Book Review* on 29 October 1944, with influential follow-ups in *Saturday Review* and the *Southern Review*. Cowley argued his case with almost evangelical conviction: 'It is time to make a plea for the work of William Faulkner. More than that of any other living American author it has been misinterpreted by the critics and, in recent years, ignored by the public at large.' The conclusion was even more emphatic: 'It is time for [his] work to be more widely read. We haven't so many good novelists in this country that we can afford to neglect one of our more distinguished talents.'[38] The essay cast Faulkner as a type of artist audiences find irresistible. Once rightly famous, now unjustly forgotten, he was ripe for that most fabled of second acts in America, the comeback.

All he had to do now was get out of Hollywood. Warner Bros had already granted him two lengthy furloughs: from August 1943 to February 1944 and January to June 1945, Faulkner worked on *A Fable* at Rowan Oak. In September 1945 he took leave again, this time unauthorized. From Oxford he begged Jack Warner for his freedom: 'I feel that I have made a bust at moving picture writing and therefore have mis-spent and will continue to mis-spend time which at my age I cannot afford.'[39] Warner seemed to delight in keeping his catch wriggling on the contractual hook. Studio lawyers ordered him to return by March 1946 or face legal consequences. As that deadline neared, Ober and Bennett Cerf suddenly intervened and persuaded Warner to relent. Cowley's essays had created unanticipated demand for Faulkner's fiction, with American literature now needing him more than the movies did. To ensure he never again had to go west for a living, Random House promised a monthly $500 stipend.

The previous August, as Faulkner dreamed of escaping Hollywood, Cowley shared a declaration Jean-Paul Sartre made famous throughout post-war France: 'Pour les jeunes en France, Faulkner c'est un dieu.' The time had come for readers in his homeland – readers both young and old – to recognize Faulkner as a god.

7

Aiming for the 'Magnum O'
(1946–54)

Ironically, Random House didn't publish the book that proved the 'Faulknaissance' was real. In 1940, when Robert Haas insisted his sales couldn't justify larger advances, Faulkner attempted to leave the firm for the Viking Press. Its founder, Harold Guinzburg, had courted the author of *Sanctuary* when Cape & Smith went into receivership in 1931 and now promised $6,000 for the collection that became *Go Down, Moses*. At the last minute Bennett Cerf intervened, scaring off Guinzburg by insisting Viking would owe Random House for the printing plates and unsold stock of *The Hamlet*, making the investment unfeasible. Three years later, Guinzburg produced a literary anthology for soldiers called *As You Were* that sold well and earned praise for its patriotism. Pleased, he turned the format into a series devoted to individual authors. By war's end, Viking Portable Library entries on Twain, Thoreau and Poe provided affordable editions 'built like a Jeep: compact, efficient, and marvelously versatile' for 'the convenience of [readers] who are mostly on the move and must travel light'.[1] Entries on Steinbeck and Hemingway served as victory laps after the gargantuan successes of *The Grapes of Wrath* (1939) and *For Whom the Bell Tolls* (1940), while *The Portable F. Scott Fitzgerald*, edited by Dorothy Parker in 1945, helped reestablish the reputation of *The Great Gatsby*'s author, who died prematurely in 1940.

Having edited *The Portable Hemingway* (1944), Malcolm Cowley understood how the series elevated literary reputations. As his essays on Faulkner appeared, he convinced Guinzburg that a volume devoted to the fallen-from-favour author was needed. Cowley's design for the collection was ingenious. Most Viking Portables surveyed a writer's career from beginning to end, but the critic organized a chronological overview of Yoknapatawpha history, beginning in 1820 with Ikkemotubbe's rise over his Chickasaw tribe in 'A Justice' and ending with 'Delta Autumn' in the 1940s. With excerpts from *The Sound and the Fury, Absalom, Absalom!, The Unvanquished* and *Go Down, Moses*, the collection gave equal attention to Faulkner's four fallen aristocracies (the Compsons, Sutpens, Sartorises and McCaslins), counterpointing them to the Snopeses with 'Spotted Horses' (albeit the version from *The Hamlet*, which many find dramatically inferior to the 1931 short story). If the selections had a single failing it was the absence of *As I Lay Dying* and 'Barn Burning', but Cowley emphasized the underappreciated short stories with both obvious choices ('A Rose for Emily' and 'The Bear') and surprises ('Ad Astra' and 'Death Drag'). For readers who still liked the sensational Faulkner, he included the gangster Red's wickedly absurd funeral scene from *Sanctuary* and Percy Grimm's castration of Joe Christmas in *Light in August*.[2]

Faulkner appreciated Cowley's selections but deflected biographical queries for his introduction. 'I'm old fashioned and probably a little mad too,' he warned the editor. 'I don't like having my private life and affairs available to just any and everyone who has the price of the vehicle it's printed in, or a friend who bought it and will lend it to him.'[3] In particular, he objected to references to his mythical career as a First World War aviator. In his research Cowley had relied on a 1942 reference book called *Twentieth Century Authors* that suggested the writer had been wounded on the front – a fair enough assumption given that variations on his crash had appeared in both the *New Yorker* in 1931 and the *Sewanee Review* a year later, citing 'two [downed] enemy planes to his credit'.[4] Enduring several requests for specifics, Faulkner vented his frustration: 'You're going to bugger up a fine dignified distinguished book with that war business. The only point a war reference or anecdote could serve would be to reveal me a hero, or (2) to account for the whereabouts of a male of my age on Nov. 11, 1918 in case this were a biography . . . Say only what Who's Who says and no more: "Was a member of the RAF in 1918."'[5]

Cowley continued to press for details, believing Faulkner's wound made him a bona-fide member of the Lost Generation profiled in *Exile's Return* (1934), his autobiographical chronicle of the First World War's effect on modernist literature. Faulkner's convoluted response admitted none of the fibs that had ended up in print, such as the *New Yorker*'s description of him hanging upside down in a cockpit in France with two broken legs. 'The mishap was caused not by combat,' he conceded, 'but by (euphoneously) "cockpit trouble"; i.e., my own foolishness; the injury I suffered I still feel I got at bargain rates.'[6] Much later, when Cowley published his Faulkner correspondence, he asked, 'Why didn't he say flatly that he hadn't served in France during the war?'[7] The answer seems obvious: Faulkner feared being outed as a liar. But at a deeper level his aversion defended the artist's right not to be judged by literal standards of truth. Whether on the page or in life, Faulkner's flagrant inventions insist that a writer may spin stories that *could be* true, even if they never truly happened. That so many in the literary community assumed on the strength of his depiction of aviators that he saw combat testifies to his prowess in making stories convincing.

Cowley had better luck persuading Faulkner to contribute to the anthology. He wanted a simple summary of *The Sound and the Fury* to introduce the novel's excerpted fourth section, in which Dilsey takes Benjy to Reverend Shegog's Easter Sunday service. Faulkner was too inventive for such a basic exercise. Instead, he produced a genealogy called '1699–1945 The Compsons' that mimicked the language of heraldry to lend grandeur to Yoknapatawpha County history – and to parody that gravity.

The appendix updates the Compsons' fates since the 1929 novel. Strangely, Caddy is banished to Vichy France, where she is last seen 'cold serene and damned' riding alongside a Nazi general. During a Q&A in the late 1950s, a University of Virginia student asked if a sequel might rescue Caddy from what seems a flippant fate for such a tragic character. 'I think that would be a betrayal of Caddy,' Faulkner replied, without acknowledging that he was the one who consigned his 'heart's darling' to such an ignoble end. 'If she were resurrected there'd be something a little shabby, a little anti-climactic about it, about this.'[8] The appendix also reveals Jason committed Benjy to a mental institution after their mother's death. The chronicle is notable less for any knowledge it adds to *The Sound and the Fury* than for its form. Like part four of 'The Bear' in which Faulkner mimics the language of plantation ledgers, the curious addendum demonstrates how the author often adapted the language of official documents to undermine their authority.

The Portable Faulkner earned rave reviews upon publication in April 1946 and sold 20,000 copies over the next two years. One practical effect of including excerpts from the novels was to whet appetites for rediscovering the texts *en toto*. Faulkner books were extremely hard to procure at the time. Three of his publishers were out of business (Liveright, Cape & Smith, Smith & Haas), and not even his old mentor Phil Stone had preserved copies of *The Marble Faun* in case of future interest. Faulkner himself didn't own a copy of *The Sound and the Fury* when Cowley quizzed him on details. All of his books except *Sanctuary* were out of print, and only a handful of libraries across the country shelved copies. A new fan in 1946 would have to send off for British editions published by Chatto & Windus.

Yet the situation was rapidly changing. As *The Portable Faulkner* arrived in bookstores, plans were afoot for a Modern Library volume pairing *The Sound and the Fury* with *As I Lay Dying*. Faulkner nixed as 'bad taste' a possible preface from Hemingway. As he told Random House's Robert Linscott, the editor compiling the volume, that was akin to 'asking one race horse in the middle of a race to broadcast a blurb on another horse in the same field'.[9] Faulkner was wise not to stoke competition. Although Hemingway had outgrown the churlish gibes in *Death in the Afternoon*, he never would have stated publicly the praise he shared privately with Cowley when he admitted Faulkner 'has the most talent of anybody . . . How beautifully he can write and as simple and as complicated as autumn or as spring.'[10] At Faulkner's recommendation, Random House rejected any introduction and reprinted instead the Compson appendix, lending that text added importance but doing little to contextualize the novels. Nevertheless, the Modern Library edition introduced more readers to these masterpieces than their first printings had (as would new editions of *Light in August* and *Absalom, Absalom!* in the early 1950s). Meanwhile, Cowley urged Faulkner to collect his best short stories in a single volume. The project would take four years to realize, by which point other hard-to-find works, including *Sanctuary*, *Pylon* and *The Wild Palms* were available in cheap paperback editions.

Suggesting any downside to the rediscovery of Faulkner that began in 1945–6 may seem the very definition of Negative Nellyism. Yet the renewed attention put the middle-aged writer in the uncomfortable position of competing against former glories. It was one thing to cash in on forgotten efforts, as when Harold Ober sold RKO Studios the movie rights to the barnstormer stories 'Honor' and 'Death Drag' for $6,600. More daunting was remaining productive knowing the world wondered, a half-decade after his last book, whether his talent was intact as he neared fifty. As *The Portable Faulkner* amassed kudos, Faulkner buckled down and spent eighteen straight months labouring over *A Fable*. To Cowley he insisted the book would be his 'magnum o'. To Haas he said it would be a '*War and Peace* close enough to home, our times, language, for Americans

As Faulkner was canonized in colleges and universities from the late 1940s, the era's exploding paperback market also played a role in his rediscovery, their covers selling the salaciousness he had been associated with since *Sanctuary*.

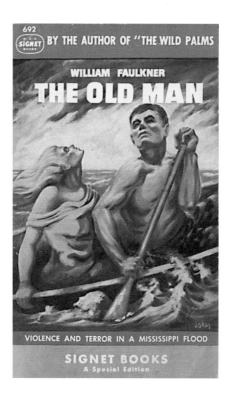

to really buy it'.[11] Despite these grand professions, the writing did not go smoothly.

Part of the problem was Faulkner's uncertainty over the 'locale and the matter'. Not only was *A Fable*'s French geography alien, but the style required more deliberation than he was used to. In early 1945 he claimed the novel forced him to mature; no longer could he write by instinct and 'illimitable courage for rhetoric'. Forced to 'weigh every word' he couldn't 'bang it on like an apprentice paper hanger and never look back'. 'I have grown up at last,' he insisted.[12] By 1946–7, weighing every word felt laborious and inhibiting. Allegory by definition requires an attentiveness to symbolism and imagery that borders on the overdetermined; without it, intended parallels between the mutiny of his French infantrymen in 1918 and the Passion of Christ simply wouldn't stand out. Yet the intensity of focus *A Fable* required rendered his writing process self-conscious instead of spontaneous. What once felt like an escape now felt imprisoning.

Compounding his frustration was the $500 Cerf and Haas mailed each month. The stipend made him acutely aware that *A Fable* had to pay off, creatively and financially. As if to reassure himself, Faulkner blamed his crippled progress on ageing instead of his creaky premise. 'There's nothing wrong with this book,' he insisted in autumn 1947. 'I am just getting older and don't write fast anymore. I always did do a lot of rewriting; I just make my mistakes slower now – and correct them slower.'[13] Maturity no longer meant artistic growth but the onset of senescence.

As if to tether the storyline to more familiar terrain he digressed into a subplot about an unlikely trio. A white British soldier, a black American preacher and the preacher's teenaged grandson steal a champion horse so it can continue racing despite a crippling injury. Known as *Notes on a Horsethief*, it would be inserted whole within *A Fable*, despite its departure in tone (it reads like a tall tale) and time and setting (it takes place in the u.s. before the First World War). Faulkner allowed Harold Ober to submit the 'novelette' to *Partisan Review*, the literary journal of New York intellectuals, which sought a contribution. To his dismay, the editors rejected it, spiralling him into self-doubt.

Beleaguered, he looked for distractions wherever he could find them. He tended to Greenfield Farm, wrote letters to the local newspaper, and even agreed to a rare public appearance, speaking to several English classes at the University of Mississippi for $250. The Q&A sessions were supposed to be informal, but university publicity 'jumbled' him 'head over heels' in 'high-pressure ballyhoo'.[14] Asked to rank his contemporaries, Faulkner placed Hemingway fourth after Thomas Wolfe, himself and John Dos

Passos because 'he has no courage, has never climbed out on a limb. He has never used a word where the reader might check his usage by a dictionary.'[15] The *New York Herald Tribune* republished the offhand remarks, upsetting Hemingway, who asked the general whose regiment he shadowed during the Second World War, Gen. Charles T. 'Buck' Lanham, to post a reprimand to Oxford. After Lanham passed along Faulkner's apology, the authors mended fences, though privately Hemingway insulted his rival's alcoholism. The incident confirmed for Faulkner that writers should stay out of the spotlight, letting their work speak for them.

By January 1948 only four hundred of *A Fable*'s projected thousand pages were finished. Exasperated, Faulkner set the novel aside, convinced that if he didn't produce something soon Random House would discontinue his stipend. ('I've been on Random H's cuff a long time now,' he lamented.)[16] To his delight, the new project took only three months to write, a pace unmatched since *Pylon* thirteen years earlier. Several elements expedited its completion. First, Faulkner returned to the familiar confines of Yoknapatawpha County. Except for when he finally completed *A Fable* in 1953–4, his fiction remained rooted within its borders from this point on. Second, he took up a genre whose well-defined structure spared him plot worries. As he wrote to Ober, 'The story is a mystery-murder . . . a Negro in jail accused of murder and waiting for the white folks to drag him out and pour gasoline over him and set him on fire, is the detective, solves the crime because he goddamn has to to keep from being lynched.'[17] Finally, Faulkner drew from another favourite plotline, the coming-of-age story, employing as his main protagonist a sixteen-year-old Tom Sawyer figure, Charles 'Chick' Mallison. As Chick investigates the crime, he must confront the South's animosity towards African Americans and the unlikelihood of racial reconciliation, leaving him immeasurably saddened.

The most challenging part of the book was the title. Faulkner had a prepositional phrase he liked – *in the Dust* – but he couldn't decide on the right noun. He entertained rather silly possibilities (*Skullduggery*, *Jugglery*) along with abstract options (*Malfeasance*, *Malaprop*) before settling on *Intruder in the Dust*. It referred to the crime's solution, which involved twice digging up a grave. For Faulkner aficionados, the main interest was the return of familiar faces. The wrongly accused man was Lucas Beauchamp, as proud of his McCaslin heritage as in *Go Down, Moses* and just as unwilling to bow down to whites. Representing the voice of justice was Gavin Stevens, the all-purpose attorney from serious efforts (such as *Moses*'s title story) and potboilers (1932's 'Smoke'). Giving Chick a black sidekick (Aleck Sander) and a grandmotherly protector (the Dickensian-named Eunice Habersham), Faulkner even recalled the Bayard–Ringo–Granny Millard trio from *The Unvanquished*.

Intruder in the Dust is the Faulknernian equivalent of a B-movie. The plot is serviceable but not suspenseful. The tension of lynching fictions like 'Dry September' and *Sanctuary* is nowhere to be found, and a reader with a rudimentary appreciation of Arthur Conan Doyle or Agatha Christie can predict the real killer. Whether in spite or because of its flaws, the novel was a popular success when published on 27 September 1948, selling 23,000 copies. The film rights brought in $50,000, finally paying back Random House's investment in Faulkner. MGM's faithful screen adaptation, filmed the following spring in Oxford, is entertaining but not morally challenging. Only a modest box-office success in 1950, the movie, directed by Clarence Brown (known for *National Velvet* and *The Yearling*), is regarded as the best of a late 1940s spate of films condemning Southern violence against African Americans. Yet what Ralph Ellison wrote of the movie is true of the novel: it is 'not *about* Negroes at all; it is about what whites think and feel about Negroes.'[18]

The novel's popularity bore two effects on Faulkner's reputation. The first was to catapult him to the frontline of authorities on the

South the media turned to for reactions to the burgeoning Civil Rights Movement. It was not a role Faulkner was suited for, and his positions both outraged segregationists and disappointed progressives. As Gavin Stevens insists, by ardently opposing desegregation, the South is 'really defending . . . the privilege of setting [blacks] free ourselves: which we will have to do for the reason that nobody else can since going on a century ago now the North tried it and have been admitting for seventy-five years now that they failed'.[19] At several points in *Intruder* Stevens asserts this 'gradualist' stance in rhetoric so windy critics wonder how seriously Faulkner intended his pontifications. As Noel Polk notes, *Intruder* 'provides sufficient evidence of Stevens's shortcomings to make us wary of accepting his words at face value'. This is truest whenever the lawyer refers to African Americans as 'Sambo', a retrograde term even by the late 1940s. Yet 'the distressing extent to which Faulkner seems to have endorsed Stevens's opinions' in

Faulkner's disdain for publicity is evident in this 1948 photo by J. R. Cofield celebrating the publication of *Intruder in the Dust* (1948). The novel's brisk sales finally gave the writer the financial security he had sought for twenty years.

coming years makes it difficult to read any irony in the author's own 'moderate point of view'.[20]

The second effect may seem paradoxical given the book's subject-matter. *Intruder* was the novel that finally redefined its author from a 'mere' Southern writer into a commentator on all humanity. As the headline to Horace Gregory's *New York Herald Tribune Weekly* review declared, Faulkner was a 'Regional Novelist of Universal Meaning'.[21] When Faulkner read Cowley's first essay in 1944 he objected to being identified as a spokesman for his homeland: 'I'm inclined to think that my material, the South, is not very important to me. I just happen to know it, and don't have time in life to learn another one and write at the same time.'[22] Occasional critics agreed that his fiction dramatized universals instead of concerns only relevant below the Mason–Dixon line. In 1939 George Marion O'Donnell insisted in *Kenyon Review* that the conflict between the Sartorises and the Snopeses was mythological, not sociological, marking 'fundamentally a struggle between humanism and naturalism'. That made Faulkner 'a traditional moralist' using a 'universal conflict' to promote 'ethically responsible will' and 'vital morality'.[23] A few years later, reviewing *The Portable Faulkner*, Robert Penn Warren objected to Cowley's emphasis on 'the Southern elements' and outlined various 'issues common to our modern world' that demonstrated Faulkner's 'legend is not merely the legend of the South' but also 'a legend of our general plight and problem'.[24] This stance became increasingly common as Faulkner was canonized. Encouraging the argument was the onset of the Cold War, which led criticism to define American authors as ambassadors of Western democratic values rather than social critics. Faulkner's own language likewise grew preoccupied more by man's fate than the South's.

Faulkner's critical and commercial rehabilitation provided recognition and much-needed financial stability, but it did nothing to resolve family tensions. Bill and Estelle continued to drink and argue to excess. The now-teenaged Jill shouldered the brunt of the malice; once when she begged her father to stop bingeing, Faulkner replied, 'Nobody remembers Shakespeare's children.'[25] Servants at Rowan Oak learned to scatter when tempers flared; neighbours avoided the family. Screenwriter A. I. 'Buzz' Bezzerides, who looked after Faulkner during Hollywood drinking binges from 1942 to 1945, recalled overhearing a disturbing incident while visiting Oxford:

> I awoke about two or three o'clock in the morning and I heard the fierce, vicious whisper of Estelle's voice: 'Don't touch me, Bill, I don't want you to touch me. Don't you touch me.' I woke up my wife, and she heard Estelle's protest, and in the middle of all this, there was a sound I'll never forget: that sharp, intense striking of a hand against flesh. He had apparently slapped her in the face. Just to hear that slap inflicted pain; and then silence. Shortly after that, we became aware of a sexual encounter on the other side of the door . . . Next morning, Estelle was as cheerful as she possibly could be when we sat down to eat with her and Bill.[26]

In these post-Hollywood years Faulkner complained of romantic and sexual loneliness. Inevitably, his critical rediscovery provided extramarital opportunities. In late 1948 while visiting New York he made a pass at Ruth Ford, a Mississippi actress he first met when she dated his brother Dean in the 1930s. He and Ruth later socialized in Hollywood, where she was a contract player at Warner Bros. When Ford politely declined his advances, Faulkner drank so heavily Ford had him hospitalized. Still, the pair remained close, with the author promising to tailor his next project, an unlikely stage play, as a vehicle for her. In July 1949 another potential mistress entered the scene when 21-year-old Joan Williams sought advice on her fiction. After publishing a stopgap collection of Gavin Stevens mystery stories (*Knight's Gambit*), Faulkner invited Joan to collaborate on his play, hoping to seduce her.

As with *A Fable*, writing *Requiem for a Nun* (1951) – a title first toyed with in 1933 – proved arduous. The plot explored the fate of Faulkner's most notorious heroine, Temple Drake, some eight years after her rape in *Sanctuary*. Married to the alcoholic cad who abandoned her to Popeye, Gowan Stevens, Temple has suffered another tragedy: her nanny, Nancy Mannigoe (revived from 'That Evening Sun'), has smothered the Stevens's youngest child to stop Temple from running off with Pete, the younger brother of the gangster Red, murdered by Popeye. Covering the interval between Nancy's murder conviction and her execution, *Requiem* wants to be a philosophical disquisition on guilt, complicity and suffering, but the dialogue is leaden and the staging contrived. In encouraging Temple to confess her responsibility for Nancy's actions, the drama twice resorts to the gimmick of Gowan hiding behind a desk to learn things his wife cannot admit to him. The theme that humanity must inevitably suffer to understand justice bears some affinities with existential thinking, which is why Albert Camus was attracted to the material, staging it in France in 1956. But Faulkner doubted the project from the start and felt abandoned to it when Joan Williams's participation proved perfunctory throughout spring 1950.

In hopes of adding import, he came up with the idea of introducing each act with a prose-poem on the history of the institutions governing justice's administration: the courthouse, Mississippi's state capital in Jackson and the jailhouse. The first of these prose meditations was sold to *Harper's* under the title 'A Name for the City'. Finishing the prologues to Acts II and III took more time, but the three pieces eventually became the most compelling elements of what Faulkner decided was an unconventional novel, adding many details to Yoknapatawpha County history. In September 1951 reviewers agreed *Requiem for a Nun* was an 'interesting experiment in form', as Faulkner described it, but found little to commend in characterization or dialogue.[27]

While struggling with *Requiem*, Faulkner again found himself competing against past accomplishments when the long-deferred *Collected Stories of William Faulkner* finally appeared in August 1950. As with *The Portable Faulkner*, the table of contents eschewed chronology for a thematic organization that documented the sweep and scope of Faulkner's contribution to a genre that he considered a mere revenue stream. As early as 1948 Faulkner came up with a plan for dividing its 42 stories into six sections that ranged from the agrarian countryside into Jefferson, then outward to 'The Wasteland' with war stories, 'The Middle Ground' with a mixture of Yoknapatawpha and non-Yoknapatawpha selections, and finally into 'Beyond' with supernatural and experimental efforts. As Faulkner wrote to Cowley about the divisions, 'Even to a collection of stories, form, integration, is as important as to a novel – an entity of its own, single, set for one pitch, contrapuntal in integration, toward one end, one finale.'[28] The literary establishment agreed: *Collected Stories* won the National Book Award – no mean feat considering that two of the year's judges, Maxwell Geismar and Granville Hicks, were frequent detractors.

In November 1950 there came word that Faulkner had won the Nobel Prize in Literature. Rumours circulated for years that his name was on the shortlist. When no prize was given the previous year, many guessed he was the top vote-getter but failed to garner unanimous support. (The speculation was true; Faulkner actually received the 1949 award alongside the 1950 recipient, philosopher Bertrand Russell.) Faulkner initially declined to attend the December ceremony but relented after pressure from Random House, the American State Department and Jill Faulkner. It was fortunate that he did, albeit with Jill but not Estelle accompanying him. Among the dozen American writers to receive the prize (including the most recent, Bob Dylan), Faulkner delivered the most stirring and best-remembered address. Many audiences today have never heard of Pearl Buck (1938), or have no clue what remarks Saul

Bellow (1976) or Toni Morrison (1993) delivered, but they are likely to recognize Faulkner's statement, 'I decline to accept the end of man . . . I believe that man will not merely endure: he will prevail.' The speech was a *cri de cœur* for artists to reject apocalyptic fear in the Atomic Age ('Our tragedy today is a general and universal physical fear so long sustained by now that we can even bear it. There are no longer problems of the spirit. There is only the question: When will I be blown up?') and re-engage 'the problems of the human heart in conflict with itself'. For decades, phrases from the address were culturally inescapable, cited endlessly in public oratory. With its deliberate abstraction and insistent rhythms, the speech established once and for all that William Faulkner was more than a Southerner or a modernist, more even than a representative American. He was a humanist who stood for 'the old verities and truths of the heart, the old universal truths . . . courage and honor and hope and pride and compassion and pity and sacrifice which have been the glory of his past'.[29]

Faulkner returned from the ceremony convinced he had to finish *A Fable*. Wrapping up *Requiem for a Nun* intruded on his plans: the novel was no sooner scheduled for publication than Ruth Ford introduced him to a producer interested in staging it. The second half of 1951 was lost to rewrites and rehearsals, which Faulkner found exasperating. The work was wasted when financing failed to materialize for different stagings in New York and Paris. Other diversions also kept him from writing: a trip to France to accept the Legion of Honour, an address to students at Jill's high-school graduation and his off-and-on pursuit of Joan Williams, which was consummated, unsatisfactorily for them both, in summer 1952. Joan was not Faulkner's only adulterous interest – in this period he reconnected with Meta Carpenter one last time and slept as well with Else Jonsson, the widow of a Swedish journalist who promoted him for the Nobel Prize. Yet Joan was the lover whose affections he sought most vigorously, even after Estelle discovered their

Faulkner and Oxford drugstore proprietor Mac Reed in the early 1950s, posing during the filming of a Ford Foundation documentary on the author. Reed stocked his friend's novels, from the outset of his career, as a personal favour.

incriminating letters, leading to a showdown. Faulkner hoped that Joan's youth would recharge his waning energies, but her insistent doubts over their thirty-year age difference and his physical condition hastened his flagging.

In truth, Faulkner's health was rapidly deteriorating. Beginning in mid-1952 he was hospitalized repeatedly for back pain, drinking binges and seizures. After visiting Rowan Oak that October at Estelle's request, his editor, Saxe Commins, sent first his wife and then Random House dire reports: Faulkner was completely incapacitated, 'mumbling incoherently and . . . totally incapable of controlling his bodily functions . . . This is more than a case of acute alcoholism. It is the complete disintegration of a man.'[30] Faulkner consented to electroshock therapy and psychiatric sessions in New York, to little effect. Estelle suffered her own reversals, including blurred vision, haemorrhaging and a heart attack.

As Faulkner struggled to complete *A Fable* in the early 1950s, he famously outlined the allegorical action on the walls of a downstairs bedroom at Rowan Oak. The outline is preserved to this day and remains one of the highlights of touring the house.

Amid these crises, it is remarkable Faulkner summoned the strength to complete *A Fable* in November 1953. Nine years in the making, the book remains the least read of his nineteen novels, with even *Soldiers' Pay* and *Mosquitoes* attracting more attention. Despite several powerful descriptive passages building up to the execution of Corporal Stefan, the novel's Christ figure, the narrative feels at once abstract in characterization and locale and yet reductively obvious in its biblical parallels. The interpolated *Notes of a Horsethief* (which old friend Ben Wasson's Levee Press also published independently in 1951) muddles the critique of military and bureaucratic callousness towards human life. Other ancillary tall tales dilute the already anaemic drama.

The best way to understand *A Fable* is historically. It belongs to a series of novels by major writers published in the 1950s that Dwight Macdonald derisively dubbed 'midcult'. These were books aimed at educated, middle-class audiences that, in the critic's acidic phrase, were 'advanced enough to impress midbrows without worrying them'. Whereas modernist literature is disruptive and despairing, midcult fictions are sentimental reaffirmations of humanity's ultimate good. Their literariness comes from straining for what Macdonald called 'universal significance' through 'fake Biblical prose' and Christological symbols, but their morality remains uncomplicated. In this way, 'midcult' works are both 'ultra-simple and grandiose'.[31] Macdonald's chief examples were *The Old Man and the Sea* (which won Hemingway the Nobel Prize in 1954) and Thornton Wilder's *Our Town*, but other examples include John Steinbeck's *The Pearl* (1947) and Bernard Malamud's debut novel *The Natural* (1951). Such books reflect again the Cold War dualism, flattering Western readers that their values were timeless and noble. *A Fable* is more ironic than many of these earnest works, yet it eschews the contradiction and paradox that makes major novels such as *Light in August* and *Absalom, Absalom!* richly unrelenting in confronting moral issues.

The novel's reception was mixed. Supporters hailed it for its lofty ambitions; detractors found it pretentious and convoluted. No matter: *A Fable* won both the National Book Award and the Pulitzer Prize. Commentators agreed that the judges rewarded the career, not the novel.

8

Breaking the Pencil (1955–62)

Faulkner's final years found him living out a paradox. A fiercely private man, he opposed inquiries into his personal life with 'On Privacy (The American Dream: What Happened to It?)'. The diatribe, twice delivered to university audiences before appearing in *Harper's* in July 1955, vents his annoyance at Robert Coughlan's unauthorized biography *The Private World of William Faulkner* (1954). Around the same time, he adamantly rejected Random House's request to sit for another *Time* magazine profile and supposedly called for his shotgun when journalist William Emerson arrived uninvited on his doorstep for a *Newsweek* cover story. Yet Faulkner also enjoyed the perks of adulation and politely tolerated fans who, as Coughlan and Emerson had, trekked to Oxford to catch a glimpse of the famous writer. Sometimes he even tolerated the visitors at home. The Alabama novelist William Cobb recalls in his 2015 memoir *Captain Billy's Troopers* unexpectedly happening upon the author while strolling the grounds at Rowan Oak as a young man at Estelle's invitation: 'He glared at me with coal-black eyes . . . Then he smiled and winked and walked off down to the edge of the lawn and stood smoking his pipe.'[1]

With fame came opportunities to travel, as when old friend Howard Hawks invited Faulkner on an extended jaunt through Europe and Egypt to write a script called *Land of the Pharaohs*, material hardly simpatico with Yoknapatawpha County. Faulkner also accepted invitations from the u.s. State Department to speak at international destinations on both his fiction and his hopes for humanity. He even briefly chaired a commission of writers for President Dwight D. Eisenhower's People to People Program, exploring how the arts might promote American values abroad.

The rewards for hard-won renown relieved the pressure to write. Faulkner could still produce intriguing work: the autobiographical prose-poem 'Mississippi' for the travel magazine *Holiday*; the short story 'Race at Morning', which brought his highest price ever from the *Saturday Evening Post* ($2,500) and which closed a selection of his best hunting stories that Random House issued in October 1955 called *Big Woods*; a pair of unlikely articles on hockey and the Kentucky Derby for *Sports Illustrated*. Yet the exhaustion from completing his 'magnum o' left him pining for new pleasures to replace writing's drudgery. One vivid phrase appears in his correspondence as early as 1951 as he longed to complete *A Fable*: 'I have a feeling that I shall be through,' Faulkner wrote to Else Jonsson, 'can break the pencil and cast it all away, that I have spent 30 years anguishing and sweating over, never to trouble me again.'[2] The phrase 'break the pencil' reappears throughout the 1950s as his literary powers diminished.

The anguish wasn't simply from exhausted creativity. Faulkner's poor health made travel a dicey proposition. In August 1955 he embarked on a goodwill tour of Japan. On his second day he missed a luncheon in his honour attended by two hundred professors and students in Tokyo. Severe back pain nearly immobilized him at a reception that same afternoon, and before the following day he was in emergency treatment, nearly scrubbing the entire month's itinerary. Thanks to the assistance of the U.S. Information Service officer charged with his caretaking, Dr Leon Picon, Faulkner rallied out of a sense of duty and patriotism. Although he referred to Picon as his 'wet nurse' and 'control officer', he found the press conferences and seminars arranged for him endurable if not exactly enjoyable. His answers to sometimes reductive, sometimes repetitive questions about symbols and images in his fiction, his thoughts on peers like Hemingway and Thomas Wolfe and the state of mankind were unerringly polite. Yet Faulkner also indulged his more fabulist side. To one group he described his career when he met Sherwood Anderson in New Orleans: 'I was working for what we called a bootlegger . . . I ran a boat that would go down into the Gulf of Mexico and bring back the rum to make into the bottled whiskey. I didn't need very much money in those days and I would be paid a hundred dollars for each trip, which was a lot of money in 1921, so I would loaf until I ran out of money again, and I would write.'[3] No one in his audience pointed out that he spent most of 1921 living with his parents on the Ole Miss campus, his only employment house painting.

After the tour, Faulkner returned to the States via Italy, where he reconnoitred with the new woman in his life. The affair with Joan Williams ended in late 1953; like Helen Baird nearly thirty years earlier, Joan rejected him to marry a more conventional man – in her case, a man her own age. The following month, while travelling with Hawks for their *Land of the Pharaohs* project, Faulkner met another nineteen-year-old, Jean Stein, the wealthy daughter of a co-founder of the entertainment company MCA. Much worldlier than Joan, Jean was ambitious and sophisticated. She would go on to pioneer the genre of oral biography in American non-fiction and edit the prestigious literary journal *Grand Street* before committing suicide in 2017 by leaping from a Manhattan apartment building. For the moment, she happily played the adoring daughter/caretaker role Faulkner desired of female companions. A diary entry by Christopher Isherwood's long-time partner, Don Bachardy, captures the relationship: Faulkner 'was brought to our table by Jean Stein in such a glow of triumph that a fanfare might have accompanied the scene. Small, impassive and inaudible, if in fact he said anything at all at our table, Faulkner has a remote air and his dark, hooded eyes suggest a blind man with Jean as his seeing-eye dog.'[4]

Bookending his time abroad was controversy back home. Earlier that spring Faulkner wrote several letters to the *Memphis Commercial Appeal* arguing that racial integration was inevitable in the wake of the Supreme Court's 1954 Brown vs Board of Education ruling. Segregation, he insisted, made little economic sense, especially in regard to education. Because Mississippi's public schools were below par, maintaining separate but equally inferior institutions hurt both whites and blacks and kept the state impoverished. Faulkner's letters sparked a landslide of public and private opprobrium, including midnight phone calls denouncing him as a 'nigger lover'.

Shortly after he arrived in Rome at the end of summer, news broke from Money, Mississippi, 120 kilometres (75 mi.) southwest of Oxford, of the murder of Emmett Till. A fourteen-year-old African American child from Chicago, Till was viciously beaten and dumped in the Tallahatchie River after a woman named Carolyn Bryant fabricated claims he had disrespected her. A pivotal moment in the Civil Rights crusade, the killing incited a firestorm of condemnation. Faulkner issued a press release that challenged segregationists to admit the inhumanity of violence: 'If we in America have reached that point in our desperate culture where we must murder children, no matter for what reason or what color, we don't deserve to survive, and probably won't.'[5]

Returning home, Faulkner spoke at a riotous meeting of the Southern Historical Association, urging Southerners to accept desegregation with 'dignity and goodwill'. His remarks bewildered his family. Long-simmering tensions with his youngest surviving brother, John, boiled over. For years John and his family had relied on Bill's financial generosity. He also cashed in on his brother's fame, adding the 'u' to his surname and publishing his own novels. Faulkner almost certainly means John when he complains in a 1952 letter of supporting 'parasites who do not even have the grace to be sycophants'.[6] A card-carrying member of the White Citizens' Council, John now fired off his own letter to the *Commercial Appeal*

accusing desegregation advocates of being Communist dupes.[7]
The brothers barely spoke.

Faulkner's position had not evolved since *Intruder in the Dust.*
He was not a progressive; to him the South either desegregated
on its own or the federal government would intervene and occupy
the region as in 1865. Faulkner believed that African Americans
had no interest in entering white people's world, only in economic
equality. Unfortunately, his state of mind wasn't always stable
when articulating his position. In a late February 1956 interview
with reporter Russell W. Howe he spoke against federal intervention
with ill-advised bravado: 'I don't like enforced integration any more
than I like enforced segregation. If I have to choose between the
United States and Mississippi, then I'll choose Mississippi . . .
I'd fight for Mississippi against the United States, even if it meant
going out into the street and shooting Negroes.'[8]

The remark caused a furore when it appeared in late March in
the periodical *The Reporter*. The meeting with Howe occurred while
Faulkner suffered deep anxiety over the fate of Autherine Lucy, a
25-year-old African American whose admission to the University
of Alabama had been mandated by the federal courts. Convinced
Lucy would be murdered, he drank heavily before the interview,
something he subtly acknowledged in a *mea culpa* issued to news
outlets. The words attributed to him, he claimed, were 'statements
no sober man would make, nor it seems to me, any sane man
believe'.[9]

The damage was done, however. Progressives denounced
Faulkner. NAACP co-founder W.E.B. Du Bois, a generation older
than the writer, challenged him to a debate on the courthouse
steps in Sumner, Mississippi, where a jury acquitted Till's
murderers. James Baldwin, a generation younger, eviscerated
him in *Partisan Review*, asking what exactly he had done for
blacks that entitled him to speak on their status. The only thing
that could possibly unite Civil Rights advocates and obstructionists,

it seemed, was their mutual disdain for William Faulkner. The condemnation didn't silence him. An essay written before the controversy, 'On Fear: The South in Labor', appeared in *Harper's* that June, and Faulkner reiterated his plea for moderate change to any interviewer who asked. Yet any serious credibility he had on the issue was gone.

As racial unrest roiled the South, Faulkner sought refuge in his craft. More than a decade and a half after *The Hamlet*, he returned to his Snopes chronicle, labouring over its second instalment, *The Town*, throughout 1956. The novel follows Flem Snopes and his wife, the former Eula Varner, as they move to Jefferson from Frenchman's Bend in 1909. Over the subsequent two decades, Flem rises through the middle class to seize control of the Sartoris Bank (based on the bank grandfather J.W.T. Falkner founded during the writer's childhood). As with the first Snopes book, the novel incorporates previously published short stories, including another of Faulkner's best, 1932's 'Centaur in Brass', as well as 1934's 'Mule in the Yard'. Both stories had been reprinted recently in *Collected Stories*; that fact and the familiar cast of characters – Chick Mallison, Gavin Stevens, Gowan Stevens, V. K. Ratliff and, of course, Flem himself – made the material seem a retread to some readers. 'It is only when we compare it with Faulkner's earlier work that the novel disappoints us,' wrote Granville Hicks (who had often critiqued those earlier novels). 'Alas, that is the comparison that has to be made. I read it with great though not continuous pleasure.'[10] By the mid-1950s younger novelists such as Saul Bellow, Arthur Miller, Sloan Wilson and John Cheever were preoccupied with what Governor Adlai Stevenson called the post-war crisis of 'collectivism colliding with individualism'.[11] They protested the rise of corporations, white-collar alienation, the emergence of deceptively idyllic suburbs and the stifling cultural conformity creeping across America. Amid such pressing concerns, episodes in *The Town* involving mule trading, prohibition whisky, smutty French postcards and blackmail over adultery seemed almost quaint, throwbacks to the 'revolt from the village' fiction of the 1910s and early 1920s.

One particular reader took almost malicious glee in the novel's mixed reception. When the *Commercial Appeal* published a trenchant review that dismissed *The Town* as a '300-page wallow' in a 'Slough of Despond', Phil Stone wrote its author, Jim Dan Hill, an appreciative letter. 'It was certainly a relief to read your article,' Faulkner's 64-year-old former mentor said. 'I am tired of the nauseating obsequiousness that proclaims an indication of genius everything that Bill does and writes and every little remark he makes (usually borrowed from someone else).'[12] Stone spent his later years bitterly declaring Faulkner 'overrated' to any correspondent who wrote to Oxford seeking background information. Not even the fact that Faulkner had dedicated *The Town* to him – all three Snopes novels are, in fact, dedicated to Stone – stopped him from disparaging his former charge's literary development.

Despite its folk humour, *The Town* exudes a distinctly autumnal melancholy. In *The Hamlet* Eula Varner is a Venus figure, sensual and alluring. In adulthood, as Mrs Flem Snopes, she embodies the sorrows of the heart, committing suicide in 1927 to avoid public revelation of her eighteen-year affair with Manfred de Spain, Jefferson's mayor and the bank president Flem dethrones.

Another poignant plot thread concerns Gavin Stevens's 'avuncular' feelings for Eula's daughter, Linda, who learns in her teen years that Flem is not her biological father. Linda and Gavin's May–December relationship reflects Faulkner's own dependency on the approval of young women like Joan Williams and Jean Stein. As the second Snopes novel made its way into print, Stein ended their affair. Cynical observers said she encouraged the old man's affection as a stepping stone to her own writing career. Although Joan was the one who would publish a *roman-à-clef* of her time with Faulkner – her second novel, *The Wintering* (1971) – Jean capitalized more immediately on their relationship. With the writer's assistance, she compiled from their correspondence the most insightful interview Faulkner ever gave about his work and sold it to the *Paris Review* in mid-1956. Their exchange remains the source of the author's most-cited quotations about his art, including his description of Yoknapatawpha County as his 'little postage stamp of native soil'.[13] When Stein broke off the affair only six months later, Faulkner was devastated and, predictably, binged until he was hospitalized.

His recovery coincided with a new opportunity. In winter 1957 he accepted a post as writer-in-residence at the University of Virginia. The Faulkners began visiting Charlottesville a year earlier when Jill relocated there with her husband, Paul D. Summers, whom she wed in August 1954. With the birth of their first grandchild in 1956, Bill and Estelle enjoyed long forays outside of Oxford. Their marriage reached a quiet détente: Estelle was now a member of Alcoholics Anonymous, and while Faulkner continued drinking, the loss of Jean Stein appears to have ended his adulterous streak, which he had flaunted to hurt his wife. Charlottesville was for the couple, if not a new start, at least a chance to escape memories of their domestic misery at Rowan Oak. As one biographer notes, the new setting allowed Faulkner to 'cut away much of the baggage of his Mississippi past. No one [in Charlottesville] called him "little Billy" or even "Billy," no hint of Count No 'Count, and no history of past due bills and charges that in his writing he had slandered his land and his people for profit.'[14] Instead, he surrounded himself with professors like his future biographer Joseph Blotner, who recognized the immensity of his contribution to American literature.

His duties at the university involved discussing his work in formal question-and-answer sessions with students and faculty. The discussions were so successful Faulkner returned in winter 1958 for a second appointment. Transcripts from both years, published in 1959 as *Faulkner in the University*, provided yet another invaluable

record of his intentions and ambitions. There was only one drawback
to the residency. When Blotner and colleague Frederick Gwynn
petitioned UVA president Colgate Darden to appoint the Nobel
laureate to a permanent position, Darden demurred, leery of both
Faulkner's reputation for drinking and his stance on integration.

The Faulkners maintained ties to Charlottesville even after
the writer-in-residence position for the 1958–9 school year went
to Katherine Anne Porter. Eventually they bought a second home
and talked of acquiring additional property, including a farm.
The recent birth of their second grandchild (a third would follow)
wasn't the only reason for remaining. Faulkner had always enjoyed
horseback riding. In Oxford he kept a mare named Tempy, short
for Temptress. In Virginia, through Jill, he befriended Grover
Vandevender, the owner of a 300-acre horse farm and the huntsman
since 1929 of the Farmington Hunt Club of fox hunters. Nearly thirty
years earlier Faulkner had expertly borrowed the rituals of the sport
as a metaphor for marital manipulation in his story 'Fox Hunt', but
the ceremonial formalities in Virginia were even more ornate. With
Vandevender schooling him, Faulkner became a regular at both
Farmington hunts and at those of its friendly rival, the Keswick
Hunt Club. He acquired his own horse in Albemarle County, dubbed
Powerhouse, and soon sported the colours of the Farmington club.
Donning the official uniform of pink coat, black derby and top
boots, he commissioned a formal portrait of himself from Oxford
photographer J. R. Cofield, replete with crop, whip and spurs. It
remains a defining image of the writer, to this day hanging over
the mantel at Rowan Oak for tourists to admire.

Faulkner's obsession with horseback riding and fox hunting
coincided with the final entry in the Snopes trilogy, *The Mansion*.
The focus this time is only nominally Flem Snopes. Instead, front
and centre is his cousin Mink, who spends 38 years at Parchman
Prison planning for the day he will murder Flem for not helping
him elude conviction for killing Jack Houston, a crime first narrated

in the 1931 story 'The Hound' then revised for *The Hamlet* and retold again in *The Town*. Abetting Mink's revenge plot is Linda Snopes Kohl, Flem's 'adopted' daughter and now the widow of a Spanish Civil War volunteer. Also returning, inevitably, is Gavin Stevens, whom Linda encourages to embrace and engage life, offering Faulkner a final resolution to the Prufrockian fate of the faun/Horace Benbow character isolated from his passions. The plot takes significant sojourns to New York City and the POW camp in Belgium where Chick Mallison is interred during the Second World War (details of which Faulkner borrowed from Joseph Blotner's experiences as a captured bombardier). Despite these atypical settings, *The Mansion* borrows characters and events from *The Sound and the Fury* (Jason Compson returns as a foil to Flem), *Sanctuary*, 'Knight's Gambit', 'Shingles for the Lord' and many other works. Unfortunately, these echoes never threaten to overshadow their source material. As with its predecessor, the novel feels dutiful rather than inspired.

For Random House, the main concern was resolving discrepancies with *The Hamlet* and *The Town* so the trilogy might one day appear in a single volume. Because Faulkner's editor, Saxe Commins, died of a heart attack in mid-1958, reconciling inconsistencies in chronology and character names fell to his replacement, Albert Erskine. Faulkner lost patience with the minutiae. 'If what I wrote in 1958 aint better than what I wrote in 1938,' he snapped when Erskine wanted to change details to match the earlier books, 'I should have stopped writing twenty years ago.'[15] Both men well understood that the work of 1958 was a far cry from that of 1938. Rather than correct the discrepancies, Faulkner insisted on adding an odd author's note claiming they occurred because over decades of writing about the same characters he had grown to know them better.

The Mansion appeared in the waning months of the 1950s. As the new decade began William Faulkner was more of an institution than a working writer. Reminders of his legacy were constant. Movie

Invited to wear the coat and colours of the Farmington Hunt Club in Virginia, Faulkner commissioned a portrait of himself in his stately uniform. An oil painting from this series hangs today above the mantel at Rowan Oak.

adaptations came and went, some impressive (*The Long Hot Summer* with Paul Newman and Joanne Woodward, based very loosely on 'Barn Burning' and *The Hamlet*), some terrible (*The Sound and the Fury*, starring Yul Brynner as Jason Compson). Thanks to Ruth Ford's persistence, *Requiem for a Nun* finally enjoyed a New York run in 1959. A constant stream of awards and honours came Faulkner's way. Interviewers published sometimes testy responses to tired questions; newspapers reported on his unenthusiastic trip to Venezuela on behalf of the u.s. State Department in 1961 and a more rousing appearance at West Point a year later.

Mostly what the new decade brought were reminders that time was running out. In October 1960, just weeks before 43-year-old John F. Kennedy won the presidency and became a symbol of the era's burgeoning obsession with youth, Maud Falkner died slightly shy of ninety. The Young Colonel's youngest son, J.W.T. Falkner, Jr, passed away fifteen months later, not quite eighty. Almost as if challenging his own mortality, the sexagenarian Faulkner pushed his body to extremes riding and fox hunting, often for hours on end, and often wracked with back pain from constant falls. At various points he broke his collarbone, fractured his clavicle, compressed his spine, pulled and bruised his groin and wound up pinned to the ground under a horse. Frederick R. Karl suggests that the 'break the pencil' image, which 'comes back ominously' into his correspondence in these final years, reflects a suicidal impulse: 'There is little question that something of a death wish, or flirtation with death, lies just below the surface [of these injuries]; for his failure to heed medical advice and his disregard for certain signs of deterioration are indication of a submission to final things.'[16]

Yet he did not submit – at least not as dramatically as Hemingway did. By the time his main surviving rival ended his life by shotgun on 2 July 1961 – an act that deeply shook Faulkner – he had returned to fiction, rallying for one final novel. Originally called *The Horse Stealers: A Reminiscence*, it repeated the scenario of *Notes of a Horsethief* by teaming up a white man (or at least a half-white one), a black man and a young boy in a plot involving horse racing. Faulkner soon seized upon an arcane spelling for an obscure Scottish word for 'thief' and retitled the story *The Reivers* (1962). This time the boy was Lucius 'Loosh' Priest, the black man Ned McCaslin (a cousin of Lucas Beauchamp) and the other man Boon Hogganbeck, the part-Native American hunter revived from 'The Bear'. The book was an opportunity to heal at least one lingering family wound. Older now than Murry Falkner had been when he died in 1932, the author drew a sympathetic portrait of his father as Loosh describes the livery stable Maury Priest operates in Jefferson. The narrative's fly-in-amber tone is likewise obvious in its depiction of a setting that in *Sanctuary* had been treated as acerbic and nightmarish. As Loosh embarks on a series of adventures to reacquire his grandfather's Winton Flyer automobile after Ned trades it for a horse to pay off a friend's debt, the trio ends up at Miss Reba's bordello in the Memphis Tenderloin. No Popeyes or Reds haunt the hallways anymore. The whores have hearts of gold, including the love of Boon's life, Everbe Corinthia, or 'Miss Corrie'.

As a picaresque, *The Reivers* makes for an amiable read. If nothing else, it demonstrates once again Faulkner's attachment to coming-of-age narratives. With its charm and happy ending (Boon and Everbe have a child they name after Loosh), the novel mainly seems a gift in the form of a crowd-pleaser to Random House, a token of appreciation for its 25 years of support. Faulkner's publishers arranged for excerpts to appear in both the *Saturday Evening Post* and *Esquire*, and the Book of the Month Club selected it as a featured recommendation. As if apologizing for his wrongheaded dismissal of *Absalom, Absalom!* years earlier, Clifton Fadiman wrote a glowing review for BOMC members.

All seemed set for Faulkner to enjoy one final victory lap. Then, only two weeks after *The Reivers* was published on 4 June

When photographer Martin Dain visited Faulkner months before his death, he captured how worn the writer's clothes were from hours of riding his beloved horses. With Faulkner is Victoria Fielden Johnson, his step-granddaughter.

1962, the writer suffered another agonizing fall when a recently acquired horse named Stonewall bucked him onto the ground just past Bailey's Woods. Faulkner lay paralysed in the red dirt before managing to rise. Once home at Rowan Oak he insisted on remounting Stonewall to prove that as a rider he was unconquerable. Over the subsequent days, when the back pain refused to heal, Faulkner mixed alarming amounts of alcohol and tranquilizers. On 5 July, after he drank a fifth and a half of whisky, his speech grew confused. Estelle and other family members decided to check him into Wright's Sanitarium in Byhalia, his usual recourse for drying out from a binge. Later commentators would question whether a sanitarium was the appropriate facility for a man complaining of chest pains, but those around him had been through the cycle of alcohol dependency so many times the symptoms did not seem unusual. When doctors checked him in at 6 p.m. that night, his blood pressure and heartbeat were normal. Only a few hours later, however, around 1:30 a.m. on 6 July, William Faulkner sat up, let out a groan, and died of a massive heart attack at the age of 64.

Amid the shock of his passing, some time would pass before commentators recognized the significance of the date: 6 July was the birthday of the Old Colonel, the original William Falkner, whose swaggering ways inspired his great-grandson's imagination to heights none of the Mississippi clan he founded could ever have expected.

More than fifty years later, the coincidence still seems too symmetrical to be believed, closing not just one man's life but one of the most dominating literary legends of twentieth-century America in a perfect circle.

Afterword:
'To Think of Myself
Again as a Printed Object'

In 2011, as fans of William Faulkner began commemoration plans
for the following year's semi-centennial of his death, the pay-TV
platform HBO announced an intriguing collaboration with the
writer's estate. In conjunction with one of its most acclaimed writer/
directors, David Milch, the channel revealed plans to weave plots
and characters from various works into an episodic series chronicling
Yoknapatawpha County.[1] The decision to adapt Faulkner to the small
instead of the big screen seemed ingenious. The announcement came
at a time when scripted television had surpassed the cinema in
prestige and inventiveness. Like the man himself, Faulkner films
have always been constrained by the Hollywood medium. The
lone exception is arguably 1933's *The Story of Temple Drake*. This
controversial rendering of *Sanctuary* is often cited as one impetus
for the Motion Picture Producers and Directors of America's
decision to implement the rigid strictures against sex and violence
known as the Hays Code, which lasted from the Great Depression
into the 1960s. Otherwise, adaptations have jettisoned his
experiments in style and form, reducing his plots to oversimplified
melodrama. (See, for example, the 1957 version of *The Sound and the
Fury*, which focuses on Jason Compson, or 1972's *Tomorrow*, based on
the 1940 Gavin Stevens detective story of the same name.) In theory,
episodic television would provide the breadth possible to create
something as inventive and epic as Malcolm Cowley's *The Portable
Faulkner*, in which chronologically arranged short stories and

excerpts from Faulkner novels dramatize the transformation of Yoknapatawpha County – and therefore the American South – from the early nineteenth century to the mid-twentieth. Upon hearing HBO's announcement, Faulkner devotees immediately wondered which memorable characters would make their way into the tapestry of TV storylines. Almost certainly the series would feature Benjy Compson and Flem Snopes, and probably Thomas Sutpen and John Sartoris. But what about Joanna Burden, or Addie Bundren? Whither Lucas Beauchamp and Ike McCaslin?

Even more intriguingly, commentators wondered whether William Faulkner himself might appear in the series. In recent years the rise of the literary 'biopic' has offered award-winning actors the opportunity to tackle the formidable task of portraying authors as diverse as Truman Capote, Virginia Woolf, Iris Murdoch, Sylvia Plath, William Shakespeare, Leo Tolstoy, Jane Austen, Beatrix Potter and even Robert E. Howard, the inventor of Conan the Barbarian. In the years since HBO's announcement, Thomas Wolfe, Allen Ginsberg, Christopher Marlowe, David Foster Wallace and even Emily Dickinson have joined this already long list. The performances frequently walk a fine line between inhabiting these writers' public images and parodying them. The most critically adored movie at the time of the HBO deal – Woody Allen's *Midnight in Paris* – charmed audiences with affectionate caricatures of Ernest Hemingway and F. Scott Fitzgerald, playing up to admirers' romantic notions of how these icons would behave if contemporary audiences travelled back in time and encountered them in the expatriate Paris of the 1920s. The popularity of the film reminded many Faulkner advocates that, compared to his two main rivals, fictional depictions of the South's most famous bard are few and far between. Indeed, one can only readily identify a single portrayal. In 1991, filmmakers Joel and Ethan Coen released *Barton Fink*, which features, in addition to a main character based on playwright Clifford Odets, an obvious Faulkner stand-in in the form of soused writer W. P. Mayhew (played by John Mahoney). The representation is far more cutting and cruel than Allen's gentle ribbing, though. Drawling like Foghorn Leghorn, signing copies of his pretentiously named *Absalom, Absalom!*-manqué masterpiece, *Nebuchadnezzar*, and slurring through verses of Stephen Foster's 'Old Black Joe', Mayhew is a cartoon image of Faulkner's 1940s nadir in Hollywood, drunk and bitter, without a hint of the man's humour, charisma or gentility. By the time W. P. Mayhew is berating his secretary/mistress (based on Meta Carpenter, Faulkner's real-life lover in the late 1930s) for condescendingly calling him a genius, then smacking her around, one feels one's protective instincts kick in.[2] If this is how Hollywood views Faulkner, it is probably just as well other depictions do not exist.

For various reasons, the HBO series never went further than the press release announcing the deal. (In 2013–14, however, the Faulkner estate did authorize a pair of hastily produced and quickly forgotten film versions of *As I Lay Dying* and *The Sound and the Fury*, proving once again that Faulkner is too expansive for the movies.) To a certain extent, the lack of fictionalized Faulkners in popular culture before and after this aborted project is a testament to the enigma of the author's personality. William Faulkner was a man of masks who kept himself at a certain remove from emotions, making him difficult to typecast. Aspects of his public facade are every bit as iconographic as Hemingway's, Fitzgerald's or any other celebrated writer. His moustache (which a psychologist told him in the 1950s he hid behind), his pipe, his hawkish nose, his thatch of white hair are all instantly recognizable, even by people who only know his name and not a single one of his books. Yet these attributes cannot be made to stand for an ethos or stance in the way that Hemingway's puffed chest symbolizes his outsized masculinity or Fitzgerald's baby face encapsulates his youthful, perishable glamour. If anything, the obvious characteristic that photos and portraits radiate of Faulkner is his inscrutability, formal to the point of iciness.

Everything about his glare tells readers to look elsewhere for signs of what his books are about. Perhaps to the books themselves, he would no doubt say to scholars studying him.

The flipside of his authorial aloofness is that it can promote the fallacy that his biography has no real relevance to his writing at all. Reviewing Jay Parini's 2004 biography *One Matchless Time: A Life of William Faulkner*, *Washington Post* columnist Jonathan Yardley wondered why after so many earlier accounts of the life by Joseph Blotner, David Minter, Frederick R. Karl and the much-maligned Stephen B. Oates, just to name a few, we need one more: 'Understanding Faulkner's work . . . doesn't seem to require knowing the details of his life . . . Apart from his writing – which in Faulkner's mind seems to have taken place in its own separate universe, a point Parini makes with some care and skill – he really didn't do much.'[3] As Yardley insists, Faulkner drank to excess, remained in an unhappy marriage, had affairs, 'puttered' around Oxford and 'worried obsessively' about money. (Interestingly, the reviewer says nothing about Hollywood.) For Yardley, the fact that 'there isn't much of a story to tell' should point readers – including future chroniclers of the writer's life – to a succinct moral they would do well to abide by: 'Read Faulkner, not about Faulkner.'

Rather crankily, Yardley takes here a purist stance: to 'know' a writer, just crack open a book, and the meaning is self-evident for readers who have taste, intuition and a modicum of training and history. Additional resources are part of an unnecessary apparatus – including literary scholarship, which the critic contemptuously dismisses *en toto*: 'The amount of scholarship (mostly pedantry) devoted to his work almost literally defies calculation . . . Many university careers have been built on the foundation laid by Faulkner, and professors by the scores owe their tenure to him, but astonishingly few books of real merit have emerged from all this scholarly hairsplitting.' In other words, academic criticism is sound and fury, signifying nothing. Yet in reality, the human interest that biography generates often sparks readers' curiosity about the writing. If audiences were not interested in the private life of authors, there would be no steady stream of tourists visiting Oxford, Mississippi, each year to tour Rowan Oak, Faulkner's estate. Nor would there have been a half-century plus of personal reminiscences by Falkner family members, beginning with brother John Faulkner's *My Brother Bill* (1963) and culminating with niece Dean Faulkner Wells's *Every Day by the Sun: A Memoir of the Faulkners of Mississippi* (2011). Readers want to know who writers were so they can appreciate the struggles and triumphs of creating art.

In the case of a 'difficult' writer, knowing the life story is a necessary entry point into the fiction. Recognizing the resentment that Faulkner felt towards his parents, for example, helps explain the sense of generational disaffection and historical disconnect that haunts the Compson children in *The Sound and the Fury.* These resentments are only one crowbar for prying one's way into a house of fiction whose floorplan can seem a hall of mirrors. Similarly, appreciating the despair Faulkner felt over losing Meta Carpenter in 1937 renders comprehensible the debunking, disillusioning aggression towards romance and passion that makes 'The Wild Palms' sections of *If I Forget Thee, Jerusalem* so caustic. Biographical inspirations are stepping stones to understanding attitudes and anxieties in the text, leading us to broader realms of significance that are more cultural than personal.

Other biographical issues are equally illuminating. As easy as it is to say Faulkner's writing declined precipitously after 1942, we have barely begun to reckon with alcoholism's effect on his prose. Ever-advancing scientific explanations for how alcohol affects the brain, both freeing inhibitions in the short term and enfeebling perception in the long, have made scholars leery of proposing beyond generalities how drinking may have helped Faulkner to discover his style before it stranded him in endless convolutions of his trademark mannerisms.

The literary marketplace is another biographical context that is extremely important to understanding his books. Faulkner benefited from working with publishers who printed whatever manuscript he posted to them, with only modest editorial interference. His one stinging rejection when Horace Liveright declined *Flags in the Dust* in 1927 allowed him to ensconce himself in his imagination and drill deep into technical innovation, leading directly to *The Sound and the Fury*, a novel so confident and self-assured it could only have come from a writer unconcerned with whether anyone understood or enjoyed it. But the autonomy publishers granted Faulkner had a downside. Some of his novels – *Pylon, Intruder in the Dust*, certainly the torturous *A Fable* – could have benefited from an editor/collaborator who, like Maxwell Perkins with Thomas Wolfe or later Nan Talese with the late Pat Conroy, might have challenged him to more fully articulate if not realize their potential. With literary freedom, furthermore, came financial dependency. Faulkner spent the peak years of his creativity (1929–42) reliant upon advances and loans from the firms that printed his books (at least when not working in the salt mines of cinema). His constant, sometimes consuming need for money to support his extended family left him frazzled and bitter at the boundaries of support that men like Harrison Smith, Bennett Cerf and Robert K. Haas could extend without jeopardizing the solvency of their companies. How Faulkner made money influenced his own, sometimes wrong-headed, perceptions of his art. His accomplishments in the short story are ironically enriched by his dismissive view of short fiction as a quick-cash remedy for monetary woes. Simply put, Faulkner never appreciated his own achievements in the genre, which are many. So too his resentment towards Hollywood, where with a collaborator like Howard Hawks he should have toyed with narrative structure and devices for exploring consciousness as he did in his novels, if only he did not see movies as a means to a financial end.

The point is that too often we think of biography as factoids instead of contexts: who lived where and travelled to what destination to work, who knew whom and benefited from the connection, who feuded with whom, who slept with whom (and how often). Measured according to such basic details, Faulkner's life can seem distinctly less exciting than those of his contemporaries, who variously globetrotted, paraded in the public eye, wound up crushed by mental illness or became political pariahs. Such events are the stuff of high drama, and they make for far more vivid narrative trajectories than the static image of a writer in a room at a desk letting his imagination do his peregrinating. Yet the 'actual and psychological connections between Faulkner's life and work' are neither as 'separate' nor as 'distinct' as Yardley insists. Faulkner may have borrowed names from Phil Stone or a mentally disabled brother from his teacher Annie Chandler or even his biographer Joseph Blotner's experiences as a Second World War POW for *The Mansion*, but his family's history in the South was the germinating seed of his fictional universe. Nor was he shy about announcing this fact. If he had been, he never would have identified himself as 'Great-grandson of William Faulkner, C.S.A., author of "The White Rose of Memphis"' in the author's note of his first book, *The Marble Faun*. Nor would he have allowed reporters such as Marshall J. Smith and Robert Cantwell to mention Falkner family history in their personality profiles of him in *The Bookman* and *Time* magazine respectively if he truly believed what in his later years he insisted: 'The artist is of no importance. Only what he creates is important.'[4] That 'u' he either accidentally or intentionally slipped into the spelling of his great-grandfather's name in his short history of himself in *The Marble Faun* is likewise telling. Faulkner may have wanted to link himself to his grandfather's romantic-but-fraught legend, but not as an adjunct to it. Whether he could admit it or not, he set out to create a body of art that would subordinate W. C. Falkner to *his* literary renown. (He succeeded.) This tension between Falkner and Faulkner may be the most obvious fault line by which to trace the writer's seismic ambitions: William Faulkner knew he was from a specific place and had inherited a unique history, but he wanted to be his own self-made man, too.

In the end, Faulkner may be our best reminder among his generation that literary biography should tell the story of a writer's creativity: where ideas come from, how they transmogrify into art. As Faulkner's far-fetched tales of being shot down in the First World War or bootlegging out of New Orleans during his Sherwood Anderson period demonstrate, invention and licence from the truth are tools in the book of life as on the printed page. It seems telling that when Faulkner in 1932 told the story of writing *Sanctuary* for his Modern Library introduction he spoke of himself and his work as inseparable: 'I began to think of myself again as a printed object', he says – not 'I began to think of *my work* as a book.'[5] Part of Faulkner's genius was to intrigue us with the background sources of his fiction, if only to make us appreciate the audacity of how he metamorphosed them. In this way, details of the life are important, not as conclusive explanations but as catalysts. The writer may be less important than the art, but that does not make the writer unimportant.

Accordingly, readers hoping to understand William Faulkner should tweak Yardley's dictum ever so slightly:

Read Faulkner, read about Faulkner, then reread Faulkner again. And so on.

References

Introduction

1 Joseph Blotner, ed., *Selected Letters of William Faulkner* (New York, 1977), p. 354. 'The Man Behind the Myth' was the title given to the second part of Coughlan's article, which appeared in *Life* on 5 October 1953. The first part, 'The Private World of William Faulkner', appeared in the previous week's issue, dated 28 September, and was reprinted in book form in 1954.

2 Blotner, ed., *Selected Letters*, p. 182.

3 William Faulkner, 'Interview with Jean Stein Vanden Heuvel', in *Lion in the Garden: Interviews with William Faulkner*, ed. James B. Meriwether and Michael Millgate (Lincoln, 1968), p. 255.

4 Blotner, ed., *Selected Letters*, p. 282.

5 T. S. Eliot, 'Tradition and the Individual Talent', in *Selected Essays: 1917–1932* (New York, 1932), p. 9.

6 Blotner, ed., *Selected Letters*, p. 282.

7 Robert Coughlan, *The Private World of William Faulkner* (New York, 1954), p. 20.

8 William Faulkner, 'On Privacy (The American Dream: What Happened to It?)', in *William Faulkner: Essays, Speeches and Public Letters*, ed. James B. Meriwether, updated edn (New York, 2004), p. 75.

9 John A. Pope, 'Some Facts on William Faulkner', *The Harvard Crimson*, www.thecrimson.com, 28 October 1954.

10 Coughlan, *The Private World of William Faulkner*, pp. 17–18.

11 Blotner borrows the phrase 'impenetrable man' from a Merrill Peterson quote about Thomas Jefferson to describe his frustrations with capturing Faulkner's personality during the writing of his biography. See Joseph Blotner, Foreword to *Faulkner: A Biography; One-volume Edition* (New York, 1984), p. xi. (As with most Faulkner

critics, I refer, except when noted, to Blotner's two-volume biography published a decade before this one-volume condensation and update.) For more on Faulkner's evasiveness, see Blotner's 'Did You See Him Plain?', in *Fifty Years of Yoknapatawpha: Faulkner and Yoknapatawpha 1979*, ed. Doreen Fowler and Ann J. Abadie (Jackson, MS, 1980), pp. 3–22.

12 Frederick R. Karl, *William Faulkner: American Writer* (New York, 1989), p. 17.

1 Backgrounds and Futures (1839–1913)

1 The caption appears in the first instalment of Coughlan's essay, 'The Private World of William Faulkner', *Life* (28 September 1953), p. 128.

2 Robert Coughlan, *The Private World of William Faulkner* (New York, 1954), p. 26.

3 Joel Williamson was the first Faulkner biographer to demonstrate persuasively that W. C. Falkner fathered a second family. See *William Faulkner and Southern History* (New York, 1993), pp. 64–71.

4 William Faulkner, *Requiem for a Nun*, in *Novels: 1942–1954* (New York, 1994), p. 535.

5 Dennis J. Mitchell, *A New History of Mississippi* (Jackson, MS, 2014), p. 261.

6 John Faulkner, *My Brother Bill: An Affectionate Reminiscence* (New York, 1963), p. 97.

7 William Faulkner, 'Artist at Home', in *Collected Stories of William Faulkner* (New York, 1950), p. 640.

8 James E. Fickle, *Mississippi Forests and Forestry* (Jackson, MS, 2001), pp. 92–119.

9 William Faulkner, Dedication to *Big Woods* (New York, 1955), pp. 4–5.

10 Williamson, *William Faulkner and Southern History*, p. 156.

11 W. C. Falkner, *The Little Brick Church* (Philadelphia, PA, 1882), p. 68.

12 James K. Vardaman, quoted in Anon., 'Some Lynching Distinctions', *The Clarion-Ledger* (30 June 1903), quoted in Albert D. Kirwan, *Revolt of the Rednecks: Mississippi Politics, 1876–1925* (Lexington, KY, 1951), p. 152.

13 William Faulkner, *The Town*, in *Novels: 1957–1962* (New York, 1999), p. 36.
14 William Faulkner, 'Mississippi', in *William Faulkner: Essays, Speeches and Public Letters*, ed. James B. Meriwether, updated edn (New York, 2004), p. 13.
15 See, respectively, Theresa M. Towner, *The Cambridge Introduction to William Faulkner* (New York, 2008), p. 2; Williamson, *William Faulkner and Southern History*, p. 141.
16 Joseph Blotner, ed., *Selected Letters of William Faulkner* (New York, 1977), p. 212.
17 David Minter, *William Faulkner: His Life and Work* (Baltimore, MD, 1981), p. 15.
18 Williamson, *William Faulkner and Southern History*, pp. 111–38.
19 Jay Parini, *One Matchless Time: A Life of William Faulkner* (New York, 2004), p. 20.
20 Jay Martin, 'Faulkner's "Male Commedia": The Triumph of Manly Grief', in *Faulkner and Psychology: Faulkner and Yoknapatawpha 1991*, ed. Donald M. Kartiganer and Ann J. Abadie (Jackson, MS, 1994), pp. 149–50.
21 Joseph Blotner, 'The Sources of Faulkner's Genius', in *Fifty Years of Yoknapatawpha: Faulkner and Yoknapatawpha 1979*, ed. Doreen Fowler and Ann J. Abadie (Jackson, MS, 1980), p. 252.
22 Judith L. Sensibar, *Faulkner and Love: The Women Who Shaped his Art, A Biography* (New Haven, CT, and London, 2009), p. 167.
23 William Faulkner, 'Interview with Jean Stein Vanden Heuvel', in *Lion in the Garden: Interviews with William Faulkner*, ed. James B. Meriwether and Michael Millgate (Lincoln, NE, 1968), p. 255.

2 Birth of a Faun (1914–21)

1 Susan Snell, *Phil Stone of Oxford: A Vicarious Life* (Athens, GA, 1991), pp. 3, 38.
2 Phil Stone, 'William Faulkner: The Man and His Work', *Oxford Magazine* 3 (1934), reprinted in James B. Meriwether, 'Early Notices of William Faulkner by Phil Stone and Louis Cochran', *Mississippi Quarterly*, XVII/3 (Summer 1964), p. 163.

3 Quoted in Joseph Blotner, *Faulkner: A Biography* (New York, 1974), vol. I, p. 85.

4 See Joel Williamson, *William Faulkner and Southern History* (New York, 1993), p. 16.

5 Stone, 'William Faulkner', in Meriwether, 'Early Notices', p. 162.

6 Quoted in Snell, *Phil Stone of Oxford*, p. 101.

7 Ben Wasson, *Count No 'Count: Flashbacks to Faulkner* (Jackson, MS, 1983), p. 25.

8 William Faulkner, *Light in August*, in *Novels: 1930–1935* (New York, 1985), p. 590.

9 Stephen B. Oates, *William Faulkner: The Man and the Artist; A Biography* (New York, 1985), p. 20.

10 John Faulkner, *My Brother Bill: An Affectionate Reminiscence* (New York, 1963), p. 133.

11 Ibid.

12 Quoted in Blotner, *Faulkner: A Biography*, vol. I, p. 195. The fact that these lines are a translation of French lyrics to a song was not discovered until 1989. See Donald P. Duclos, '"A Song" for Estelle', *Faulkner Journal*, V (Autumn 1981), pp. 61–5.

13 F. Scott Fitzgerald, 'F. Scott Fitzgerald's Ledger: 1919–1938', p. 170, available at library.sc.edu/digital.

14 Carlos Baker, ed., *Ernest Hemingway: Selected Letters, 1918–1961* (New York, 1981), p. 25.

15 Judith L. Sensibar, *Faulkner and Love: The Women Who Shaped his Art, A Biography* (New Haven, CT, and London, 2009), p. 299. The letters are reprinted in James G. Watson, ed., *Thinking of Home: William Faulkner's Letters to his Mother and Father, 1918–1925* (New York, 1992), pp. 19–44.

16 Frederick R. Karl, *William Faulkner: American Writer* (New York, 1989), p. 109.

17 David Minter, *William Faulkner: His Life and Work* (Boston, MA, 1981), p. 29.

18 Philip Weinstein, *Becoming Faulkner: The Art and Life of William Faulkner* (New York, 2009), p. 241.

19 See his 7 June 1918 letter to Murry and Maud in Watson, *Thinking of Home*, p. 63.

20 Blotner, *Faulkner: A Biography*, vol. I, p. 221.

21 Faulkner, *My Brother Bill*, p. 108.

22 Wasson, *Count No 'Count*, p. 30.

23 Murry C. Falkner, *The Falkners of Mississippi* (Baton Rouge, LA, 1967), pp. 90–91.

24 'Interview in the *New Yorker* (1931)', in *Lion in the Garden: Interviews with William Faulkner*, ed. James B. Meriwether and Michael Millgate (Lincoln, 1968), p. 12.

25 Karl, *William Faulkner*, p. 117.

26 Preston Lauterbach, 'A Cheap Idea', *Virginia Quarterly Review*, XCI/1 (Winter 2015), www.vqronline.org.

27 William Faulkner, 'L'Apres-midi d'un faune', in *William Faulkner: Early Prose and Poetry*, ed. Carvel Collins (New York, 1963), p. 124.

28 Edna St Vincent Millay, 'First Fig', in *A Few Figs from Thistles* (New York, 1920), p. 9.

3 Foaling Season (1921–7)

1 William Faulkner, *Vision in Spring*, ed. Judith L. Sensibar (Austin, 1984), p. 25.

2 Phil Stone, 28 December 1931 letter to Louis Cochran, reprinted in James B. Meriwether, 'Early Notices of William Faulkner by Phil Stone and Louis Cochran', *Mississippi Quarterly*, XVII/3 (Summer 1964), p. 139.

3 William Faulkner, 'The Hill', in *William Faulkner: Early Prose and Poetry*, ed. Carvel Collins (New York, 1963), p. 92.

4 William Faulkner, 'Adolescence', in *Uncollected Stories of William Faulkner*, ed. Joseph Blotner (New York, 1979), p. 465.

5 Joseph Blotner, *Faulkner: A Biography* (New York, 1974), vol. I, p. 121.

6 Julius Weis Friend, '*The Double Dealer*: Career of a "Little" Magazine", *Mississippi Quarterly*, XXXI/4 (Autumn 1978), p. 599.

7 Quoted in Blotner, *Faulkner: A Biography*, vol. I, pp. 336–7.

8 William Faulkner, *The Marble Faun and The Green Bough* (reprint, New York, 1965), pp. xlvi and xxxv.

9 Phil Stone, Preface, *The Marble Faun and The Green Bough* (reprint, New York, 1965), p. xii.

10 Monte Cooper, 'The Book of Verses', in *William Faulkner: The Contemporary Reviews*, ed. M. Thomas Inge (New York, 1995), p. 5.

11 William Faulkner, 'Verse Old and Nascent: A Pilgrimage', in *William Faulkner: Early Prose and Poetry*, pp. 114–15.

12 Blotner, *Faulkner: A Biography*, vol. I, p. 118.

13 Sherwood Anderson, 'A Meeting South', *Dial*, LXXVIII (April 1925), p. 269.

14 Blotner, *Faulkner: A Biography*, vol. I, p. 135.

15 William Faulkner, 'Interview with Jean Stein Vanden Heuvel', in *Lion in the Garden: Interviews with William Faulkner*, ed. James B. Meriwether and Michael Millgate (Lincoln, NE, 1968), p. 255

16 William Faulkner, 'Sherwood Anderson', in *William Faulkner: Essays, Speeches and Public Letters*, ed. James B. Meriwether (New York, 2004), updated edn, p. 249.

17 Cleanth Brooks, *William Faulkner: The Abstract and the Actual* (Baton Rouge, LA, 1989), pp. 167–8.

18 William Faulkner, *Soldiers' Pay*, in *Novels: 1926–1929* (New York, 2006), pp. 208–10.

19 E. Hartley Grattan, 'A Book of Hatred', in Inge, ed., *The Contemporary Reviews*, p. 11.

20 Elizabeth Anderson and Gerald R. Kelly, *Miss Elizabeth: A Memoir* (Boston, MA, 1969), p. 131.

21 Quoted in Judith L. Sensibar, *Faulkner and Love: The Women Who Shaped his Art, A Biography* (New Haven, CT, and London, 2009), pp. 422–3.

22 William Faulkner, 'Elmer', *Mississippi Quarterly*, XXXVI/3 (Summer 1983), p. 376.

23 Joseph Blotner, ed., *Selected Letters of William Faulkner* (New York, 1977), p. 17.

24 Donald Davidson, 'William Faulkner', in Inge, ed., *The Contemporary Reviews*, p. 12; Thomas Boyd, 'Review', in *William Faulkner: The Critical Heritage*, ed. John Bassett (London, 1975), p. 57.

25 William Faulkner, *Mosquitoes*, in *Novels: 1926–1929*, pp. 371–2.

26 Ibid., p. 538.

27 Ibid., p. 540.

28 Blotner, ed., *Selected Letters*, p. 32.

29 Faulkner, *Mosquitoes*, in *Novels: 1926–1929*, p. 408.

30 Donald Davidson, 'The Grotesque', in Inge, ed., *The Contemporary Reviews*, p. 20.

31 Quoted in James B. Meriwether, 'Sartoris and Snopes: An Early Notice', *Library Chronicle of the University of Texas*, VII (Summer 1962), pp. 36–7.

32 Quoted in William Faulkner, 'A Note on Sherwood Anderson', in *Essays, Speeches and Public Letters*, p. 7.

33 Blotner, ed., *Selected Letters*, p. 38.

4 Driving the Nails Straight (1928–31)

1   Quoted in Joseph Blotner, *Faulkner: A Biography* (New York, 1974), vol. I, p. 205.

2   Quoted in Tom Dardis, *Firebrand: The Life of Horace Liveright* (New York, 1995), p. 245.

3   William Faulkner, 'The Composition, Editing, and Cutting of *Flags in the Dust*', in *William Faulkner: Essays, Speeches and Public Letters*, ed. James B. Meriwether, updated edn (New York, 2004), p. 262.

4   William Faulkner, *Flags in the Dust*, in *Novels: 1926–1929* (New York, 2006), p. 875.

5   Ibid., pp. 559–60.

6   Ibid., p. 566.

7   Ibid., pp. 870–71.

8   William Faulkner, 'Introduction to *The Sound and the Fury*, 1933', in *Essays, Speeches and Public Letters*, p. 293.

9   William Faulkner, 'A Justice', in *Collected Stories of William Faulkner* (New York, 1950), p. 360.

10 William Faulkner, 'Interviews in Japan', in *Lion in the Garden: Interviews with William Faulkner*, ed. James B. Meriwether and Michael Millgate (Lincoln, NE, 1968), p. 147.

11 William Faulkner, *The Sound and the Fury*, in *Novels: 1926–1929*, p. 880.

12 William Faulkner, quoted in *Faulkner in the University: Class Conferences at the University of Virginia, 1957–1958*, ed. Frederick L. Gwynn and Joseph L. Blotner (Charlottesville, VA, 1959), p. 31.

13 Philip Weinstein, *Becoming Faulkner: The Art and Life of William Faulkner* (New York, 2009), p. 55.

14 William Faulkner, *The Sound and the Fury*, in *Novels: 1926–1929*, p. 909.

15 Faulkner, *Faulkner in the University*, p. 32.

16 Faulkner, *The Sound and the Fury*, in *Novels: 1926–1929*, p. 992.

17 Ibid., p. 935.

18 Ibid.

19 Faulkner, 'Interviews in Japan', in *Lion in the Garden*, p. 146.

20 Faulkner, *The Sound and the Fury*, in *Novels: 1926–1929*, pp. 1079, 947 and 1053 respectively.

21 Ibid., p. 1106.

22 Ibid., p. 1124.

23 Quoted in Robert Cantwell, 'The Faulkners: Recollections of a Gifted Family', in *Conversations with William Faulkner*, ed. M. Thomas Inge (Jackson, MS, 1999), p. 35.

24 Joseph Blotner, ed., *Selected Letters of William Faulkner* (New York, 1977), p. 41.

25 Faulkner, 'The Composition, Editing, and Cutting of *Flags in the Dust*', in *Essays, Speeches and Public Letters*, p. 262.

26 Ben Wasson, *Count No 'Count: Flashbacks to Faulkner* (Jackson, MS, 1983), p. 89.

27 Ibid., p. 90.

28 Quoted in Carl Rollyson, 'Faulkner's First Biographers', in *Faulkner and Print Culture: Faulkner and Yoknapatawpha*, ed. Jay Watson, Jaime Harker and James G. Thomas (Jackson, MS, 2017), p. 53.

29 Henry Nash Smith, 'In His New Novel William Faulkner Broadens His Art', and Mary Ellen Chase, 'Some Intimations of Immortality', in *William Faulkner: The Contemporary Reviews*, ed. M. Thomas Inge (New York, 1995), pp. 25 and 28.

30 Joseph Blotner, *Faulkner: A Biography*, revd edn (New York, 1984), p. 240.

31 Blotner, ed., *Selected Letters*, p. 43.

32 William Faulkner, *Sanctuary*, in *Novels: 1930–1935* (New York, 1985), p. 182.

33 William Faulkner, *Sanctuary: The Original Text*, ed. Noel Polk (New York, 1981), p. 3.

34 William Faulkner, *Sanctuary*, in *Novels: 1930–1935*, p. 376.

35 Blotner, *Faulkner: A Biography*, vol. I, p. 237.

36 Blotner, ed., *Selected Letters*, pp. 44–5.

37 Henry Nash Smith, 'Three Southern Novels', and Clifton Fadiman, 'Hardly Worth While', in Inge, ed., *The Contemporary Reviews*, pp. 33

and 38 respectively. Evelyn Scott, 'On William Faulkner's *The Sound and the Fury*', in *William Faulkner: The Critical Heritage*, ed. John Bassett (London, 1975), p. 78.

38 William Faulkner, 1946 introduction to *The Sound and the Fury*, in *Essays, Speeches and Public Letters*, p. 297.

39 William Faulkner, *As I Lay Dying*, in *Novels: 1930–1935*, p. 178.

40 Ibid., pp. 120—21.

41 Ibid., p. 54.

42 Ibid., p. 116.

43 'Interview with Dan Brennan', in *Lion in the Garden*, p. 48.

44 'Interview with Ralph Thompson', in ibid., p. 61.

45 William Faulkner, 'A Rose for Emily', in *Collected Stories of William Faulkner* (New York, 1950), pp. 119–30.

46 William Faulkner, 'Thrift', in *Uncollected Stories of William Faulkner*, ed. Joseph Blotner (New York, 1979), pp. 382–99.

47 Both letters are printed in full in James B. Meriwether, 'Faulkner's Correspondence with *The Saturday Evening Post*', *Mississippi Quarterly*, xxx/3 (Summer 1977), pp. 465 and 474 respectively.

48 Unsigned review, in Bassett, *The Critical Heritage*, p. 94.

49 Henry Nash Smith, 'A Troubled Vision', in Inge, ed., *The Contemporary Reviews*, p. 49.

50 Sinclair Lewis, 'The American Fear of Literature', www.nobelprize.org, 12 December 1930.

51 Arnold Bennett, Review of *Soldiers' Pay*, in Bassett, *The Critical Heritage*, p. 62.

52 Sherwood Anderson, 'They Come Bearing Gifts', *The American Mercury* (October 1930), pp. 129–30.

53 William Faulkner, 'Introduction to the Modern Library Edition of *Sanctuary*', in *Essays, Speeches and Public Letters*, p. 178.

54 Polk, 'Afterword', in *Sanctuary: The Original Text*, p. 304.

55 Quoted in Blotner, *Faulkner: A Biography*, vol. I, p. 613. Ben Wasson has Faulkner declaiming this line in person, but the dialogue feels paraphrased from the letter Blotner cites. See *Count No 'Count: Flashbacks to Faulkner* (Jackson, MS, 1983), pp. 115–16.

56 Faulkner, *Sanctuary*, in *Novels: 1930–1935*, p. 396.

57 Henry Seidel Canby, 'The School of Cruelty', in Inge, ed., *The Contemporary Reviews*, p. 56.

58 Maurice Coindreau, *The Time of William Faulkner: A French View of Modern American Fiction* (Columbia, SC, 1971), p. 26.

59 Quoted in Rollyson, 'Faulkner's First Biographers', p. 54.

60 For the parody and caricature, see Corey Ford, *In the Worst Possible Taste* (New York, 1932), pp. 84–99. For Lewis's dismissal, see 'William Faulkner, the Moralist with a Corn Cob', in *Men Without Art* (London, 1934), pp. 42–64. For the 'corncob man' quote, see Blotner, *Faulkner: A Biography*, vol. II, p. 1002.

61 Faulkner, 'Dry September', in *Collected Stories*, p. 169.

62 Quoted in James B. Meriwether, 'Faulkner's Correspondence with *Scribner's Magazine*', *Proof*, III (1973), pp. 268–9.

63 Quoted in Blotner, *Faulkner: A Biography*, vol. I, p. 702.

64 Faulkner, 1946 Introduction to *The Sound and the Fury*, in *Essays, Speeches and Public Letters*, p. 298.

65 William Faulkner, *Light in August*, in *Novels: 1930–35*, p. 604.

66 Howard Mumford Jones and Walter Rideout, eds, *Letters of Sherwood Anderson* (Boston, MA, 1953), p. 252.

67 Ellen Glasgow, 'Opening Speech of the Southern Writers Conference', in *Friendship and Sympathy: Communities of Southern Women Writers*, ed. Rosemary M. Magee (Jackson, MS, 1992), p. 10.

68 Quoted in Ann Waldron, *Close Connections: Caroline Gordon and the Southern Renaissance* (Knoxville, TN, 1989), p. 105.

69 Quoted in 'Interview in University of Virginia *College Topics*', in *Lion in the Garden*, pp. 17–18.

70 Blotner, ed., *Selected Letters*, p. 53.

71 Blotner, *Faulkner: A Biography*, vol. I, p. 726.

72 Blotner, ed., *Selected Letters*, p. 61.

73 Faulkner, *Light in August*, in *Novels: 1930–1935*, p. 589.

74 Ibid., p. 740.

75 Blotner, *Selected Letters*, p. 202.

5 Rushing from Pillar to Post (1932–8)

1 For an account of the Faulkner/Hawks friendship from the latter's perspective, see Todd McCarthy, *Howard Hawks: The Grey Fox of Hollywood* (New York, 1997), pp. 176–9.

2 J. Donald Adams, 'Mr. Faulkner's Astonishing Novel', in *William Faulkner: The Contemporary Reviews*, ed. M. Thomas Inge (New York, 1995), p. 87.

3 Frederick L. Gwynn and Joseph L. Blotner, eds, *Faulkner in the University: Class Conferences at the University of Virginia, 1957–1958* (Charlottesville, VA, 1959), p. 45.

4 Ernest Hemingway, *Death in the Afternoon* (New York, 1932), p. 173.

5 Quoted in Michel Gresset, *A Faulkner Chronology*, trans. Arthur B. Scharff (Jackson, MS, 1985), p. 40.

6 Joseph Blotner, ed., *Selected Letters of William Faulkner* (New York, 1977), p. 78.

7 Ibid., p. 79.

8 Ibid.

9 Ibid.

10 Peter Monro Jack, 'William Faulkner Presents a Mixed Sheaf of Short Stories' and 'Another Batch of Faulkner Stories', in Inge, ed., *The Contemporary Reviews*, pp. 107 and 115 respectively.

11 Blotner, ed., *Selected Letters*, p. 84.

12 Ibid., p. 87.

13 William Faulkner, *Pylon*, in *Novels: 1930–1935* (New York, 1985), pp. 908–9.

14 Janann Sherman, *Walking on Air: The Aerial Adventures of Phoebe Omlie* (Jackson, MS, 2011), p. 92.

15 Faulkner, *Pylon*, in *Novels: 1930–1935*, p. 876.

16 Laurence Stallings, 'Gentleman from Mississippi', in John Bassett, ed., *William Faulkner: The Critical Heritage* (London, 1975), p. 176; John Crowe Ransom, 'Faulkner, South's Most Brilliant but Wayward Talent, Is Spent', in Inge, ed., *The Contemporary Reviews*, p. 120; 'Torrid Tomes', *Snappy* magazine (September 1935), quoted in David M. Earle, *Re-covering Modernism: Pulps, Paperbacks, and the Prejudice of Form* (New York, 2009), p. 196.

17 Dean Faulkner Wells, *Every Day by the Sun: A Memoir of the Faulkners of Mississippi* (New York, 2011), p. 111.

18 Meta Carpenter Wilde and Orin Borsten, *A Loving Gentleman: The Love Story of William Faulkner and Meta Carpenter* (New York, 1976), pp. 75–6.

19 Quoted in Joseph Blotner, *Faulkner: A Biography* (New York, 1974), vol. II, p. 927.

20 Ibid., p. 938.

21 William Faulkner, *Absalom, Absalom!* in *Novels: 1936–1940* (New York, 1990), p. 215.

22 Ibid., p. 182.

23 See, for example, Richard Godden's ground-breaking essay '*Absalom, Absalom!*, Haiti, and Labor History: Reading Unreadable Revolutions', in *Fictions of Labor: William Faulkner and the South's Long Revolution* (New York, 1997), pp. 49–79, and, as a rejoinder, Wanda Raiford, 'Fantasy and Haiti's Erasure in William Faulkner's *Absalom, Absalom!*', *South*, XLIX/1 (Autumn 2016), pp. 101–21.

24 Godden, '*Absalom*', p. 154.

25 Ibid., p. 293.

26 Ibid., p. 311.

27 Frederick R. Karl, *William Faulkner: American Writer* (New York, 1989), p. 558.

28 Faulkner, *Absalom, Absalom!* in *Novels: 1936–1940*, p. 311.

29 Mary-Carter Roberts, 'Faulkner's Style Dwarfs Material in New Novel', and Max Miller, '*Absalom, Absalom!*' in Inge, ed., *The Contemporary Reviews*, pp. 149–50 and 151 respectively.

30 Clifton Fadiman, 'Faulkner, Extra-special, Double-distilled', *New Yorker* (31 October, 1936), p. 64.

31 Wallace Stegner, 'New Technique in Novel Introduced', in Bassett, ed., *The Critical Heritage*, p. 211.

32 Quoted in Lise Jaillant, *Modernism, Middlebrow and the Literary Canon* (London, 2014), p. 126.

33 Blotner, ed, *Selected Letters*, p. 338.

34 Quoted in Jaillant, *Modernism, Middlebrow and the Literary Canon*, p. 130.

35 William Faulkner, *The Unvanquished*, in *Novels: 1936–1940*, p. 454.

36 Ibid., p. 449.

37 Ibid., p. 490.

38 Blotner, ed, *Selected Letters*, p. 106.

39 Ibid., p. 96.

40 Allen Maxwell, Review of *The Wild Palms*, *Southwest Review*, XXIV/3 (April 1939), p. 360.

6 'The Best in America, By God' (1939–45)

1   Robert Cantwell, 'When the Dam Breaks', *Time* (January 23, 1939), p. 45.
2   Joseph Blotner, *Faulkner: A Biography* (New York, 1974), vol. II, p. 1015.
3   Robert Cantwell, 'The Faulkners: Recollections of a Gifted Family',
    in *Conversations with William Faulkner*, ed. M. Thomas Inge (Jackson,
    MS, 1999), p. 30.
4   Cantwell, 'When the Dam Breaks', pp. 46–8.
5   Conrad Aiken, 'William Faulkner: The Novel as Form', in *William
    Faulkner: The Critical Heritage*, ed. John Bassett (London, 1975),
    pp. 243–50.
6   Cantwell, 'When the Damn Breaks', p. 45.
7   Ibid., p. 46.
8   William Faulkner, *If I Forget Thee, Jerusalem,* in *Novels: 1936–1940*
    (New York, 1990), p. 529.
9   Ibid., p. 726.
10 Ibid., p. 1091.
11 William Faulkner, 'Interviews in Japan', in *Lion in the Garden: Interviews
    with William Faulkner*, ed. James B. Meriwether and Michael Millgate
    (Lincoln, NE, 1968), p. 132.
12 Joseph Blotner, ed., *Selected Letters of William Faulkner* (New York,
    1977), pp. 107–8.
13 Don Stranford, '*The Beloved Returns* and Other Recent Fiction',
    in *William Faulkner: The Contemporary Reviews*, ed. M. Thomas Inge
    (New York, 1995), p. 224.
14 Malcolm Cowley, 'Faulkner by Daylight', in Inge, ed., *The Contemporary
    Reviews*, p. 216.
15 Stephen Vincent Benét, 'Flem Snopes and His Kin', *Saturday Review
    of Literature* (6 April 1940), p. 7.
16 Blotner, ed, *Selected Letters*, p. 124.
17 Ibid., p. 128.
18 See Daniel J. Singal, *William Faulkner: The Making of a Modernist*
    (Chapel Hill, NC, 1999), p. 262.
19 William Faulkner, 'Delta Autumn', in *Novels: 1942–1954* (New York,
    1994), p. 268.
20 Blotner, ed, *Selected Letters*, p. 135.
21 William Faulkner, 'The Old People', in *Novels: 1942–1954*, p. 137.

22 William Faulkner, 'The Bear', in *Novels: 1942–1954*, p. 141.

23 For a fascinating study of the real-life records that inspired this scene, see Sally Wolff, *Ledgers of History: William Faulkner, an Almost Forgotten Friendship, and an Antebellum Plantation Diary: Memories of Dr. Edgar Wiggin Francisco III* (Baton Rouge, LA, 2010).

24 William Faulkner, 'The Bear' [*Saturday Evening Post* version], in *Uncollected Stories of William Faulkner*, ed. Joseph Blotner (New York, 1979), pp. 293–4.

25 Faulkner, 'The Bear', in *Novels: 1942–1954*, pp. 220–21.

26 Faulkner, Dedication to *Go Down, Moses*, in *Novels: 1942–1954*, p. 2.

27 Jeannette Greenspan, 'Faulkner at his Best', in Inge, ed., *The Contemporary Reviews*, p. 241.

28 William Faulkner, 'Classroom Statements at the University of Mississippi', in *Lion in the Garden*, p. 54.

29 Blotner, ed., *Selected Letters*, p. 153.

30 Ibid., p. 122.

31 Ibid., p. 154.

32 Ibid., p. 113; Blotner, *Faulkner: A Biography*, vol. II, p. 1134.

33 Blotner, ed, *Selected Letters*, p. 178.

34 Meta Carpenter Wilde and Orin Borsten, *A Loving Gentleman: The Love Story of William Faulkner and Meta Carpenter* (New York, 1976), p. 279.

35 Tom Dardis, *Some Time in the Sun: The Hollywood Years of F. Scott Fitzgerald, William Faulkner, Nathanael West, Aldous Huxley, and James Agee* (New York, 1976), p. 119.

36 Blotner, ed., *Selected Letters*, p. 182.

37 Ibid., p. 168.

38 Malcolm Cowley, 'William Faulkner's Human Comedy', *New York Times Book Review* (29 October 1944), p. 5.

39 Blotner, ed, *Selected Letters*, p. 204.

7 Aiming for the 'Magnum O' (1946–54)

1 Alexander Woollcott, Introduction to *As You Were: A Portable Library of American Prose and Poetry Assembled for Members of the Armed Forces and the Merchant Marine* (New York, 1944), p. XI.

2 For a useful reconsideration of Cowley's design, see Michael Millgate, 'Defining Moment: *The Portable Faulkner* Revisited', in *Faulkner at 100: Retrospect and Prospect* (Jackson, MS, 2000), pp. 26–44.

3 Joseph Blotner, ed., *Selected Letters of William Faulkner* (New York, 1977), p. 215.

4 A. Wigfall Green, 'William Faulkner at Home', *Sewanee Review*, XL (Summer 1932), p. 300.

5 Blotner, ed., *Selected Letters*, p. 219.

6 Ibid.

7 Malcolm Cowley, *The Faulkner–Cowley File: Letters and Memories, 1944–1962* (New York, 1966), p. 65.

8 Frederick L. Gwynn and Joseph L. Blotner, eds, *Faulkner in the University: Class Conferences at the University of Virginia, 1957–1958* (Charlottesville, VA, 1959), p. 1. For the appendix itself, see 'Appendix: Compson, 1699–1946', in *William Faulkner A to Z*, ed. A. Nicholas Fargnoli and Michael Golay (New York, 2002), pp. 313–19.

9 Blotner, ed., *Selected Letters*, pp. 229–30.

10 Carlos Baker, ed., *Ernest Hemingway: Selected Letters, 1917–1961* (New York, 1981), p. 604.

11 Blotner, ed., *Selected Letters*, pp. 233 and 238 respectively.

12 Ibid., p. 188.

13 Ibid., pp. 256–7.

14 Ibid., p. 249.

15 'Classroom Statements at the University of Mississippi', in *Lion in the Garden: Interviews with William Faulkner*, ed. James B. Meriwether and Michael Millgate (Lincoln, NE, 1968), p. 58.

16 Blotner, ed., *Selected Letters*, p. 262.

17 Ibid.

18 Ralph Ellison, 'The Shadow and the Act', in *Shadow and Act* (New York, 1964), p. 277.

19 William Faulkner, *Intruder in the Dust,* in *Novels: 1942–1954* (New York, 1994), p. 400.

20 Noel Polk, 'Faulkner and the Southern White Moderate', in *Children of the Dark House: Text and Context in Faulkner* (Jackson, MS, 1998), p. 224.

21 Horace Gregory, 'Regional Novelist of Universal Meaning', in *William Faulkner: The Contemporary Reviews*, ed. M. Thomas Inge (New York, 1995), p. 257.

22 Blotner, ed., *Selected Letters*, p. 185.

23 George Marion O'Donnell, 'Faulkner's Mythology', in *William Faulkner: The Critical Heritage*, ed. John Bassett (London, 1975), pp. 238–40.

24 Robert Penn Warren, 'Cowley's Faulkner', in Bassett, ed., *The Critical Heritage*, pp. 316–17.

25 Joseph Blotner, *Faulkner: A Biography* (New York, 1974), vol. II, p. 1204.

26 Quoted in Louis Daniel Brodsky, 'Reflections on Faulkner: An Interview with Albert I. Bezzerides', *Southern Review*, XXI/2 (1985), pp. 384–5.

27 Blotner, ed., *Selected Letters*, p. 303.

28 Ibid., p. 278.

29 William Faulkner, 'Upon Receiving the Nobel Prize for Literature', in *William Faulkner: Essays, Speeches and Public Letters*, ed. James B. Meriwether, updated edn (New York, 2004), pp. 119–21.

30 Saxe Commins, Letter to Dorothy Commins, 8 October 1952, in *Faulkner: A Comprehensive Guide to the Brodsky Collection, vol. II*, ed. Louis Daniel Brodsky and Robert W. Hamblin (Jackson, MS, 1982), p. 89.

31 Dwight Macdonald, 'Masscult and Midcult', in *Masscult and Midcult: Essays Against the American Grain* (New York, 2010), p. 38.

8 Breaking the Pencil (1955–62)

1 William Cobb, *Captain Billy's Troopers: A Writer's Life* (Tuscaloosa, AL, 2015), p. 94.

2 Joseph Blotner, ed., *Selected Letters of William Faulkner* (New York, 1977), p. 314.

3 William Faulkner, 'Interviews in Japan', in *Lion in the Garden: Interviews with William Faulkner*, ed. James B. Meriwether and Michael Millgate (Lincoln, NE, 1968), p. 118.

4 Don Bachardy, 'A Life Open to Art', in *The Isherwood Century: Essays on the Life and Work of Christopher Isherwood* (Madison, WI, 2001), p. 92.

5 William Faulkner, 'Press Dispatch on the Emmett Till Case', in *William Faulkner: Essays, Speeches and Public Letters*, ed. James B. Meriwether, updated edn (New York, 2004), pp. 222–4.

6 Blotner, ed, *Selected Letters*, p. 339.
7 John Faulkner's 4 December 1955 letter is reprinted in Eileen Gregory, 'Faulkner's Typescripts of *The Town*', *Mississippi Quarterly*, xxvi/3 (Summer 1973), p. 383.
8 'Interview with Russell Howe', in *Lion in the Garden*, pp. 260–61.
9 'To the Editor of *The Reporter*, April 19, 1956', in *William Faulkner: Essays, Speeches and Public Letters*, p. 225.
10 Granville Hicks, 'The Question of William Faulkner: His New Novel, *The Town*, as Test', in *William Faulkner: The Contemporary Reviews*, ed. M. Thomas Inge (New York, 1995), p. 444.
11 Adlai Stevenson, 'A Purpose for Modern Woman', *Woman's Home Companion* (September 1955), pp. 29–31.
12 Phil Stone, Letter to Joe Dan Hill, in *Faulkner: A Comprehensive Guide to the Brodsky Collection, vol. II*, ed. Louis Daniel Brodsky and Robert W. Hamblin (Jackson, MS, 1982), p. 215.
13 William Faulkner, 'Interview with Jean Stein Vanden Heuvel', in *Lion in the Garden*, p. 255.
14 Joel Williamson, *William Faulkner and Southern History* (New York, 1993), p. 316.
15 Blotner, ed., *Selected Letters*, p. 429.
16 Frederick R. Karl, *William Faulkner: American Writer* (New York, 1989), p. 995.

Afterword: 'To Think of Myself Again as a Printed Object'

1 Lesley Goldberg, 'HBO Pacts with 'Luck's' David Milch for William Faulkner Adaptations', *The Hollywood Reporter*, www.hollywoodreporter.com, 30 November 2011.
2 *Barton Fink*, dir. Joel and Ethan Coen (Twentieth-century Fox, 1991).
3 Jonathan Yardley, review of *One Matchless Time: A Life of William Faulkner* by Jay Parini, *The Washington Post*, www.washingtonpost.com, 21 October 2004.
4 William Faulkner, 'Interview with Jean Stein Vanden Heuvel', in *Lion in the Garden: Interviews with William Faulkner*, ed. James B. Meriwether and Michael Millgate (Lincoln, NE, 1968), p. 284.

5   William Faulkner, 'Introduction to the Modern Library edition of *Sanctuary*', in *William Faulkner: Essays, Speeches and Public Letters*, ed. James B. Meriwether, updated edn (New York, 2004), p. 177.

Select Bibliography

Works by Faulkner

The Marble Faun (Boston, MA, 1924)

Soldiers' Pay (New York, 1926)

Mosquitoes (New York, 1927)

Sartoris (New York, 1929)

The Sound and the Fury (New York, 1929)

As I Lay Dying (New York, 1930)

Sanctuary (New York, 1931)

These Thirteen (New York, 1931)

Idyll in the Desert (New York, 1931)

Light in August (New York, 1932)

A Green Bough (New York, 1933)

Dr. Martino and Other Stories (New York, 1934)

Pylon (New York, 1935)

Absalom, Absalom! (New York, 1936)

The Unvanquished (New York, 1938)

The Wild Palms [*If I Forget Thee, Jerusalem*] (New York, 1939)

The Hamlet (New York, 1940)

Go Down, Moses (New York, 1942)

The Portable Faulkner (New York, 1946)

Intruder in the Dust (New York, 1948)

Knight's Gambit (New York, 1949)

Collected Stories of William Faulkner (New York, 1950)

Notes on a Horsethief (Greenville, MS, 1951)

Requiem for a Nun (New York, 1951)

The Faulkner Reader (New York, 1954)

A Fable (New York, 1954)

Big Woods (New York, 1955)
The Town (New York, 1957)
Three Famous Short Novels (New York, 1958)
New Orleans Sketches (New Brunswick, NJ, 1958)
Faulkner in the University (Charlottesville, VA, 1959)
The Mansion (New York, 1959)
The Reivers (New York, 1962)
William Faulkner: Early Prose and Poetry (New York, 1962)
William Faulkner: Essays, Speeches and Public Letters (New York, 1966)
Flags in the Dust (New York, 1973)
Uncollected Stories of William Faulkner (New York, 1979)
Sanctuary: The Original Text (New York, 1981)

Letters

Blotner, Joseph, ed., *Selected Letters of William Faulkner* (New York, 1977)
Cowley, Malcolm, ed., *The Faulkner–Cowley File: Letters and Memories, 1944–1962* (New York, 1966)
Watson, James G., ed., *Thinking of Home: William Faulkner's Letters to his Mother and Father, 1918–1925* (New York, 1992)

Biographical and Critical Studies

Bleikasten, André, *William Faulkner: A Life through Novels* (Bloomington, IN, 2017)
Blotner, Joseph, *Faulkner: A Biography*, 2 vols (New York, 1974); updated edn 1 vol. (New York, 1984)
Brodsky, Louis Daniel, *William Faulkner, Life Glimpses* (Austin, TX, 2013)
Brooks, Cleanth, *William Faulkner: The Yoknapatawpha Country* (Baton Rouge, LA, 1963)
Clarke, Deborah, *Robbing the Mother: Women in Faulkner* (Jackson, MS, 1994)
Cullen, John B., and Floyd C. Watkins, *Old Times in the Faulkner Country* (Chapel Hill, NC, 1961)
Duvall, John N., ed., *Faulkner and his Critics* (Baltimore, MD, 2010)

Falkner, Murry C., *The Falkners of Mississippi: A Memoir* (Baton Rouge, LA, 1967)

Fargnoli, A. Nicholas, and Michael Golay, *William Faulkner A to Z: The Essential Reference to his Life and Work* (New York, 2001)

Faulkner, John, *My Brother Bill: An Affectionate Reminiscence* (New York, 1963)

Fowler, Doreen, *Faulkner: The Return of the Repressed* (Charlottesville, VA, 1997)

Hamblin, Robert W., *Myself and the World: A Biography of William Faulkner* (Jackson, MS, 2016)

Hickman, Lisa C., *William Faulkner and Joan Williams: The Romance of Two Writers* (Jefferson, NC, 2006)

Inge, M. Thomas., *The Dixie Limited: Writers on William Faulkner and His Influence* (Jackson, MS, 2016)

Karl, Frederick R., *William Faulkner: American Writer* (New York, 1989)

Matthews, John T., ed., *William Faulkner in Context* (New York, 2015)

Millgate, Michael, *The Achievement of William Faulkner* (Lincoln, NE, 1966)

—, *Faulkner's Place* (Athens, GA, 1997)

Minter, David, *William Faulkner: His Life and Work* (Baltimore, MD, 1980)

Moreland, Richard C., *Faulkner and Modernism: Rereading and Rewriting* (Madison, WI, 1990)

—, ed., *A Companion to William Faulkner* (Malden, MA, 2008)

Parini, Jay, *One Matchless Time: A Life of William Faulkner* (New York, 2004)

Porter, Carolyn, *William Faulkner: Lives and Legacies* (New York, 2007)

Robinson, Owen, *Creating Yoknapatawpha: Writers and Readers in Faulkner's Fiction* (New York, 2013)

Rollyson, Carl, *Uses of the Past in the Novels of William Faulkner* (New York, 1998)

Schwartz, Lawrence H., *Creating Faulkner's Reputation: The Politics of Modern Literary Criticism* (Knoxville, TN, 1988)

Sensibar, Judith L., *Faulkner and Love: The Women Who Shaped his Art, A Biography* (New Haven, CT, and London, 2009)

Singal, Daniel J., *William Faulkner: The Making of a Modernist* (Chapel Hill, NC, 1997)

Towner, Theresa M., *The Cambridge Introduction to William Faulkner* (New York, 2008)

—, and James B. Carothers, *Reading Faulkner: Collected Stories* (Jackson, MS, 2006)

Volpe, Edmond L., *A Reader's Guide to William Faulkner: The Novels*
    (Syracuse, NY, 2003)
Wagner-Martin, Linda, ed., *William Faulkner: Six Decades of Criticism*
    (East Lansing, MI, 2002)
Watson, James G., *William Faulkner: Self-presentation and Performance*
    (Austin, TX, 2000)
Wells, Dean Faulkner, *Every Day by the Sun: A Memoir of the Faulkners of
    Mississippi* (New York, 2011)
Williamson, Joel, *William Faulkner and Southern History* (New York, 1993)

Journals and Websites

Digital Yoknapatawpha, http://faulkner.iath.virginia.edu/
Kreiswirth, Martin, ed., *The Faulkner Journal* (Orlando, FL, 1981–)
The William Faulkner Society, www.faulknersociety.com

Acknowledgements

My thanks go first and foremost to my colleague and fellow Hemingway Society trustee, Verna Kale of Penn State University. Verna wrote the excellent *Hemingway* volume in Reaktion Books's Critical Lives series and recommended me when her publisher asked if she knew of anyone who might contribute a Faulkner entry to the project; I appreciate her thinking of me and hope someday to return the favour. I'm also deeply grateful to the fine folks at Reaktion Books, particularly editorial director Vivian Constantinopoulos, who was extremely patient with my ever-renegotiated deadlines. Halfway into this project, I was transferred to a campus 45 minutes from home and put in charge of supervising an additional fifty faculty members. For the first time in my career, I discovered how precious writing time was; Vivian's willingness to work around my new circumstances made the adjustment a lot less stressful. The seasoned Faulkner scholar Deborah Clarke was very kind to provide feedback on the manuscript. I also owe my mother, Beverly, a huge debt for her positivity and presence in my life. Over the course of completing this book I became a grandfather not once but twice, so to Zayd and Sara I wish to say: 'This one's for you.'

Photo Acknowledgements

Cofield Collection, Archives and Special Collections, University of
Mississippi Libraries: pp. 15, 24, 33, 41, 44, 102, 131, 150, 165, 171, 184;
collection of the author: pp. 51, 62, 66, 74, 88, 146, 161, 172; Dain Collection,
Archives and Special Collections, University of Mississippi Libraries: p. 187;
Library of Congress, Prints and Photographs Division: pp. 6, 82 (Historic
American Buildings Survey), 92, 95, 113.